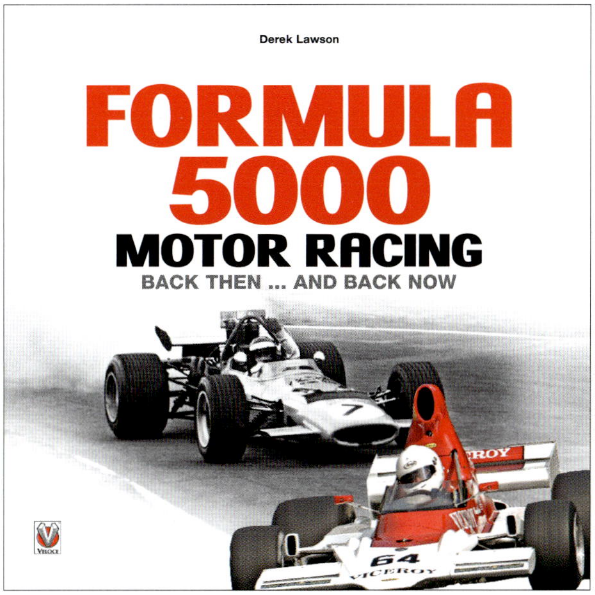
Derek Lawson
FORMULA 5000
MOTOR RACING
BACK THEN ... AND BACK NOW
VELOCE

First published in October 2009 by Veloce Publishing Limited, 33 Trinity Street, Dorchester DT1 1TT, England. Fax 01305 268864/e-mail info@veloce.co.uk/web www.veloce.co.uk or www.velocebooks.com.
ISBN: 978-1-84584-216-1 UPC: 6-36847-04216-5



Readers with ideas for automotive books, or books on other transport or related hobby subjects, are invited to write to the editorial director of Veloce Publishing at the above address.
British Library Cataloguing in Publication Data – A catalogue record for this book is available from the British Library. Typesetting, design and page make-up all by Veloce Publishing Ltd on Apple Mac. Printed in India by Replika Press.

Derek Lawson

# FORMULA 5000 MOTOR RACING

## BACK THEN ... AND BACK NOW

VELOCE PUBLISHING
THE PUBLISHER OF FINE AUTOMOTIVE BOOKS

# CONTENTS

# ACKNOWLEDGEMENTS

Thanks must go to all the drivers, teams, sponsors and race organisers without whom this book would not have been possible. The marshals who officiated at the meetings also deserve recognition, and I extend my warmest thoughts to them.

There have been several individuals who have been particularly generous with their time, their memories and some of their personal paraphernalia, and this has assisted me in the writing of this book. In no particular order these are: Frank and Judy Lyons, Graham Livingstone, Colin Cragg, Ian Stockdale, Dan Rear, Emyr Price and Bill Aukland.

Particular acknowledgement has to be made to the photographers who have supplied me with images for this tome. The majority of them are named under their work, but I'd like to record them here as well. There are some whose name I have never known, and I would like to thank them, too. The guys I do know are as follows: Frank Hall, Norman Hayes, Eric Bryce, Graham Petch, Stuart Dent, David Lawson, Graham Etheridge, Brian Watson, Alan Cox, Richard Bunyan, Pete Taylor, Ken Grey and Rob Ryder.

My gratitude is extended to everyone and anyone I have forgotten.

**Derek Lawson**

# MY TIME IN FORMULA 5000

After a short and mistaken emigration to South Africa in November 1970, I returned to the UK in March 1971 with no drive. Sid Taylor, for whom I'd driven a Lola T70 Mk IIIB in 1969, called and asked me if I'd like to do F5000. With no other drive available, the decision was easy!

Sid had a Trojan-built McLaren M18. This was a strong but heavy car. When Frank Gardner appeared with the new, lightweight F2 Lola-based car, everything else was outdated. At Snetterton, I managed to get a good start, but Frank steadily closed the gap until he was ready to make a pass. This happened coming out of the tight right-hander after the main straight. I took the inside line and, as I moved over to the left at the exit, Frank was partway past. Neither of us gave way, and as we approached the Esses, Frank started bouncing as he was off the track on my left. We collided, and both cars went headfirst into the banking. The Lola was bent from one end to the other, but the M18 merely had suspension damage! As we walked back to the pits, Frank commented: "That were a hard one" – he'd broken a rib.

From memory I think we had a win at Brands, and also at the Dublin Grand Prix (I think it was called) at Mondello Park in the rain. Towards the end of the year we had another Brands race on the full circuit, and in this one I had about a ten-second lead over Frank with just a few laps to go when the M18 snapped sideways coming out of Clearways. A look in the mirrors showed the top link on the right rear suspension flying in the breeze. I kept going as best as I could and, again from memory, think we managed another win.

In 1972 we initially ran an old McLaren M10B – which was better than the M18 – whilst Chevron built an F5000 motor known as the B24. We had a couple of wins with this car in the UK before departing for the USA where, at Watkins Glen in July, there was $20,000 for first place. Leading by forty-five seconds from Graham McRae with five laps to go, the battery went flat. Also, we still had points in the British Championship, and brought the B24 back for a race at Oulton Park. Whilst holding a short lead from Graham, I came round Esso and, as we went up the hill before dropping down to Knicker Brook, I saw movement in the marshal's box on the right, but no flag at that time. Whistling over the top of the hill, I was confronted by two spinning cars, one of which was sideways across the track. The only choice was to go down the verge on the left; the shovel nose was damaged and we were out.

In a 1974 race in Sid Taylor's Lola T332 at Oulton Park, we had a twenty-seven-second lead over David Hobbs with two laps to go. Once again I went over the top of the hill leading down to Knicker Brook, this time the Lola snapped sideways at 150mph. The rear wing had broken its mounting brackets on the right side. At the start of the last lap David was on my tail, but somehow he failed to make it past as my T332, with no down-force at the rear, used all of the road!

Through good times and bad I greatly enjoyed my experience of Formula 5000, and I hope you enjoy reliving my time and that of all of the characters whom I regarded as friends off the track, but foes whilst on it. I'm pleased to see the cars coming back to the racetracks, and hope that they will thrill today's spectators in the same way as they did yesterday's.

This book will also provide answers to questions raised by all my memory lapses. Enjoy!

**Brian Redman**
Florida, USA

# SO WHAT IS FORMULA 5000?

Most of us are familiar with the noise a Formula 5000 car makes, but where does it come from? The 'racket' that these '5000' cars make stems from the maximum 5.0-litre (5000cc) engine capacity that they are allowed, although in their heyday, many ran with 3.5-, 4.5-, and 4.7-litre engines.

In 1965, the Sports Car Club of America (SCCA) created three new single-seater racing formulae: Formula A, for 3.0-litre racing engines, Formula B (later better known as Formula Atlantic) for 1.6-litre production-based engines, and Formula C for 1.1-litre engines. Formula A had the same regulations as Formula 1 cars of the day, but struggled to raise any worthwhile entries in its first few seasons. There were no competitors for the 1965 SCCA National Championship for Formula A, so the first national champion in that class appeared in 1966, when Harry McIntosh beat a poor field in his ex-Formula 1 Brabham BT7. The following year Chuck Kirkbride won in a Lotus 24, but was the only finisher in his class. A professional series started in 1967, but it was dominated by Formula B cars.

For 1968, the SCCA opened up Formula A to production engines of up to 5.0-litre, thus creating an opening for the 302ci Chevrolet engine, and Formula 5000 racing was effectively 'born'. In the UK and Europe, Formula 5000, matching American Formula A, was adopted in 1969, when John Webb of Brands Hatch's then-parent company, Motor Racing Developments, and Nick Syrett saw its potential. Manufacturers such as McLaren, Trojan and Lola Cars saw it, too, and were quick to provide support.

The South African, New Zealand and Australian National Championships were opened to Formula 5000 cars in 1968, 1969 and 1970 respectively.

When Britain adopted Formula 5000 for 1969, Lola Cars was already selling its T140 Formula A chassis to the Americans. Based on the T70 sports car running gear, the original T140 had been a simple and sizeable multi-tubular space frame design which proved very competitive. For 1969, the basic T140 specification was updated to create the T142 model, and further models appeared in the years that followed.

The weak pound (a result of the energy crisis) and the increasing cost of importing Chevrolet V8s caused some concern, and engine regulations for European Formula 5000 were revised to permit engines other than the big pushrod V8s – the DOHC Cosworth GA V6 (based on a unit used in Group 2 Ford Capri cars) was permitted to race at a capacity of 3500cc (rumours of a

4.0-litre SOHC BMW also persisted, but no such engine was ever seen). March 75A and Chevron B30 cars were particularly successful with a V6 power plant. The March was, in reality, little more than a March 751 Formula 1 car with minor modifications for the new engine.

The arrival of the Cosworth DFV engine in the UK meant that many teams could now afford to build their own chassis around a good engine/transmission package. Cooper, Lotus and Brabham ceased the production of customer Formula 1 cars to concentrate on the formula.

For six seasons Formula 5000 racing seemed to have taken over the world, though after that the decline was rapid. The South Africans went first, adopting Formula Atlantic for 1976; New Zealand then went the same way; the US series was dropped at the end of the year, and the British series turned into the British Formula 1 in 1977, ejecting the last Formula 5000 cars after 1978. Australia held out; its unchanged cars carried on until early 1982.

The US Formula 5000 series was replaced by Single-Seat Can-Am for 1977, giving good work to sports car-bodied Lola T330/T332 cars right up to 1986. Unlike the American series, the British Championship didn't attract many star names from Formula 1 and sports cars, and it was dominated by drivers that were usually seen in Formula 2 or at the back of Formula 1's World Championship grids. Peter Gethin, however, managed to launch his Formula 1 career, thanks to his Formula 5000 Championship titles in the UK. Andrea de Adamich, Reine Wisell, Howden Ganley, Guy Edwards, Brian Redman and a few others also made appearances in Grand Prix racing.

However, the same problem that befell US Formula 5000 happened in Europe, and in 1976, the British/European Championship was opened to Formula 1 cars, forming the basis of what would become the Aurora British Formula 1 Championship. Formula 5000 cars were still entered, but were no longer competitive against their 3.0-litre counterparts. Older Formula 5000 cars continued to be used in the British Sprint Championship.

While it was based in the United Kingdom, the British Formula 5000 series (named the Guards Formula 5000, Rothmans Formula 5000 or ShellSPORT Formula 5000 Championship, according to the year's sponsor) managed to spread across Europe. Races were held on many international circuits, including Monza (Italy), Hockenheim (Germany), and Zandvoort (Netherlands), and attracted a significant number of continental drivers, too.

In 1995, the Formula 5000 Association staged a pair of races at Lydden in England, exclusively for these cars. This was repeated the following year, again at the southern Kent venue, and another was put on at Mallory Park in 1997. Sporadic appearances in other races, mainly Formula Libre contests, followed throughout the country.

The cars made a more determined comeback to the racetracks in 2003. Since then, thanks to the Formula One Racing Car Entrants (FORCE), and the Historic Sports Car Club (HSCC), the cars have been well and truly back on the menu of many racing programmes. The Derek Bell Trophy continues to attract competitors, and their cars attract numerous fans to meetings. This book will hopefully help the reader remember many of the races, and a few of the hillclimbs, that occurred – some in the UK, a few in Europe – and others even further afield, in the early years, as well as more recently.

# CHAPTER 1
## IN THE BEGINNING

The first exclusively-Formula 5000 race in the UK was held at Oulton Park on Good Friday, 4 April 1969, and this was also the opening round of the Guards Championship for the year. The series had twelve rounds, with the Cheshire circuit holding two events and Brands Hatch hosting three. Four more rounds were held in Europe, with the British circuits Mallory Park, Silverstone and Snetterton sharing the remainder between them. Before becoming champion, a driver had to compete in at least eight rounds, with £500 and 500 points being awarded to the winner of each round. Brands Hatch was also scheduled to host a non-championship event on 27 December, but the meeting was abandoned due to thick and heavy fog.

Although the official start to the season came on Good Friday, a couple of the entrants, Mike Walker and Doug Hardwick, ran their cars at the BRSCC meeting in Cheshire on 23 March. It was Walker who came away the happiest man when he recorded a couple of wins in the day's two ten-lap Formula Libre events. Despite having to be push-started in the first of them, Hardwick was third in the second, driving a Lola-Chevrolet T142 similar to that of Walker.

When the cars were officially first unveiled to the racing public there were thirteen on the track, but not all of them were powered by 5.0-litre engines. Over 40,000 people were present to witness the event and, after qualifying, they saw that it was the 5.0-litre Chevrolet-powered Team Surtees TS5 of David Hobbs that had set the fastest time. Two-tenths of a second behind the pole-sitter was another 5.0-litre power plant supplied by Chevrolet, but this time with a McLaren M10A chassis. This was driven by Peter Gethin on behalf of Church Farm Racing, which was effectively the McLaren works team run by Derek Bell's stepfather, Bernard Hender. The highest qualifier of the smaller power plants was a Lotus 43 that had a 4.7-litre Ford engine and was driven by a private entrant, Rob 'Robs' Lamplough, from the sixth grid slot. Numbers on the starting grid were reduced by two as Hobbs' team-mate, Andrea de Adamich, had crashed his Surtees TS5 at Island in practice, and Robin Widdows experienced a problematic wheel. Also listed in the programme was Lord Cross, who was meant to be driving a 4.7-litre Ford-powered Kincraft, but he was another who did not start.

As the first of the thirty-seven laps in this one hundred-mile race got under way, it was Gethin who was first to see Old Hall corner, leaving Hobbs and Paul Hawkins (Racing) Ltd's team driver, Mike Hailwood, in a red Lola T142, to fight for second place. Mike Walker slotted his blue Lola into fourth as proceedings began, with Willie Forbes, in a yellow-coloured but mechanically identical car, chasing behind. Walker was one of the first to have problems, his Chevrolet engine began to overheat on the ninth lap and he was overtaken by virtually the whole field. Six laps later, however, Forbes' progress was halted when he crashed at Knicker Brook. Hailwood became another luckless Lola driver when he broke a drive shaft at the same place as Forbes' accident on lap twenty, which allowed Keith Holland to take over third place. Holland spun at Druids, but after recovering, he managed to overcome the whole of the remaining field to finish in that position.

*Peter Gethin leads the first ever Formula 5000 race in the UK, at Oulton Park in 1969. (Courtesy Frank Hall)*

*David Hobbs shows just how big wings were in 1969. (Courtesy Frank Hall)*

*Jock Russell lost his wing early on – a sign of things to come? (Courtesy Frank Hall)*

*But Keith Holland kept his wing intact, for this race anyway. (Courtesy Frank Hall)*

*Bev Bond felt the same way as Jock Russell and went wingless. (Courtesy Norman Hayes)*

*Ian Mitchell was part of the wingless revolution, too. (Courtesy Norman Hayes)*

As the chequered flag fell, only the orange-liveried car of Gethin and Hobbs' red and white mount had completed the full race distance, their places unchanged from the opening lap. Holland, deputising for Tony Lanfranchi, was four laps down in his blue and white version of the Huntingdon-built car. Only four other cars were running when the race finished: Hardwick in his 5.0-litre Lola, Ulf Norinder in a 4.9-litre version, and fellow Swede Horst Kroll and Mike Walker driving T142 cars that carried similar engines to that of the winner.

*Mike Hailwood was out to make a name for himself at Brands Hatch. (Author's collection)*

A few days later, on Easter Monday, the series moved on to the Grand Prix circuit at Brands Hatch. The entry list looked better than the previous meeting, but when it came to the start of qualifying, only three more cars were present. One notable absentee was Colin Crabbe, who was meant to drive a converted BRM H16.

Once again, Gethin and Hobbs were seen at the top of the grid after qualifying, but this time it was the McLaren driver who took pole position. This meant the red and white car was alongside him again, although Hobbs only managed two laps in the first session before the gearbox broke on his car. Hailwood's car had been repaired following its misfortunes at Oulton Park, and he was a close third. De Adamich, in a similarly repaired Surtees TS5, fared a lot better than on his previous outing by starting one place lower than the former motorcycle champion. Lamplough repeated his Oulton Park feat by being the quickest non-5.0-litre qualifier, but when the race started he had two more people in front of him than he had had at the opening round in Cheshire.

As the flag was waved to set them loose, the top three left the line and disputed the lead. Hobbs' Surtees broke an upright after nine of the forty laps, and he drove slowly back to the pits as lap ten began. It was Hailwood who next came to a halt with engine problems, thus leaving Gethin to ease his car to the line for the remaining distance without too much difficulty. With Holland and Norinder in their Lolas competing for the runner-up spot, the contest came to an abrupt halt when the Swede, Norinder, had to pit at the end of lap fifteen as he had punctured a tyre. That left Holland alone in second place, circulating in northern Kent in the same way as the leader, Gethin, was. The McLaren driver powered through the field and, as the chequered flag fell, only those two were on the same lap. Forbes took the remaining podium place a couple of laps down. Lamplough, who had had gear problems throughout the race, was a further two laps down in his Lotus but was the next to see the flag. Hardwick and Chris Summers were fifth and sixth respectively, whilst de Adamich recovered from a series of mishaps to finish seventh.

Before the next round of the series, Forbes returned to Scotland to ensure his car was ready to drive again, and he entered the two-part Edinburgh Charities Cup race at Ingliston on 13 April. The main opposition on the day came from Graham Birrell, who drove an Ecurie Ecosse Formula 2 Brabham BT23C, and Richard Scott's Formula 3 BT21. At the head of the results for both fifteen lappers, though, was Forbes, who won both events despite Birrell clocking the fastest lap in the first part. In the subsequent part, Forbes broke Birrell's lap record by one second and in breaking it, set a new outright lap record for the circuit; his time was 49.8 seconds, equivalent to 74.46mph.

*Willie Forbes leads Graham Birrell at Ingliston. (Courtesy Eric Bryce)*

The Kent track was also the venue for round three on 11 May, on this occasion using the Club circuit for two forty-one lappers, each with a distance of fifty miles. The results of both were amalgamated to provide the overall winner. Hobbs was otherwise employed driving for James Garner's Formula A team in America, so a former Lotus Grand Prix driver, Trevor Taylor, was drafted in to replace him at this meeting. Also making his first appearance in a Formula 5000 car in Europe was the Australian, Frank Gardner. Lanfranchi was present this time to make his Formula 5000 debut, driving the four-wheel drive, 4.5-litre Oldsmobile-powered Hepworth that Bev Bond had driven at the opening round, whilst Holland continued in the Lola that Lanfranchi was originally meant to drive in the earlier rounds.

A wet practice session meant that the drivers had only two flying laps to show what they could do. Trevor Taylor made the best impression and put his Surtees TS5 on pole with Gardner and Gethin alongside him. Taylor's joy turned to despair, however, and he didn't appear for the heats after it was revealed that he had burned out his clutch in the pre-race warm-up. This left Gethin to out-drag the Aussie as the race got under way. De Adamich and Holland kept the pressure on Gardner but, at the end of the opening heat, the top two positions remained unchanged as the flag fell. Holland started to drop back leaving de Adamich to pursue the top two, but the best he could do was to record a close third, with Holland, Mike Walker and Norinder following in that order. After an accident on lap four in the heat, when Jock Russell hit the marshal's post at Paddock Hill Bend, the Scot announced his immediate retirement from race driving.

As the cars lined up for the start of the second heat, Gardner was found on the grid without the customary wings on his Lola, as the rear wing had collapsed during the warm-up lap. Consequently, the start was delayed, which allowed Gardner's mechanics to remove the part and take off the front wing as well. This didn't seem to hamper his performance, as it was his turn to lead into Paddock Hill Bend first. Mike Walker and Holland followed the leading pair into the first turn. Lap ten, however, saw the McLaren M10A driver, Gethin, take the place at the head of the queue of cars, with Holland following him through the pack. Ten laps later it was Holland who was at the front, but he spun at Clearways just before the tenth anniversary of his lead, leaving Gethin to take the win ahead of Gardner. Holland recovered to finish third. Norinder was next to see the flag, followed by Forbes and then Lanfranchi.

When the results were combined, the top three overall were the same three that finished the second heat in front of everyone else. They were followed by, in order, Norinder, Lamplough, Lanfranchi, Mike Walker, Hardwick and John Dean in a Cooper-Shelby-Ford T66. Gethin also recorded the fastest lap of the day, 47 seconds, which equalled an average of 94.98mph, and he obviously held the championship lead. With £500 and 500 points for a race win, he and his team were £1500 better off at this stage of the season. Holland stood second, 650 points behind after his second and third places in the early rounds, with Hardwick a further 410 points in arrears.

Leicestershire was the host county for the fourth round of the inaugural championship on Bank Holiday Monday, 26 May, when it arrived at Mallory Park. It, too, had a two-heat contest with points awarded on the aggregate of both races. After qualifying, Gethin was once again on the front row accompanied by de Adamich and Hobbs, who was back after his absence. Mike Walker was alone on the second row after the Brabham BT30 driver, Peter Westbury, who had qualified fourth, was not allowed to start as it was felt his entry had not been made in time. The former British Olympic bobsleigher and the current season's Formula 2 driver, Robin Widdows, was also in the entry list in another Lola T142. He lost the nose cone after he clipped the kerb at the Devil's Elbow during the opening practice session that caused a delay to the day's proceedings.

As the first heat started it was inevitably Gethin who was the first to show. Hobbs chased his every move but was unable to prevent him from winning by over eleven seconds. Mike Walker overcame de Adamich to take third place, and he and Widdows were the next to cross the line, third and fourth respectively. De Adamich had more problems with his Surtees when lapping Carlos Avallone's T140/2, and finished sixth behind Forbes. Amongst the others, Lamplough was two laps down in seventh, Wrexham's Dave Berry was next, followed by Steve Thompson and Holland.

For the second heat, Avallone was pushed off the grid and not allowed to start. With rain falling, when the race did eventually begin it wasn't Gethin who was the first to get away this time. That particular honour went to Hobbs. As in the first heat, with these two battling against one another it was a close call to see who would emerge triumphant at the end. With the pair starting to meet backmarkers, it was the McLaren driver, Widdows, who made the best pass of one of them on lap twenty-seven. Hobbs was not to be outdone as, six laps later, it was his turn to out-brake Gethin as another, Hardwick, was encountered. As the pair approached Gerrards on the last lap, however, Hardwick was in the way yet again, and Hobbs caught Hardwick's rear wheel. Gethin made the most of the opportunity as he got past the pair of them to see the chequered flag almost one-and-a-half seconds before the Surtees man. Both drivers had lapped the entire field, and it was Mike Walker's blue Alan McKechnie Racing Lola-Chevrolet that was nearest to them. Widdows looked set for fourth, but with his wet weather tyres failing to keep grip on a drying track, he dropped back to seventh place. His finish meant that he was placed fifth overall behind Hobbs' team-mate de Adamich. New entrant Berry was tenth overall.

From Mallory Park to Silverstone isn't a terribly long way, but it was twenty days before the series reached the Northamptonshire circuit to compete for the BRSCC's Vanwall Trophy. The time and distance, however, didn't seem to bother Church Farm Racing, as it was a case of 'business as usual' in practice for the thirty-five lap race. Its driver, Gethin, posted a time of 1 minute 26.6 seconds to take a close pole position. De Adamich equalled this, and should have been alongside him for the race, but in achieving the time he had also blown his engine and, with no spare engine available to the team, he could not start the race. Mike Walker was third fastest, less than a second slower. Trevor Taylor was substituting for Hobbs again as de Adamich's team-mate, and although he was less than half a second slower than the top three, he was found next. Deputising for Widdows, and making an appearance in a Formula 2 Brabham BT30, was Alan Rollinson. His intended car was a T142 but he had been forced to start at the back of the grid after blowing up the Lola.

Tony Brooks gave a display of the car that gave the race its title before proceedings began, and Gethin was intent on making it five wins in a row. This looked a distinct possibility as he shot away from the line. On lap five though, the clutch burned out on his McLaren, and the sequence was no longer a possibility. This left the former number two to Jim Clark at the Lotus Formula 1 team, Trevor Taylor, to stretch a lead he never looked like losing until he, too, had clutch problems, four laps after Gethin's retirement. Mike Walker took up the cudgels, quickly followed by Norinder and Rollinson, and efficiently disposed of everyone in front of him. The Swede was the last one Rollinson passed, and then Forbes followed him as well, but neither could catch the blue Lola before the chequered flag was shown. Norinder held on to take fourth with Lamplough following him across the line. Holland was sixth and still the nearest to Gethin in the championship standings with 1055 points to Gethin's 2050; the extra 50 points coming from this race despite his non-finish.

The Guards Formula 5000 Championship travelled across the Irish Sea to Mondello Park for the first of its European rounds of the season on 13 July. Organised by Leinster Motor Club, together with tobacco manufacturer Rothmans and a company called Motor Racing Circuits, two forty-two lap heats constituted the Dublin Grand Prix.

This time it was Gethin who was missing from the grid, as he was a bit further across the sea. He was preparing for a Formula A event at Elkhart Lake in the USA, in which he would go on to break the lap record, but sadly fail to complete. Hobbs was back, though, from a stint that gave him a third place at Le Mans 24-Hour race. Taking full advantage of Gethin's absence, he and de Adamich set the pace in qualifying. The Englishman took pole position with Holland nearest to the two Surtees drivers. Rollinson continued in a Brabham BT30, whilst an older car from the former Formula 1 World Champion's works, a BT23, driven by Ireland's own Tommy Reid, made up the second row of the grid. John Watson was also present in a BMW-powered Lola T100, but he broke a valve in his engine during qualifying and was unable to take part in the race. After mishaps in practice, the two Mikes, Hailwood and Walker, missed qualifying and had to start from the back.

On a very hot day, Hobbs showed how good he was by streaking into a lead he never lost in the first heat, with his team colleague, de Adamich, almost twenty-five seconds behind. Holland was farther back still and, despite the close attention of Rollinson, came home third. Hailwood and Mike Walker made impressive gains and finished behind Rollinson in that order, with the latter having to be helped out of his car as the heat had got to him. Reid, however, failed to finish, as his car had gear problems that also prevented him from further competition.

In the second heat, Hobbs repeated his action of the first, but his team-mate wasn't so lucky; a broken clutch ended his race just after it had started. Holland took up the position following the Italian's misfortune. A great start by Hailwood propelled him into third place, temporarily, behind Holland, who subsequently spun on lap three. Rollinson and Mike Walker followed these two, but a broken drive shaft on the eleventh tour forced the Lola driver to retire. Two laps after that, Hobbs started to have trouble with his car, allowing Hailwood to assume the lead. Rollinson took twenty-four more laps to catch and pass the ailing TS5, but the 1600cc Brabham was unable to catch the T142 of Hailwood. Hobbs hung on to finish third in what turned out to be his last race of the 1969 Guards Formula 5000 Championship, as he was needed to compete in the American Formula A Championship instead.

Once again the results were combined, and it was the America-bound Hobbs who was the winner when they were taken as a whole. Hailwood's win in the second heat, when coupled with his fifth place in the first leg, was enough to give him the points for second place, whilst Rollinson's consistency paid off for third.

Western Europe beckoned for the next two meetings. Firstly it was Belgium that hosted these cars, potentially capable of 200mph, when a double-header of two twenty-two-lap rounds were presented in Koksijde, near Oostende, on 3 August. Both Gethin and Hobbs were away this time, at the New York state circuit in Lime Rock, and they were joined there by Lamplough, who took part in the Formula B race. In Belgium, however, and despite bad weather which curtailed the qualifying session after just twenty minutes, Surtees cars made up the front row again, with de Adamich and Trevor Taylor separated by one-and-a-half seconds in that order. A couple of seconds later followed a trio of Huntingdon's finest, piloted by Mike Walker, Norinder and Rollinson. The latter drove the car that had taken Hardwick to fourth place at the opening round, after he had been told that his Brabham cars were no longer eligible. Hailwood and Holland were a little farther back in their Lolas, too.

With the weather on race morning a big improvement on the previous day, an extra practice session was arranged which clearly delayed the start of the race. When it did finally start, however, Trevor Taylor showed why he had been chosen by Colin Chapman to drive for his Formula 1 team. With the TS5, he shot into a lead that he never lost, despite a coughing engine. De Adamich had some trouble with his car as well, but he, too, hung on to complete the race in the same position as he had started. Rollinson overcame the two in front of him to finish third, despite losing out to Hailwood early on. Rollinson's green car took the place vacated by the red one when the latter suffered electrical problems and was forced to retire at half-distance. Not that it was easy; Holland was just four-tenths behind when they passed the chequered flag.

Heat two was a slightly different variation on the theme seen in heat one. Trevor Taylor led once more as the race started, but this time it was the Italian driving a red and white Surtees who took over the lead on the second lap. Sadly, de Adamich's joy wasn't to last, as on lap five he was forced to go into the pits with a broken tyre valve. This gave the lead back to his 'new' team-mate, and the win into the bargain. De Adamich reappeared to finish sixth, and he also set a new lap record. Hailwood, Holland, Rollinson and Norinder were keen to make their mark and pressed hard, and it was the last of this quartet who came closest to Trevor Taylor as the flag fell. But Rollinson once again was third on the road. This became second to Trevor Taylor when the results of both legs were added together, with Holland in third. Local driver, Jan van Straaten, drove a 4.7-litre Lotus-Ford 24, and was classed thirteenth overall.

One week later, many of the series protagonists were at the Dutch seaside circuit at Zandvoort for two twenty-lap contests. This time pole position was taken by Hailwood, only two-tenths of a second faster than the now acceptably-entered Westbury. Another substitute appeared for Team Surtees, Derek Bell, who was racing in place of de Adamich, and he wasn't too far behind either. Van Straaten was also present to see if he could make an improvement on his previous performance. He qualified fourteenth, but failed to make the race as problems incurred in practice couldn't be repaired in time.

Very hot weather welcomed the crowd on race day, and most watched from the dunes rather than the grandstands. Westbury was consumed by Bell and Trevor Taylor as proceedings commenced, and it was these two who took the fight to Hailwood. Bell overcame the Lola man on the opening lap, but the Le Mans ace was soon overtaken himself. A problem with the car saw him retire shortly afterwards. Trevor Taylor and Westbury watched closely, waiting to pounce on any mistake their adversary made. Their patience was rewarded on lap twelve when gear selection problems beset Hailwood, who was driving for the newly formed Epstein-Cuthbert Racing team. Trevor Taylor shook the Brabham driver off his tail on lap twenty, and went on to make it three wins in a row on European soil with Westbury 4.3 seconds farther down the road. Hailwood had continued to race, and looked to have made it on to the podium until the final lap when Norinder came past the ailing Lola to take third place away from him.

Trevor Taylor scored his second double win in the Benelux countries in heat two, repeating his performance of the first heat at Koksidje the week before. Hailwood's car had been repaired and although he caught and passed Westbury, he was unable to do the same with Trevor Taylor. The top three remained in the same order as the flag fell, but Westbury was placed second on aggregate ahead of Hailwood, thanks to his second- and third-place finishes on the day.

Despite the two aggregate wins by Trevor Taylor, it was one of the absentees, Gethin, who still led the championship, on 2050 points, when it returned to Britain. Holland had edged closer, now only 345 points behind. Hobbs was drifting out of the picture but was still in third place. Trevor Taylor's fine form placed him fifth in the standings, with 955 points fewer than Gethin.

Formula 5000 cars made up almost half of the grid at the Oulton Park Gold Cup race on 16 August, the rest being a mixture of machinery from Formulas 1 and 2. De Adamich and Trevor Taylor were there in their Surtees cars, accompanied by Hailwood, Mike Walker, Holland, and Forbes. Jackie Oliver made his Formula 5000 debut in Norinder's Lola. Rollinson was also present, but drove a Formula 2 BT20. De Adamich proved the fastest of his peers, and lined up on the grid alongside Jochen Rindt's Lotus 63, having been fifth fastest overall. Oliver was next, with an identical time to the Italian, but on row three with Trevor Taylor.

As the flag fell it was the Formula 1 Brabham BT26 of Jacky Ickx that stormed into the lead, with Jackie Stewart and Rindt not too far behind. De Adamich led the Formula 5000 queue with Oliver in close attendance. Hailwood and Holland had another Formula 1 Brabham, a BT24, in front of them; this one, driven by Silvio Moser, had previously been owned by Frank Williams. Forbes spun his Lola into a ditch at Druids on the opening lap, reducing the small field even further. As the race progressed, it looked like de Adamich was giving the Formula 1 men the most to think about, particularly after Oliver spun at Old Hall as the cars began lap four. He continued, but had to rejoin at the end of the field. With Moser still between the Italian and the other Formula 5000 cars, it was Hailwood who was the nearest, with Trevor Taylor catching him up. Moser had problems with power and pitted on the ninth lap, leaving the way clear for the Brummie to attempt to get ahead of de Adamich, but also giving Trevor Taylor a sight of what might be possible. On lap sixteen this became a reality, as the second Surtees car managed to pass Hailwood's Lola. De Adamich was lapped by Ickx on lap twenty-seven, but that wasn't going to deny the Italian victory in the Formula 5000 class on the day, and with it the Sir James Scott-Douglas Trophy. Trevor Taylor tried to catch him but was unable to do so and finished a noteworthy second, whilst Hailwood took the third Formula 5000 podium position almost a minute after de Adamich and Taylor.

*Oulton Park without wings ... Jackie Oliver leads Silvio Moser. (Courtesy Eric Bryce)*

*More follow ... Keith Holland and Trevor Taylor with others behind. (Courtesy Eric Bryce)*

*Above: Mike Walker was hard at work, too! (Courtesy Eric Bryce)*

*Above right: Alan Rollinson also made an early Formula 5000 career appearance in Cheshire. (Courtesy Norman Hayes)*

*Trevor Taylor brought Surtees power to the track. (Courtesy Norman Hayes)*

Snetterton followed the non-championship race at Oulton by hosting the ninth round of the Guards series on Bank Holiday Monday, 1 September 1969, and it was Hailwood who took pole position in qualifying for the first heat of the day. Trevor Taylor had joined Team Elite but retained the same make of car as he had driven whilst abroad. This change hadn't slowed him any, and he was the closest to Hailwood on the grid after they both recorded the same practice time. Mike Walker completed the first row, with Rollinson and Holland on the second. Ian Ashley made his debut in the series driving a Kitchener K3. Gethin had hoped to take part but his team was unable to get the car ready in time, so he became an interested spectator. Berry was also a spectator, albeit an unwilling one, but having bent his car at Coram in practice, there was little else he could do.

The fastest pair each made a great start. As they passed the start-finish line, it was the new team's white car that led for the opening nine laps. The red car managed to get by and hold the lead for a short while, but Trevor Taylor was keen to show British fans what he had done abroad; he retook the place on lap twelve and maintained it for the remaining eight laps. Hailwood was content with second and reported handling problems after the race, whilst Mike Walker came home a lonely third. Rollinson admitted to gear selection problems afterwards, but still managed to finish fourth. Even after a push start, Ashley failed to finish after the differential seized on his car.

Heat two became virtually a repeat of the first, with the ex-TT motorcycle rider and the ex-Formula 1 driver taking turns to lead. It was the man who had been used to two wheels who finished ahead by less than a second, though. Once again it was Mike Walker who made it up the rostrum, and unsurprisingly it was the same three that were awarded the top points overall, with Trevor Taylor edging Hailwood for the £500 prize money after being faster in heat one than his rival had been in heat two. Regrettably, Ashley failed to start this heat, bringing his debut to an inauspicious end.

Forbes and Birrell were back at Ingliston for the weekend before the next Guards series event, but this time Birrell decided to compete in the Formula Libre event in a Formula Ford Crosslé 16F instead of the larger Brabham. As the race got under way, Forbes showed that he wanted to repeat his early season victory and he was never headed throughout the twenty-five-lap contest. Making an early career appearance in the Formula Ford category was Tom Walkinshaw, who was as dominant as Forbes and cruised to take the class win. Birrell retired after just two laps, but not until he had set another fastest lap for his class, which Walkinshaw equalled.

The Hockenheimring became the next circuit to welcome the Guards Championship just two weeks after it had been in East Anglia. Each of the two heats was given fifteen laps to show the 150,000-strong German crowds what Formula 5000 was made of. Listed among the entrants was Ferrari sports car driver, David Piper, in Doug Hardwick team's Lola, but he failed to show up. Another notable absentee on this occasion was Rollinson. He was racing a Brabham BT30 and winning both heats of the Churchman's Trophy in Ireland.

Gethin had returned from America and was keen to reprise his winning drives in the Church Farm Racing Team McLaren M10A, and ensure that Trevor Taylor's surge in form did not dent his title hopes. As if he had never been away, his was the name on pole position of the opening heat. He had, though, blown the head gasket on his McLaren whilst out setting his fastest lap, which gave his team some work to do before the race on Sunday. Trevor Taylor gave him something else to think about, too, putting his TS5 next to the McLaren and just two-tenths slower! Gethin's team wasn't the only one on late shift, though, as Mike Walker blew an engine. His Lola made it to the race only after the mechanics worked through the night fitting the spare engine that Norinder had offered him.

As the 4.2-mile opening lap started, it was Trevor Taylor who nudged ahead of his rival, but Gethin wasn't having any of it. The two traded the lead several times before a broken rocker put Gethin into safety mode. After being passed by Holland and Norinder, Hailwood recovered to take third, which then became second after he passed a gentle McLaren-nursing Gethin three laps from the end. Gethin managed to finish third despite his car's ailments. Mike Walker's replacement engine gave him some concerns, but he still finished ninth. This time, Ashley managed to cross the line, one place ahead of Walker.

The second heat was similarly unlucky for Gethin after he suffered the same problem as in the earlier contest, not that that was going to deter him. Despite a broken clutch, Trevor Taylor was again the first to show, with Hailwood and Holland settling in behind. Norinder took advantage of a first lap spin by Holland, though, and looked set for third place. Gethin, however, had other ideas, and on lap seven he passed the Swede and went on to repass a sick-sounding McLaren to finish third behind Hailwood and Trevor Taylor. Ashley's problems mounted when he was forced to retire after just one lap with a broken head gasket. Mike Walker repeated his placing of the earlier heat.

It was also the top three from the second heat who took the major points when the results from both heats had been added together. Trevor Taylor's victory had brought him to within 195 points of Gethin, who now led in the chase for the championship with 2250 points. With 1545 points, Hailwood had passed Mike Walker and was catching Holland as well, but it was a difference of 230 that separated that pair.

The penultimate round of the championship was held where it had begun, Oulton Park, just six days after the trip to Germany. This time, however, two twenty-lap heats were held instead of a single thirty-seven-lap affair. Rollinson was back in Doug Hardwick's Lola, having returned from Phoenix Park in Ireland where he had been doing rather well in his Brabham. He qualified fourth out of twenty cars, but behind Mike Walker, Gethin and pole-sitter Hailwood. Gethin's nearest title challenger, Trevor Taylor, was found in sixth, one place behind Holland after he had complained that his engine lacked power. Can-Am specialist Tony Dean brought along a Formula 2 Brabham BT23C, and qualified alongside Trevor Taylor to mark a fine first foray into Formula 5000. Farther down the grid was another pair of newcomers, Jim Charnock and Graham Eden, in a Brabham BT21A and Chevron B10 respectively.

*Mike Hailwood was also in Cheshire to compete for the Gold Cup ... (Courtesy Frank Hall)*

*Top left: ... Ulf Norinder tried as well ... (Courtesy Frank Hall)*

*Left: ... and Peter Gethin did, too, but his car blew up ... (Courtesy Frank Hall)*

*Top right: ... none of which bothered Ian Ashley. (Courtesy Frank Hall)*

*Top: Kaye Griffiths had a few outings in 1969 ... (Courtesy Norman Hayes)*

*Middle: ... as did Mike Coombs. (Courtesy Norman Hayes)*

*Bottom: Steve Thompson also began his Formula 5000 career in 1969. (Courtesy Norman Hayes)*

Gethin made the best start and led as the cars approached Old Hall for the first time, closely shadowed by Hailwood. The red car spun at Druids on lap three, though, which allowed the rest of the top six to pass by before he could rejoin. Trevor Taylor was out to take a fifth victory in succession, he made light work of those ahead until lap six when the gremlins took over and he had to retire. His bad luck gave Mike Walker the chance to chase the McLaren, and he almost overcame it as the flag fell. Holland and Rollinson had been having an intense fight for third place, but they were both passed by Hailwood as he fought to get back on terms. At the end, that place went the way of the former motorcyclist, with the other two finishing almost in unison, but as Holland was slightly in front, he was awarded third position. Such was Hailwood's determination to finish at the top of the field that he equalled the lap record set by Gethin at the season's opening meeting, lapping in a time of 1 minute 31.2 seconds, equivalent to 108.99mph!

Despite the heroic efforts in heat one, Hailwood failed to appear for heat two as it transpired that he had damaged the car whilst spinning for a second time on the penultimate lap of that event. Trevor Taylor also missed the second heat, thus harming his chances of wrestling the title from Gethin. When the flag dropped, none of this concerned Mike Walker, and it was he who got away from the line ahead of everyone else. Gethin, though, had his eye on the first place prize money as well as the championship, and he soon caught and passed the Lola driver. At half-distance, however, his efforts proved to be in vain as his engine blew up. This allowed Mike Walker to retake the lead that led to victory, with Rollinson overcoming Holland on this occasion to finish second. Norinder was fourth and Derrick Williams fifth, Ashley this time finished sixth.

Once more, the top three finishers in the second heat became the top three points scorers when the times were aggregated. Going in to the final round of the season, Gethin led the championship with 2305 points, Trevor Taylor was now 200 points in arrears and Holland was a further 205 behind. Mike Walker and Hailwood had swapped places again as a result of his win in Cheshire; Walker was 460 points behind Gethin.

Brands Hatch, on 28 September, was the venue for the season finale with only the top two drivers able to become the first Guards Formula

5000 Champion. Gethin stated his intention when he took pole position for the first of the two twenty-lap heats on the Grand Prix circuit. Hailwood intervened in the battle when he took the second grid position, with Trevor Taylor beside him. Only four-tenths of a second separated the three of them. Rollinson and Holland made up the second row, whilst the Oulton winner, Mike Walker, started from the back. He had failed to record a time due to pulling off before completing the qualifying lap as his car had had no oil pressure.

Trevor Taylor and Gethin got ahead of Hailwood as the race started, which meant that the title rivals had only themselves to worry about as the race progressed. Mike Walker failed to complete the opening lap before his engine said that it had done enough. At the sharp end, Trevor Taylor was leading Gethin on the approach to Westfield on lap nine when they came up behind a back marker, Chris Warwick-Drake, in a Cooper T90. Taylor went to the inside line and Gethin went to the other but all three tangled, and neither Taylor nor Gethin came through the ensuing melee. Drake continued to the pits, but his race was over as well. This meant that Hailwood led, with a procession of Lola drivers behind him, and he went on to take the win that had eluded him all season. Holland kept Rollinson at bay to record second place, just two-tenths of a second in front but over thirty seconds off the pace set by Hailwood.

The damage to Gethin and Trevor Taylor's cars following their accident in heat one was sufficient to render their drivers temporarily unemployed for the second. Gethin, therefore, could not be overtaken in the championship standings, and this gave him a further prize of £2000 for taking the title. The race, though, still had its own prize money to compete for, and Rollinson staked first claim for the largest share of it as he sped into the lead. Hailwood, however, had his eyes on the £500 first prize, too, and on lap six managed to pass Rollinson. It was then Rollinson's turn to give chase, and after Hailwood spun at Stirlings, he retook the lead, but 'Mike the Bike' was not about to give up, and with three laps remaining he came past again to take the flag ahead of his fellow Midlander. Holland finished third, and the overall positions were once again the same as those of this second heat. Williams, Terry Sanger and Ashley took the final points-scoring and money-earning places.

One week later, Ingliston held its last meeting of the season. Forbes was there in his Lola, looking to end the season on a high note in the forty-lap Formula Libre contest. Unfortunately, things didn't go quite as planned, and on the grid at the start of the race he found himself behind Brabham BT30 driver Reid, Scott and Mo Nunn. As proceedings began he managed to get in front of Nunn, but couldn't find a way to pass the other two, and finished over twenty seconds behind the pair with Irishman Reid being the winner.

With the drivers counting only their best eight scores towards their championship ambitions at the end of the season, the top ten of the Guards series looked like this:

| Position | Driver | Car | Engine | Points |
|---|---|---|---|---|
| 1 | Peter Gethin | McLaren M10A | 5.0 Chevrolet | 2365 |
| 2 | Trevor Taylor | Surtees TS5 | 5.0 Chevrolet | 2170 |
| 3 | Mike Hailwood | Lola T142 | 5.0 Chevrolet | 2045 |
| 4 | Keith Holland | Lola T142 | 5.0 Chevrolet | 2000 |
| 5 | Alan Rollinson | Brabham BT30<br>Lola T142 | 1.6 Ford FVA<br>5.0 Chevrolet | 1920 |
| 6 | Mike Walker | Lola T142 | 5.0 Chevrolet | 1845 |
| 7 | Ulf Norinder | Lola T142 | 5.0 Chevrolet | 1450 |
| 8 | David Hobbs | Surtees TS5 | 5.0 Chevrolet | 1275 |
| 9 | Willie Forbes | Lola T142 | 5.0 Chevrolet | 1080 |
| 10 | Robs Lamplough | Lotus 43<br>Lotus 41 | 4.7 Ford<br>1.6 Ford FVA | 795 |

# CHAPTER 2
## THE STORY CONTINUES

In 1970 the scoring system changed, as did the prize money, and the championship was renamed the Guards European Formula 5000 Championship. To earn points the drivers had to finish in the top six in the series that was now extended to twenty rounds, and the points awarded were the same as in the Grand Prix of the day, 9-6-4-3-2-1. Prize money had increased to £5000 for races of over one hundred miles, and £2500 for those of fewer than that. To count towards the title the drivers' best ten scores in the longer races, and best four in the shorter events, were used.

Thirty-six entrants were listed in *Autosport* in February 1970, a list which grew to forty-one when the magazine gave a report of Gethin's 1969 victory party on 5 March. This year there was a driver bearing the number 1 on his car which had not been the case the previous year because there had been no reigning champion. Peter Gethin was the recipient of that honour, following his overwhelming success in 1969 in what was nicknamed 'Formula Gethin'.

Gone was the McLaren M10A entered by Church Farm Racing, though, replaced by a M10B built by the New Zealand Formula 1 driver's company that Sid Taylor entered on behalf of Gethin. Charles Lucas was given number two, although in the end he didn't compete at all and Graham McRae took that number when he joined the series. The Mikes, Hailwood and Walker, were three and four respectively. After campaigning two different cars in 1969, Alan Rollinson had reportedly signed a contract with Lotus Components to drive the Colin Chapman-designed Type 70 for the new season, and he was given number seventy.

In another change to the rules, cars with engines of less than two-litre capacity were banned this year, so each engine was over 4500cc. Huge aerofoils had been outlawed mid-way through the previous season, so designers had to find other methods to make their cars go faster and maintain road holding.

Good Friday came early in 1970, on 27 March, but it was once again the date set-aside at Oulton Park for the opening round of the series in a meeting that was called the BRSCC Guards 5000 Guineas Car Races. Twenty entrants and three reserves were listed in the programme and twenty cars took part in the opening practice session, although only fifteen were present when the first heat started. Although he failed to show for the opening round, only Keith Holland from the 1969 top six kept the same car as he had campaigned in that year, as his new season car wasn't ready. Rollinson was included in the programme and he was shown as being entered by himself and not by Lotus Components, but his car was a Lotus with a 4997cc Chevrolet power plant. He didn't manage to get to the circuit in time for practice, so started from the back. There was an international feel to the grid as well, as 'Kiwi' Howden Ganley entered and drove another of his fellow countryman Bruce McLaren's M10B cars. Ulf Norinder from Sweden was also back.

The Lola T142 had been replaced with the T190 for most of the men who were in the top ten, although there were still plenty of last year's model to be seen on the grid as they lined up for qualifying for the first part of the equally-divided forty-lap race. Norinder was found in one of the new Lolas, and he entered Ian Ashley as well as himself. Ashley used the Swede's T142 from the previous year. Also making an appearance was future Indy Car team owner, Maurice ('Mo') Nunn, in a T190 provided by Doug Hardwick. Hardwick himself did not compete, but had taken over the role of team owner and, as well as Nunn, he entered Davey Powell in a Vegantune-powered T142. Trevor Taylor continued to campaign a Surtees, the TS5A this time. Gordon Spice drove a Kitchiner K3A that Tony Kitchiner himself had built, having had some small success with Ashley in a K3 the previous year.

Gethin was there to try and underline how good he was, and seemed to have done so by planting his car on pole position. Mike Walker kept him in his sights by lining up along aside him in a similar machine, but four-tenths slower than the reigning champion. Hailwood was now a works driver for Lola, and he made up the front row. Trevor Taylor continued for John Surtees' team, and he and Norinder made up row two on a 3-2-3 grid formation. Rollinson also returned, but at the back of the grid after the engine in his brand new Lotus 70 had given him some problems before qualifying which meant he was unable to set a time. Ashley, though, had a big accident at Hill Top during this period that wrote the car off, but fortunately the driver appeared unscathed. Mac Daghorn was another non-starter after he destroyed his Leda Mk 20 at Clay Hill. He, too, walked away, despite his heavy impact against the Armco and banking.

As race proceedings got under way, it was Mike Walker who led the pack with Gethin and Hailwood in hot pursuit. Trevor Taylor had clutch problems and had to have a push. Rollinson made a great start and was up to fifth on the opening lap, Avallone, however, had disappeared as the cars came round for the second lap, and palls of black smoke were seen at Clay Hill. The Lola had become airborne and burst into flames as it landed. The marshals were quick to react and the Brazilian escaped with minor burns to his legs. Back to the race, and Gethin's chase bore fruit on lap four, and on lap five Walker was down in third place as Hailwood also found a way past the Alan McKechnie Racing-entered driver at Knicker Brook. The weather played its part halfway through, and the drivers had to contend not just with rain but snow as well. This caught out Hailwood who crashed at Hill Top, but not before he passed the reigning champion on lap eleven at Knicker Brook. Gethin was having trouble keeping his car pointing ahead as well, and had Mike Walker breathing down his neck now. Walker managed to pass, and went on to record the first heat win of the new season. Gethin carried on carefully and took second place, whilst Norinder was third, a lap behind the top two. Ganley and Forbes took the next two places, whilst Spice was sixth.

Heat two was held on a damp track, and even fewer cars appeared than in the first heat. The cold and damp conditions caused Norinder to spin out at Clay Hill whilst circulating on the warm-up lap, meaning only seven cars contested the twenty-lap heat. Gethin wasn't about to make the same mistakes as he had previously, and took off at the start and into a lead he never lost. Mike Walker, however, was second, and a lot closer to Gethin than the number 1 driver had been to

Walker in the first heat, so after aggregation it was Mike Walker who gave his McLaren a winning debut to the season. Gethin was placed second overall, and Howden Ganley made it a McLaren 1-2-3 when he finished third in this heat, one place higher than in the previous one. David Prophet was fourth, whilst Forbes and Spice recorded the same finishing positions as in the opener. Rollinson was left to rue his luck after having to pit in both heats, and he went home without a point.

*Lining up for the start at Oulton Park in spring 1970, Mikes Hailwood and Walker are on the front row. (Courtesy Brian Watson)*

*Waiting to go ... Mo Nunn. (Courtesy Norman Hayes)*

*Switching to Lotus power, Mike Hailwood leads Trevor Taylor at Lodge Corner, Oulton Park. (Author's collection)*

*Below, left: Howden Ganley from New Zealand came to join the fun. (Author's collection)*

*Above: Meanwhile, Ulf Norinder returned to the Rothmans Championship. (Courtesy Frank Hall)*

Round two was another two-heat, twenty-lap affair, and was held a few days after the opening round at Oulton, at Brands Hatch, on Easter Monday. The same two dominated practice, and it was no surprise to see them on the front row. Trevor Taylor's Surtees was now a TS5A, and he used it to great effect to share the front row with the two McLarens. Although shown in the programme for the opening round, the other Kiwi, McRae, waited until this meeting before entering the

*Left: Mo Nunn finally made it onto the track. (Courtesy Norman Hayes)*

series in yet another of Bruce's cars. He qualified seventh behind Ganley, Hailwood and Norinder, whilst Daghorn, Ashley and Avallone paid the price for their incidents in Cheshire and had no cars to drive. Lingard Goulding, Holland and Fred Place were also on the entry list. Rollinson's bad luck continued when he went off hard at Hawthorn Bend; it wrote off the car but fortunately the driver was unhurt. Place failed to make the starting grid, too, when he crashed his Cooper after the brakes had locked-on.

When the cars lined up for the first heat, only two sat on a cold and windy Kentish front row. Gethin was on pole, but Trevor Taylor was an absentee due to a lack of oil pressure in his car. Mike Walker took the lead as the flag fell, with Gethin again being the nearest of his pursuers. Three laps in, however, the positions were reversed, and things got worse as first Hailwood, then Ganley and McRae found a way past. Electrical problems for the new entrant forced him to stop on lap twelve, however, and Mike Walker was back in fourth place. Hailwood and Ganley couldn't make an impression on Gethin, and the finishing order remained the same. Norinder recorded fifth place, whilst Holland's dice with Spice resulted in a sixth position for the previous championship's fourth-placed man. Gethin also set the fastest lap of the race, lapping the Grand Prix circuit in 1 minute 29.6 seconds, two seconds inside the lap record that he had set the year before.

Mike Walker and Spice made contact at Paddock Hill Bend on the opening lap of the second heat which saw the pair eliminated on the spot, giving Gethin the chance to open a lead. Hailwood kept him honest until the closing laps, when the T190 had little answer to Gethin's M10B, and he came across the line almost three-and-a-half seconds behind. McRae started from the back of the grid and got up a head of steam that had carried him up to third place. On the last but one tour, however, that steam evaporated as the electrics on the car once again failed, and he had to stop. Ganley kept the honour of New Zealand intact, however, when he was next to see the chequered flag. Norinder went one place better than in the first heat and, despite not crossing the finish line, McRae was placed fifth. Forbes was sixth.

Obviously the top three overall were the top three from each heat, with Norinder, Holland and Nunn making up the points-scoring positions in that order. Following his victory here and his second place a few days earlier in Cheshire, Gethin, however, was now in his customary position at the top of the championship standings. Mike Walker maintained second, but just 1 point behind him was Ganley.

Zolder in Belgium was the venue for round three of the European Championship, on 4 April, and Frank Gardner came along with a yellow Lola T190 for his first Formula 5000 race of the new season. He wasn't quick enough to prevent a McLaren M10B from taking pole position, although he was on the far side of the front row. Pole belonged to Gethin, with Hailwood in between the pair. McRae and Ganley made it an all-McLaren second row, whilst Mike Walker, Trevor Taylor and Norinder were on row three. Teddy Pilette was due to take part in Norinder's T142, but he failed to show up.

Snow looked likely again as race morning dawned, but this time most of the teams had prepared the cars for it, so it was no real surprise to see Gethin hit the front as soon as proceedings got under way. Gardner got ahead of Hailwood, and his fellow Southern Hemisphere driver, McRae, came through into fourth place after displacing Trevor Taylor. Early in the first heat, though, Gethin lost the lead to the Aussie, Gardner, but the reigning champion wasn't about to relinquish it easily, and around half-distance he again squeezed ahead of his rival. As the track began to dry out, however, oil-pressure problems spelled the end of Gardner's challenge on lap thirteen, leaving Hailwood, McRae and the impressive Ganley to pressure Gethin for the win. McRae got ahead of Hailwood as the laps counted down, with Ganley exercising a bit of pressure on the Englishman. Two laps from the end the pressure told as Hailwood spun on a wet patch, making a 2-3 for New Zealand behind Gethin as the flag fell.

Gethin followed his first heat victory with an equally impressive success in heat two. Hailwood made up for his disappointment, despite being passed by McRae on the second lap, but more electrical problems saw the McLaren driver's retirement half a dozen laps later. Hailwood circulated untroubled this time, and he crossed the line immediately after Gethin. Once more Ganley took third place.

At the end it was Gethin who was the 9-point earner, whilst Ganley's consistency brought him a further 6 and Hailwood was third, having earned 4 more. All of this meant that Gethin led the series with 24 points, 10 more than his nearest rival, Ganley, and 14 more than Hailwood, who lay in third position. Mike Walker lay in fourth with 9 points.

Scotland's motor racing season opened at Ingliston on 10 April, and Forbes took his Lola T142 along to contest the Edinburgh Students Charity Cup twenty-lap Formula Libre race. His biggest threat came from Graham Birrell in a Formula 2 Brabham BT30, but in the end it was the bigger car that saw the flag first. Both shared the fastest lap of the race, 50.2 seconds, equivalent to 73.86mph.

The Netherlands track at Zandvoort was the next stop on the way for the championship. Although Hailwood took pole position for the first of the two contests in the programme, his race was over early when the Lola developed gearbox trouble. Gethin moved ahead of Mike Walker, taking second place that became a lead he never lost after Hailwood's demise. On lap eleven Mike Walker, too, was forced to retire, giving Gardner the place that he was never to better or lose. McRae and David Hobbs fought for the remaining podium place, but the Englishman had to make an unscheduled pit stop near the end, handing it to McRae in a similar car to Gethin, a McLaren M10B. Ganley was fourth, followed by Spice and Prophet.

The Kiwi and the returning Hobbs had a similar fight in heat two, but this time it was for second place as none of them could catch Gethin for the lead. McRae was the nearest at the end, but Hobbs succumbed to pressure from Gardner and Hailwood and was passed by each of them as the race wore on. Gardner managed to keep the works-Lola driver behind him and claimed third place, and Hobbs recovered to finish fifth with Ganley in sixth.

Gethin was the overall winner, with the Southern Hemisphere drivers, McRae and Gardner, second and third respectively. Another antipodean, Ganley, was fourth, and Hobbs had done enough only for fifth, one place above the Kitchener K3A driver, Spice.

Gethin now led the championship, with 33 points to Ganley's 17, when the cars and drivers returned to the UK a week later on 26 April. Silverstone was the venue for the combined Formula 1 and Formula 5000 Silverstone International Trophy race, although the latter runners were competing for the GKN Trophy.

If evidence was needed of how good he was, Gethin showed it by taking pole position for his class for the first of the two twenty-six lap heats. The overall pole position was taken by Chris Amon in a March 701. The races also featured the Formula 1 cars of Jack Brabham, Bruce McLaren and Graham Hill, and it was Gethin who had these and most of the others behind him on the grid. Second fastest of the Formula 5000 runners was Hailwood, and he, too, had Formula 1 drivers behind him. Rollinson had his third car in two years when he brought an untested Lotus 70 to the circuit, but failed to qualify for the race.

As far as the Formula 5000 runners were concerned, Gethin once more proved to be the one to beat. On lap four he was well ahead of his championship colleagues, as well as Graham Hill, Bruce McLaren and Jochen Rindt. Mike Walker offered some challenge, but he spun on the track at Becketts three laps before the end allowing Hailwood and Gardner to get ahead to take the minor placings of their race within the race. Walker did recover to finish fourth with Graham Hill being one of the few Formula 1 aces behind him.

Gethin made as good a start in heat two as he had in the earlier one, even keeping the Formula 1 cars behind him for a while. Jackie Stewart was the first to pass as the superior quality cars of that series began to assemble themselves. With five Formula 1 cars in front of Gethin, the Formula 5000 race came alive as Hailwood was out to go one place better in the second heat than he had in the first. This became a possibility when Gethin was forced to retire with nine of the twenty-six laps to go. Gardner, though, had other ideas, and on the twenty-second lap managed to go past Hailwood to record a class win. Hailwood held station to take his second runner-up spot of the day, with Mike Walker behind him in third position.

Despite winning none of the heats, the consistency shown by Hailwood allowed him to take the GKN Trophy home. Although Stewart won the second heat, Chris Amon in a March 701 was the recipient of the International Trophy after the first Formula 1 win of his career. Hailwood recorded the fastest Formula 5000 race lap, 1 minute 25.4 seconds, an average of 123.39mph, which compared quite favourably to Amon's 1 minute 22.1 second trip, equal to 124.18mph. The win also meant that Hailwood had leap-frogged Ganley in the championship as the latter did not score in Northamptonshire. Gethin still led, with 33 points to Hailwood's 19.

*The start of the International Trophy Race at Silverstone. Jackie Stewart leads the pack, which includes several F5000 cars. (Courtesy Eric Bryce)*

*One of the pack was Graham McRae. (Courtesy Eric Bryce)*

One week later, the series moved from Silverstone to Brands Hatch to use the Club circuit there. Gethin's car had been repaired following its Silverstone demise with a broken rocker arm, but he was unable to prevent Trevor Taylor, in a Surtees TS5A, setting the fastest lap of 46.2 seconds in qualifying for the first of the twenty-five lap races that were held exclusively for the class. Once again, though, the pole position time was equalled later in the session by another driver, Gardner this time, but with the former Formula 1 driver being the first to achieve it, the honour was his. A lap of 46.4 seconds allowed Gethin to make up the final front row place. McRae and Hailwood were two-tenths and four-tenths slower than Gethin, but it was they who made up row two. All five had bettered Gethin's 1969 race lap record of 47 seconds.

Taylor led as the cars got away from the line, and despite insistent pressure from Gethin, held them all back until lap eight when the McLaren driver managed to squeeze by at Paddock. Two laps later it was a case of déjà-vu for Trevor Taylor, when Gardner also put his car in front. Gardner, though, only lasted until lap seventeen, when a broken fuel line robbed him of the place he looked to have secured. Hailwood had been pressing Trevor Taylor for third place, which became a battle for second following Gardner's retirement, and the Lola driver achieved his aim two laps after that. Trevor Taylor hung on to third as the flag fell, despite close attention from Hobbs. Ganley was in the top six this time behind Hobbs, and McRae followed on behind him. Despite the non-finish, Gardner recorded a new lap record; one second faster than Gethin's best mark from the previous year.

A fully repaired McLaren brought Gardner into the second heat, and it was he and Gethin who fought for the lead after the Australian moved quickly through the field. His chances were enhanced after four of his rivals, Taylor, Hobbs, Hailwood and Holland, had a coming together that eliminated their chances of winning the race. Gardner continued to press Gethin, whilst Ganley and McRae worked hard for third place, which the latter eventually claimed after passing Ganley on the sixteenth tour. Gethin lowered the lap record by a further two-tenths of a second on his way to victory.

Overall, this meant that Gethin took the 9 championship points for the win, and Ganley and Hailwood once again swopped places in the overall standings. Ganley now had half the number of Gethin's points, but 2 more than Hailwood who had failed to score. Mike Walker picked up 3 more points and was closing in on the ex-motorcycle rider.

On 9 May, loud engines returned to disturb the peace at the former wartime airfield at Castle Combe in rural Wiltshire. The meeting came too early for three of the drivers who had crashed at Brands Hatch; only Holland's car had been repaired in time. Ten thousand or so came to watch, and it was Gethin who showed them his skill; once again he set the quickest lap time in practice to take the pole for the first of the two fifteen-lap heats. McRae was next to him, with

Ganley and Mike Walker making it four McLarens up at the front. With a Ford Mustang engine, Jack Broad entered a Leda LT20 for Chris Craft which had been designed by Len Terry who also designed cars for Lotus, BRM and Dan Gurney's Eagle Formula 1 project. Mike Daghorn drove a similar car, but his used a Chevrolet power plant. Both qualified quite well; the Broadspeed version achieved a start place of sixth on the grid, and Daghorn's Malaya Garage-entered car was four places further back. Goulding had an incident that saw his car take to the grass, making it irreparable in time.

As the contest began, misfortune hit Craft's car when it refused to start and he was out of the first heat, but this didn't bother the top three qualifiers. McRae was the first across the line, but by the time they approached Quarry, it was Gethin who was in front. McRae and Ganley swapped places a few times, but Walker had had trouble starting and he was running in last place. By the fifth tour, however, he had caught up with Norinder and Holland, who were running fourth and fifth respectively. He got ahead of them both before the end of lap six and started to chase the now third-placed McRae. The New Zealander wasn't about to be caught and got past his fellow countryman, so the top three finished the heat in the same order as they had started. Walker retained his position, leaving Norinder to finish next, one place ahead of Holland.

*Derrick Williams was amongst the competitors at Castle Combe. (Author's collection)*

In the second heat, the top three shuffled themselves around, with Ganley getting the better of McRae and Gethin as proceedings began. McRae spun on lap four at Quarry leaving Gethin to take over in second place, and he lost his third place to Mike Walker as well. Despite some fierce driving by Gethin, he was unable to catch Ganley and the three crossed the line in that order. Having overtaken Holland to make it into fourth place, McRae had another spin on the twelfth lap, but he managed to maintain the place and these positions remained unchanged as the flag fell. Craft took an active part this time, finishing sixth.

Both heat winners lapped their McLarens in 56.6 seconds, equal to an average of 117.03mph, and it wasn't until 1984 that their outright lap record was broken by future Formula 5000 driver, Tony Trimmer, in a 5.7-litre Lola T330. Gethin was the overall winner again after his first and second places in the heats, with Ganley and Mike Walker in second and third. McRae was awarded 3 points for fourth, whilst Holland and Norinder had a couple and a single respectively.

Round eight of the series was held at Mallory Park, on 24 May, with two of the absentees from Castle Combe, Hailwood and Trevor Taylor, back on the grid. This time, though, Ganley and Gardner were missing, as they were otherwise employed at the London circuit in Crystal Palace. Pole position still had a familiar look, though, with the other 'G-man', Gethin, again setting the fastest time, 42.8 seconds, and making up the front row with McRae. Mike Walker had one of Wiltshire's absentees next to him, Hailwood, on a 2x2x2 grid, and Trevor Taylor was one row behind with Prophet. Despite saying that he'd retired from the sport in 1969, Jock Russell was back in a brand new Lotus 70, and he was fourteenth fastest.

The effort of qualifying must have been too much for McRae's car as it did not feature when they came on to the track. This meant that Gethin was able to make a relatively unchallenged impression as the cars headed off on the first of the twenty laps. Mike Walker, was the nearest of his pursuers, but his work came undone just over half-distance. Spinning at Shaws, Walker allowed Hailwood to take the place which he then never lost, despite some very close attention from Walker. After the twentieth lap, though, Walker had to settle himself, and finished a very close third. Trevor Taylor was fourth, with the Swede, Norinder, next, despite stalling on the grid when the starter signalled the start of the race.

With the top three on the grid for the second part of the race made up from the places achieved in heat one, Gethin was left to underline his authority when he won by over eighteen seconds. Hailwood repeated his place of the first event, but this time, Trevor Taylor overcame Mike Walker and pushed the Lola driver hard before finishing third, just two-tenths down. Prophet and a rejuvenated McRae also got past Walker, to finish fourth and fifth in that order.

Gethin's pair of wins extended his lead in the championship, and made it look like he was going to repeat his feat of the previous year. Although there were still a considerable number of points for the rest to fight for, Gethin had 60 points in the bag, compared to his nearest challenger Ganley's 27. Hailwood was a further 2 points adrift after capitalising on the New Zealander's absence at Mallory so he could compete in a Formula 2 race at Crystal Palace, but unfortunately the chassis on his BT30 was slightly twisted and he decided not to race there either.

More travelling was needed by the series a week later when it shifted across the Irish Sea again for the two forty-two-lap races held at Mondello Park. Malaya Garage replaced Daghorn in its Leda car with a young American, Roy Pike, but he could not stop Gardner, back from his Touring Car racing in London, from doing well. Along with Gardner, Gethin set the fastest time in practice. Gardner was awarded pole position, though, and it was he that led for the first couple of laps until Gethin got ahead. Gethin made an uncharacteristic mistake on lap twenty-six, and the hard charging Trevor Taylor took the lead that remained unchallenged to the chequered flag. Gardner and Ganley had also made it past Gethin, and they took second and third respectively, though the series leader was able to recover his car to finish in fourth position. Pike was one who failed to finish, with Mike Walker being one of the others.

Trevor Taylor failed to make the best use of his qualifying position for the second heat, although in the end he managed to finish ahead of most of his pursuers. Gethin was the only one to be ahead of him in this heat, and with Gardner and Ganley immediately behind him, it was he who took the 9 points for the overall win. David Prophet, in another McLaren M10B, equalled Trevor Taylor's best racing lap of 55.2 seconds, and picked up the last point of the weekend when he was sixth overall. Although he lined up on the grid, Mike Walker recorded another 'DNF' when Fred Saunders' Crosslé clipped the stricken McLaren after it had previously spun in avoidance of Derrick Williams' Lola at Shell. Gethin added 6 points to his tally, whilst Gardner earned 4 for his efforts. Ganley was fourth overall, followed by Holland and Prophet.

Round ten of the Guards European Formula 5000 Championship on 6 June visited Silverstone for a pair of eighteen-lap heats that would gain the winner the Martini Trophy, as well as the 9 points. Gethin was again the fastest driver in a sixteen-car field. McRae was the next best, a few tenths in front of Gardner and Walker. Trevor Taylor's car was down on power and he posted a 'DNS', and Rollinson was in yet another car, a Surtees TS5A this time, but had to start from the back. Hailwood didn't have a car available so didn't race, whilst Ganley withdrew as a mark of respect following the death of his friend and fellow countryman, Bruce McLaren, at Goodwood a few days earlier.

With the top two qualifiers out of sight battling for the lead, it was a question of who would be bravest. McRae got in front on lap eight, but Gethin had the measure of his rival and took the place back on the following lap. The two continued to joust for the remaining nine laps before Gethin took the win. The competition behind them was just as intense, and at first it seemed that Gardner would be third, but problems with the car allowed Mike Walker and Prophet to pass. Prophet got ahead of his fellow McLaren driver shortly afterwards, and Mike Walker's misery was complete when he then spun out of the race. With Gardner now in fourth, it was Pike, at his second Formula 5000 meeting, who kept the pressure on, but he couldn't find a way to promote himself any higher up the order. Powell took sixth place in a misfiring Lola. Rollinson crawled into the pits at the end of the opening lap with a split oil tank.

A similar story existed for the second heat until McRae spun on the twelfth trip around the circuit, dropping him behind the advancing Gardner. The top three positions remained static for the remaining distance, so Gethin recorded his seventh win of the season so far. McRae was second and Gardner third, whilst Mike Walker came back to finish fourth. With the top three finishers achieving the points-winning places, newcomer Pike was fourth when the times were aggregated. Powell was fifth, whilst Forbes took the final point. Russell just missed out on the points, two laps down in seventh.

*Before the accident with Derrick Williams in Sweden, Fred Saunders in a Crosslé. (Author's collection)*

The next three rounds were held on continental Europe with Monza, Anderstorp and the Salzburgring being the venues. On 21 June at the Italian circuit where Gethin was later to record a famous Grand Prix victory, Derek Bell drove the series leader's McLaren. Gethin was driving a Formula 1 version in the Netherlands for the works Grand Prix team. Bell showed how good he was when he set the pole position time for the opening heat, and it was he who was the first to see the chequered flag after twenty laps. Mike Walker was next, followed by Ganley. For heat two, though, Bell's car broke down before the race had completed ten laps, leaving Ganley to take the lead. Mike Walker was in close attendance for the following nine, and he finally got ahead on the last lap to take victory, with Spice in third, but some way back. Only three other cars finished the heat, Saunders, Kaye Griffiths and Bob Miller, regular runners who hadn't finished in the higher placings before. Mike Walker was the overall winner, with Ganley and Pike second and third in that order.

One week later, in Sweden, Gethin was back, and it was he who was the overall winner this time in his repaired M10B. Mike Walker was second, and Pike copied the same result as at Monza. During the race, however, tragedy struck. Williams lost control of his Lola during the first lap of the second heat. He made contact with Saunders' Crosslé that sent Williams' car flying into the air, and it crashed heavily on to the track. The car burst into flames on impact and, despite the attention of the BRSCC Rescue crew and local fire marshals, they were unable to get Williams out.

Two weeks after that, Austria was the next country to be visited. Trevor Taylor, who had missed the previous two rounds, was involved in a high-speed crash when a tyre burst whilst travelling at 160mph in practice at the Salzburgring. Fortunately he emerged from the wreckage unhurt, but the car was written off so Team Surtees decided to bring its campaign to an end for 1970. When the racing started, Hailwood was the winner of both heats after he and Gethin had enjoyed some terrific dices, and Gethin had retired. Ganley was second in both, and so second overall, whilst Pike continued his sequence of third places. After this meeting, Norinder announced his retirement from the sport for personal reasons, and Tony Lanfranchi took over driving the car for the rest of the season.

With a more-than-eventful series of races behind them, Gethin still led the championship chase with 84 points. Ganley had half that amount and was second, with Mike Walker a further 6 points adrift. Hailwood was 1 behind Mike Walker in fourth, and 16 in front of McRae. Trevor Taylor and Gardner were joint sixth, on 18 points apiece.

Following the European adventures, the championship returned to British shores on 9 August, to Thruxton in particular. This was Gethin's last Formula 5000 race of the season as he was due to drive in a few Formula 1 and Can-Am events later that year, so he was out to make his mark in an attempt to extend his championship lead. Trevor Taylor was back in a racing car following his Austrian accident, and for this meeting he used a Lola, provided by Doug Hardwick, that had been previously driven by Mo Nunn and Davey Powell earlier in the season. Using a new car but with the Chevrolet engine which had been salvaged from his Lola T142 that was wrecked at Castle Combe, was Goulding, in a Beattie P1100. Rollinson was also back in a Surtees TS5A, but Mike Walker was missing as his car was having some work done to it.

Gardner made sure that Gethin wasn't about to get things all his own way when he registered a time of 1 minute 13.6 seconds in his Lola T190, to take pole position for the first of the two fifteen-lap heats. Next to him was the sometime McLaren Formula 1 driver, two-tenths down, followed by the similar car of Ganley a further two-tenths behind. McRae hurt his back when his car had an off-road excursion, and he also had to start low down on the grid.

Gardner made a poor start which allowed Gethin, Ganley and Rollinson to get ahead as the first two laps were ticked off. He was close behind Gethin, though, on lap three, and then got into the lead two laps later. Gethin wasn't about to give up, however, and with one lap remaining, retook the lead to finish six-tenths in front of the Lola. Ganley was third, followed by Rollinson and then Hailwood. Trevor Taylor led the pack behind these, but his race was over near the end when a bolt sheared on the back of his car. This meant that Prophet finished sixth, but someway behind the top five.

Gardner's fortunes changed in the second event, and it was he who saw the flag first after passing Gethin with three laps remaining, and, crucially, two-tenths quicker than his rival in the opener. Hailwood beat Ganley and Rollinson to finish third this time. Rollinson finished one place lower than in the first heat, whilst Prophet made no gains or losses.

With Gardner and Gethin on the first two steps on the podium in that order, it was Ganley, the other 'G', who made things look symmetrical. The difference between the top two was once again just two-tenths of a second. Trevor Taylor's change in car owner, however, didn't prove fruitful, and he failed to score any points on the day. Hailwood, Rollinson and Prophet in that order were the other points-scorers.

The next date that the drivers had circled on their calendars was 15 August, and with Silverstone the venue for round fifteen of the series, it looked increasingly likely that Gethin was to be champion. The Swedish driver, Reine

Wisell, was here to stand in for him whilst he was away on Grand Prix duty again, in Austria this time, but his 90-point haul so far looked unbeatable. The nearest driver to him in the championship was Ganley, and he was keen to impress everyone that came to watch. Gardner, too, was trying to make everyone take notice, and it was his Lola that lay at the top of the time sheets after qualifying finished for the first of the two ten-lap heats. Ganley was next fastest, followed by McRae. Wisell's appearance was marred by a faulty fuel pump, but he managed to qualify the Chevrolet-powered McLaren on the second row alongside McRae. Rollinson and Prophet were next.

Frank Gardner came out to play at Silverstone ... (Courtesy Alan Cox)

... and so did Roy Pike. (Courtesy Alan Cox)

As the race started, Gardner repeated his qualifying performance and sped off into a lead that he never lost. Prophet, though, was unable to get his engine to start, and was pushed away from the track. The two New Zealanders tried to catch Gardner, but succeeded only in racing each other, with Wisell in hot pursuit of them both. When they failed to dispose of a backmarker at Club, the Swede saw his chance and took second place from the pair. Third place became the temporary 'property' of Mike Walker when Ganley's avoidance manoeuvre put him on to the grass and McRae spun, but Ganley recovered to overtake Walker and finish third. McRae also found a way past the Alan McKechnie-entered M10B on lap seven, to come home fourth.

When the second heat started, Wisell looked to have inherited the Gethin style of driving, as well as his car, as he raced into the lead approaching Copse. Gardner, Ganley, McRae and Mike Walker were in close attendance, though, but then the latter came to an abrupt halt at Woodcote on the second lap, and McRae overtook Ganley as the race progressed. The work done on Mike Walker's car before the meeting became unimportant after this mishap, leaving the driver shaken and the car a write-off. Gardner pressed hard and overcame Wisell on lap four, but was demoted again on lap eight as McRae took second. The positions remained unchanged then for the remaining two laps, giving the 9 winning points to Gardner. Wisell justified his inclusion in the field, and had the satisfaction of gaining second place overall with McRae in third. Ganley earned 3 points for fourth, placing him just 31 points behind Gethin with five rounds of the championship to go. Rollinson recorded fifth place, over one minute slower than the drivers in front of him, whilst a similar gap existed between him and sixth-placed Lanfranchi.

The 5.0-litre-engined cars combined with five contemporary Formula 1 cars again in a clash for Oulton Park's coveted Gold Cup on 22 August. Jackie Stewart was the reigning World Champion of that series, and was given the number 1 for his Ken Tyrrell team March Ford. Gethin was absent again so there was no conflict of the two series' reigning champions. Representing the world of the Formula 1 World Championship were the works teams of Lotus, BRM, and Surtees, and the drivers were Jochen Rindt, Jackie Oliver, and John Surtees respectively. Graham Hill was also there, to act for the privateer team of Brooke Bond Oxo Racing, as the first of the two-part, one hundred and ten-mile race got under way. Andrea de Adamich was entered to drive a Formula 5000 version of his McLaren Alfa Romeo M14D Formula 1 car, after spending much of the year as part of the works team, but he failed to show up as the team didn't have a spare engine! Mike Walker was another absentee as his car hadn't been repaired in time. Chris Summers was present, though, and he drove a Lola T142 that Sid Taylor had entered in earlier competitions and that had been used by Gardner, Robin Widdows and Lanfranchi. The Formula 5000 entry also had two newcomers to Oulton Park, Goulding and Bob Miller, with the latter in a Dulon LD8.

During practice the rain came down, so times weren't as fast as they had been earlier in the year. Leading the way in his class, though, was Gardner's Lola, who made it to the front row overall, followed by Prophet. He should have lined up next to Jackie Stewart, but the Formula 1 driver used a new car for the race and was relegated to the back of the queue. The third row was made up entirely of Formula 5000 machinery, with Trevor Taylor and Wisell on each flank. In between the pair of them should have been McRae, but in qualifying he hit the banking at the top of Deer Leap and spun across the line, finally stopping opposite the control tower. The left front wheel was ripped off and the bodywork damaged which rendered the car irreparable and he registered a 'DNS'. Rindt was on the next row with Ganley next to him. The other Formula 5000 cars took the remaining places. There was a mystery driver called 'Ippocastano', in a Cooper, who was really Peter Hawtin.

The weather had improved when Gardner was the first Formula 5000 driver into Old Hall, followed by Wisell, both of them having John Surtees and Jackie Oliver in front of them with Rindt breathing down their respective necks. Ganley passed Wisell on the second lap, with Hailwood doing the same just as quickly. The Swede was hanging on the tail of the Midlander, and managed to pass whilst Ganley was pulling away trying to catch Gardner. At half-distance, Ganley locked-up going into Cascades, and when he rejoined he was behind Wisell and Hailwood. Hailwood got in front of Wisell on lap eleven and went after the class leader. On lap fifteen Gardner slowed, and a lap later he retired to the pits with a broken rear wishbone. Wisell crashed two laps before the end, making Hailwood the next target for Ganley but the Lola was too far ahead. This meant that it was Hailwood who took victory of his class in the first of the Formula 5000 sections of the two-part race. Third position in Formula 5000 was claimed by Trevor Taylor, with all three ahead of Stewart in the previously-unsorted Tyrell.

For any chance of being champion, Ganley had to overcome Hailwood, Gardner and Wisell on his way to the chequered flag in the second heat. The pressure of this eased partially after Gardner had to start from the back in his now-repaired car. Ganley was the first Formula 5000 driver to show, with Trevor Taylor and Prophet the nearest of his pursuers, and Saunders was next. Prophet's chances of victory all but disappeared when he was forced to pit on lap three after his gear lever came away, leaving him stuck with just top gear. Gardner was making rapid progress through the field, and on lap five he passed Trevor Taylor to take second place in this 'race within the race'. Then, in his fully-restored Lola T190, he showed that he was the superior of his peers when he guided his car past Ganley's at Old Hall on lap ten. Crossing the line he also set a new lap record for the class of 1 minute 29.6 seconds, an average of 112.19mph.

This didn't bother Ganley, though, as he proved to be the fastest overall and was judged to be the winner on the day. Trevor Taylor's consistency added 6 points to his total so far, with Irish deep-sea diver, Saunders, in a Rover V8-engined Crosslé 15F, in third position. Trevor Taylor was £10 worse off, though, after being fined for dangerous driving. During the warm-up lap for one of the heats there was a spillage of oil at Knicker Brook, and he decided to try and avoid it by changing his line through the area. A marshal, who was standing by the track ready to deal with the oil, wasn't spotted by the driver, and although the two didn't meet any closer than a whisker, the Observer reported the incident and Trevor had to open his wallet to the Clerk of the Course.

*Bob Miller was another out to see if he could win a F5000 race ... (Courtesy Frank Hall)*

*... whilst Howden Ganley already had. (Courtesy Eric Bryce)*

*Lingard Goulding was yet another driver waiting for a win. (Courtesy Frank Hall)*

One week later, the Formula 5000 cars were back on their own with the BARC hosting the Guards European Formula 5000 Championship at Snetterton. McRae was back, and so were Mike Walker and Pike. With rain falling during qualifying, Ganley could do no better than fifth on the grid. Pole position was achieved by

*A few weeks later Fred Saunders was back in England, also trying for a win. (Courtesy Norman Hayes)*

Hailwood as he managed to get some times in before the rain, and Rollinson achieved his best placing of the season thus far alongside him. Trevor Taylor was next, with Pike in Len Terry's newly-designed Leda LT22 making up the top five. Wisell was sixth. Of the other returnees, Mike Walker managed a few laps near the end of the session and started towards the back of the grid, but McRae didn't record a time, only driving a few laps in the untimed warm-up session. The Kiwi, though, withdrew from the event after being given a ten-second penalty for practicing out of session. Gardner was back in a Touring car at Brands Hatch and did not appear.

Rollinson showed his intentions by taking off into the lead as proceedings got under way, but he was quickly caught by Hailwood on the second tour. He was then further demoted by the advancing Trevor Taylor, and again by Ganley as the fifth lap began. These positions remained unchanged as the flag dropped at the end of the twelfth lap, with Wisell as a close fourth, having passed Rollinson who had pitted to sort out a handling problem.

It was Wisell who showed first in the second heat, and he built a lead that he extended, lap after lap, to finally win by over fifteen seconds at the finish, setting an average speed of 117.26mph. Of the twelve who started the race, Ganley was closest to him, two-tenths ahead of Hailwood. Trevor Taylor couldn't make any impact on these three, and he finished a distant fourth. The race, however, wasn't accident-free, as on lap eight Chris Summers' Lola had a tyre lose pressure and the car went flying off the track at the end of the Norwich Straight. The driver was thrown out of the vehicle, injuring him critically, and tragically those injuries cost him his life as he died on the way to hospital.

Wisell's efforts were good enough to give him the overall victory, and he was followed onto the podium by Hailwood. Ganley came up next, having added just 1 extra point in his quest to be champion, and therefore making Gethin the series winner for 1970. Trevor Taylor, Prophet and Pike took the 3, 2 and 1 points-paying places in that order.

Two weeks later, it was another overseas trip and a European driver who took the first prize money and points. With Gethin away, in Canada this time, Wisell was once again driving the McLaren that proved to be the class of the field after two heats of fifteen laps apiece of Hockenheim. Gardner was second in heat one, and Mike Walker third. McRae was second in heat two, but with Gardner third in that heat, the overall second-placed driver was Gardner. Mike Walker marked his return with a fine third place. Prophet was fourth overall following fourth and fifth places, whilst McRae finished one place ahead of Pike. Ganley failed to finish either heat, but Hailwood had decided not to travel to Germany so Ganley's second place in the championship was as secure as Gethin's title win.

Wisell was proving a more-than-capable deputy for Gethin, and was on substitute duty again when the penultimate meeting of the season came to Oulton Park, on 19 September. He came to Cheshire with hopes of making it a hat trick of wins but his chances looked slim when Gardner and McRae were split by just two-tenths of a second in the Aussie's favour in the battle for pole position. Next fastest, and on the new 2x2 grid, was Hailwood in a race test for his new car for 1971, a Lola T192. Wisell made it onto row two, with Mike Walker and Prophet behind. A new Australian appeared on the fourteen-car grid for the first time; Dave Walker, in a Lotus 70 possessing a Ford Mustang V8 engine similar to the one that had previously been driven by Rollinson. He qualified ninth. Another Taylor appeared on the grid as well, Robert, who drove a 4.7-litre Kitchiner K3A that started from the final grid slot.

As the race was on the long circuit, just twelve laps were given to the two heats, and it was Gardner who showed first when the cars were released from the grid. Hailwood, Wisell, Mike Walker and a confident Ganley got ahead of the Tasmanian, McRae, as did Prophet's M10B. Both the Walkers' day came to an end on lap two; first of all Mike retired at Esso (nowadays called Shell) with an engine that was being starved of fuel because the pump feeding it had failed, Dave's Lotus made it to Knicker Brook before he gave up without a clutch. McRae's day became worse on the second lap after he lost control of his car and temporarily left the track at Knicker Brook, but he rejoined, albeit without his front aerofoils. Two laps later, Wisell looked to have lost his chance when he locked up all four wheels at Lodge, but he managed to maintain momentum and a lap after that he overtook Hailwood and began to catch Gardner. With laps running out, though, the best he could do was to finish runner-up, one second behind the winner. Hailwood was having trouble with his new motor, and both Ganley and Trevor Taylor managed to pass him before the flag fell and they finished the heat in that order.

Just eleven cars made it to the start for the second heat, and the crowd saw the first two from the earlier contest swap places at Knicker Brook on the fourth tour. The pair continued to the flag in that order, with Wisell equalling the outright lap record for the circuit. Gardner wasn't about to give in, though, and he equalled the time, 1 minute 26.6 seconds, that was even faster than the Formula 1 cars had gone. Once more Ganley, Trevor Taylor and Hailwood were third, fourth and fifth respectively, which was also their overall positions. Wisell was faster than Gardner when both of his times were added together, and so his hoped-for hat trick had been achieved. Trevor Taylor was placed fourth, whilst Rob Taylor's debut gave him an overall placing of eleventh. Hailwood and McRae made up the top six in that order. Dave Walker was awarded a placing two below the K3A driver.

With the championship already secure, Gethin was again absent for the final meeting on 27 September at Brands Hatch, and Gardner and Ganley were in contention for the runner-up spot. Wisell had already secured a big prize though; he had been selected by Colin Chapman to drive for the Lotus Formula 1 team in the last two races of 1970 and for the 1971 Grand Prix season, replacing John Miles. He made his debut for the team the week after the Brands Hatch Formula 5000 event, when he was third to new team-mate Emerson Fittipaldi, at the US Grand Prix at Watkins Glen. Ironically, another former-Formula 5000 driver was also due to make a first entry in Formula 1 in that race, Peter Westbury, who was down to drive for the works-BRM team, but he failed to qualify for the race.

Before that though, in Kent, Gardner showed that he knew the circuit as well as anyone, and he took pole position on the Grand Prix configuration in a time of 1 minute 27.4 seconds. That was almost three seconds faster than Gethin's pole-winning time a little under six months earlier. Mike Walker came next, with Trevor Taylor making up the front row. McRae followed, but shortly after setting his best time during the first practice session, a 'moment' at Druids saw him lose a wheel, thus curtailing his hopes of a faster rotation of the Grand Prix layout. Sunday's session saw a rebuilt car and a slightly faster time, but he still started fourth. Wisell was next, followed by Ganley, Hailwood and the rest.

Gardner, though, failed to complete a racing lap when his diff' cracked and retirement beckoned as the opening lap came to a close. As the second lap started, it was Mike Walker who led followed by Wisell, Trevor Taylor, McRae, Ganley and Hailwood, whilst Gardner was nowhere in sight. The lead became a difficult thing to hang on to as Mike Walker's McLaren developed clutch trouble after he took over at the front. He retired at the end of lap two to allow Wisell into the lead, but then he, too, had car trouble, and his M10B came to a halt four laps before the end of the fifteen-lap heat. The seemingly poisoned chalice was then picked up by McRae, and he broke the jinx to win by over seventeen seconds. Ganley came home a solitary second, whilst Hailwood had managed to deal with Trevor Taylor's efforts and took third place.

With the Sid Taylor-backed McLaren engineers able to repair the broken drive shaft on Wisell's McLaren in time for the second heat, he was able to achieve third place before a broken oil pump forced his second retirement of the day. With only Ganley ahead of him, McRae took over in front on lap seven, and he carried on to record a second win of the day. Second and third places were taken by the same two as had finished in those places in the earlier contest, Ganley and Hailwood in that order. Trevor Taylor finished fourth in the heat. Those were also the overall podium places as the season came to a close, with Trevor Taylor also fourth overall and Ray Calcutt, in a Lola T142, and Fred Saunders' Rover-powered Crosslé filling the next two gaps.

Despite his absences in the season, Gardner finished third in the championship, 9 points behind Ganley's 61, with Gethin still on 90. Hailwood was fourth, 2 points behind the Australian.

The championship top ten looked like this:

| Position | Driver | Car | Engine | Points |
|---|---|---|---|---|
| 1 | Peter Gethin | McLaren M10B | 5.0 Chevrolet | 90 |
| 2 | Howden Ganley | McLaren M10B | 5.0 Chevrolet | 61 |
| 3 | Frank Gardner | Lola T190 | 5.0 Chevrolet | 52 |
| 4 | Mike Hailwood | Lola T190<br>Lola T192 | 5.0 Chevrolet<br>5.0 Chevrolet | 50 |
| 5 | Mike Walker | McLaren M10B | 5.0 Chevrolet | 42 |
| 6 | Graham McRae | McLaren M10B | 5.0 Chevrolet | 36 |
| 7 | Trevor Taylor | Surtees TS5A<br>Lola T190 | 5.0 Chevrolet<br>5.0 Chevrolet | 33 |
| 7 | Reine Wisell | McLaren M10B | 5.0 Chevrolet | 33 |
| 9 | Roy Pike | Leda LT20<br>Leda LT22 | 5.0 Chevrolet<br>5.0 Chevrolet | 17 |
| 10 | David Prophet | McLaren M10B | 5.0 Chevrolet | 11 |

# CHAPTER 3

## CONCENTRATION WORKS!

In 1971, Rothmans took over the sponsorship of the European Formula 5000 Championship, and with three fewer rounds in which to compete, a new champion would be found. Peter Gethin had become a full time Grand Prix driver after he had been recruited by the McLaren Formula 1 team. His place in Sid Taylor's McLaren car was taken by the former Chevron test and works race driver, Brian Redman, who had reversed his 1970 decision to go and live in South Africa. This year the team was using an M18 version of the popular manufacturer's cars in place of the M10s from the last two years. Frank Gardner joined Lola as its full-time works and test driver, having previously used a car provided by Motor Racing Research Ltd. In *Autosport* on 14 January 1971, Lotus Racing announced that Mike Walker would be its works driver for the new season, making it the third different marque of car he would drive since the inception of the formula in the UK. Mike Hailwood abandoned plans to return to motorcycle racing, and instead joined John Surtees' team to drive a TS8.

Before the championship got under way in Britain, some drivers took advantage of the Tasman series in Australia and New Zealand to test themselves and their vehicles. Two of the British competitors and their cars from the forthcoming series were rushed out to South America for the Argentine Grand Prix meeting on 24 January. David Prophet and Gordon Spice went with their McLaren M10Bs to fill the places left on the grid, following Ferrari's withdrawal from the main race. Jo Bonnier also entered a Formula 5000 Lola T190 that he had previously raced at Sebring. In common with most of the Rothmans European Formula 5000 Championship races run in the 1971 season, two heats were held. When the results of each were amalgamated it was Prophet who came out best of the Formula 5000 runners, with only three Formula 1 cars in front of him. Spice was eighth and Bonnier was two places farther back, despite retiring after twenty-two laps of the first twenty-five-lap heat.

Tony Dean and John Myerscough were others who had some pre-championship rehearsal time, but they went to Cheshire rather than Buenos Aires. One week before the opening race of the series, Dean was entered in an old Formula 1 M7A that had won the 1969 Italian and Mexican Grand Prix with Denny Hulme at the wheel, but had now been converted for Formula 5000 use. In a Formula Libre race at Oulton Park, and after completing ten laps in 16 minutes 20.6 seconds, Dean was declared the winner. Myerscough was half a lap down in Mike Walker's old M10E, but still finished second in a race that also featured some Formula Fordsters amongst the entrants.

A new rule introduced for the 1971 championship meant that only cars that had qualified within ten per cent of the pole position driver's time would be allowed to start the race. Another change saw Mallory Park as the first venue of the season, instead of Oulton Park. This round took place on 28 March 1971, and featured fourteen cars in the now-familiar two-heat format. Mike Hailwood proved to be the man to beat after he set the fastest qualifying time for the first of the twenty-five-lap contests in Leicestershire. Dean benefitted from his workout the previous week as he was next on the grid, one place ahead of Redman but two in front of a Lola T192 driven by Mike Walker, after the Lotus deal he had been offered was bettered by Doug Hardwick's Huntingdon-based and works-backed team. Another new car to make it to the grid was Terry Sanger's Harrier, but after having gear selection problems, the best he could do was over five seconds slower than Hailwood and he started three places from the back. Spice was also at the back with all sorts of problems, and only completed the required three qualifying laps, but he was allowed to start despite the ten per cent rule as it was considered too early in the season to apply it.

Dean showed a clean, but cold, set of wheels to Hailwood but then spun exiting Gerards which Mike took advantage of, taking over and off into the lead as the race got under way. Sadly, the Leicestershire crowd rarely saw Dean in this heat, as he had little or no grip after that and his car never made it to the second corner. This gave the debutant, Redman, second place, with Keith Holland managing to pass David Prophet and a slow starting Mike Walker to slot into third. Walker, though, recovered on lap fourteen as Prophet started to have problems with gears, and he got in front of the M10B driver. Despite having problems with oversteer and the attentions of a more-than-keen Holland, Redman hung on, with the rest maintaining their positions for the remainder of the race. Sanger's gear selection problems became worse when the lever broke, and he failed to finish.

Hailwood repeated his earlier feat in the second heat, and although Redman did manage to get a bit closer, he couldn't catch the works Surtees TS8 before the flag came out. Holland and Mike Walker kept the Lancastrian awake until the former made contact with Sanger's repaired car around half-distance and he found himself launched into the lake. Fortunately, although he was wet, he was unhurt. Sanger hit the wall, destroying his car. He, too, was unhurt. Mike Walker pressed on to try and catch Redman, but was only able to make up time but no places. Prophet was fourth, whilst the winner of the UK's first Formula Ford 1600 race, Ray Allen, was fifth and Fred Saunders, sixth.

The aggregate of the times proved that Hailwood was, as everyone expected, the fastest of the field. Redman had a useful debut scoring 6 points for his second place, with Mike Walker on the next step of the podium. Prophet and Allen echoed their heat two finishing places, whilst Rob Taylor's Kitchiner K3A scored the remaining point. Spice failed to finish either heat.

On Good Friday, 9 April, Snetterton was host to the second round, but Hailwood was missing from the meeting after his engine broke during testing earlier in the week. Frank Gardner was back, though, and in the works T192. Another Australian, Tim Schenken, made his first appearance in the championship. He was driving another M18 that was meant for Howard Ganley, who was away on Formula 1 duty at Oulton Park, but Redman's similar car proved to be the fastest of the field. Gardner was next up, with Mike Walker, Trevor Taylor and Prophet in the places between Redman and sixth grid-placed Schenken. Bonnier's T190 from the Argentine race was also present, but this time it was driven by a German, Roland Heiler. He proved to be slower than the former owner, and failed to make

*Trying too hard! Ray Allen spins in front of Mike Hailwood at Mallory Park. (Author's collection)*

Three days later the series moved south to use the Grand Prix circuit of Brands Hatch, and Hailwood was back. After repeating his qualifying feat of the opening round, it looked like he would be the man to beat again. Redman, Mike Walker, Holland, Allen, Gardner and Howard Ganley, who took the drive that Schenken had had in the previous round, were the next six trying to give him some opposition. At first though, it was Redman who made the best start as the cars approached Paddock Hill Bend for the first of the twenty-lappers. Hailwood and the rest gave chase, but failed to make an impression on Redman and he won by over sixteen seconds. Gardner followed Hailwood across the line in third place.

Hailwood was out to avenge his rival in the second heat and led for the first sixteen laps, but then the engine overheated and forced his retirement. This allowed Redman to record a second win of the day, followed by Gardner and then Allen, who was back at the scene of his historic victory. It was these three that took the points and the lead in the title chase. Redman was on top with 21 points, 6 ahead of Gardner and 11 more than Allen. Dean had been lapped in both heats but still took 3 points from the meeting, whilst Mike Walker scored 2, twice as many as Myerscough.

The first trip away from the United Kingdom came on 2 May when the teams crossed the Irish Sea, to race at Mondello Park, in what was called the Dublin Grand Prix. Three of the

the ten per cent time. Along with Saunders and Rob Taylor, who were also outside the margin, he was allowed to start on an eleven-car grid.

Unusually, only one race was held, and after the Union flag was waved the top two made a good start, the opening exchanges going the way of the Englishman, Redman. With just two laps left, however, Gardner saw an opening at the hairpin and took it. The McLaren driver tried to get back on terms, and they lapped closely for the rest of the race, but he failed to do so before the chequered flag signalled the end. With these two having their own race, the battle for third place raged between Trevor Taylor, Mike Walker and the new boy, Schenken. Trevor Taylor was the first to go, though, when his car developed electrical problems, and at the end of lap five he entered the pit lane. Then at the end of the very next lap, Schenken signalled he was finished when the head gasket blew on his McLaren. Allen came through in an M10B to deprive Mike Walker of third place, then started to pull away from the rest of the field leaving Prophet, Myerscough and Heiler keen to catch Walker. Although Trevor Taylor rejoined, his race was over on lap fourteen after passing the last pairing only for his engine to die after exiting the hairpin. The top six remained unchanged as the flag fell.

entrants recorded an identical qualifying time but Hailwood was first, and it was he who took the pole in front of Redman and Trevor Taylor. The race was augmented with four Irish Formula 2 runners, Ken Fildes on board a Crosslé 19F, Brian Nelson in an 18F, and a pair of Brabham BT30s driven by Tommy Reid and John Smith. Nelson and Smith lapped quicker in practice than a few of the Formula 5000 runners, Lingard Goulding, Saunders and Kaye Griffiths, and started the race in front of them.

Despite being led by Hailwood for the opening four laps, Redman remained patient and edged ahead on the next tour, keeping the lead for the remaining twenty-seven laps. Gardner came through as well, but the Surtees driver had done enough not to lose any more places. Trevor Taylor looked safe in fourth but Mike Walker had other ideas, he got past on lap seventeen after a broken valve spring caused the Formula 1 refugee's car to cough and splutter. Allen came through to take fourth three laps later, but couldn't claim a better finish before the end of the race. Trevor Taylor managed to come home sixth.

The second heat looked good for Redman until lap eighteen when a hole in his car's sump forced the end of his day. Gardner was the first to profit from this misfortune, and he was followed home by Mike Walker, Allen and a disappointed Hailwood. It was those three who took the top points-scoring positions which also allowed Gardner to jump ahead of Redman in the championship chase. Myerscough doubled his points from the previous round, leaving Dean to score just 1. Over the two heats Reid was the best of the local runners, having finished sixty-one of the sixty-four laps completed by the top four Formula 5000 runners, in front of his compatriots.

Jock Russell tries to take victory at Silverstone. (Courtesy Eric Bryce)

Northamptonshire beckoned less than a week later, and two twenty-six-lap heats at Silverstone were on the menu. The race, once again, was combined with the Formula 1 International Trophy race, and the top Formula 5000 runner was able to take the GKN Trophy home. Chris Amon was the brightest of all the drivers, and he sat on pole position. Hailwood was the fastest of his class, and lined up alongside Schenken, Pedro Rodriguez and his former Formula 5000 colleague, Gethin, who were all in Formula 1 machinery. Alan Rollinson was also in a Surtees, although his was a Formula 1 version. He was behind Hailwood, and joined on row four by Ganley and Redman. Robs Lamplough reappeared in a Formula 5000 car, a self-styled Lamplola, which in reality was a converted 1968 Formula 2 Lola T102 that used a Ford Boss engine.

Jackie Stewart led the race as the flag fell, but as far as the Formula 5000 cars were concerned, it was Hailwood who, although down in tenth place overall, led his class rivals. The TS8 was starting to develop gear problems, though, and he allowed Allen's McLaren to go through. Allen's lead was short-lived, however, as on lap four he spun on the way out of Abbey and hit the banking, damaging the rear of the car. This left Hailwood again in front, but Redman made sure he didn't stay there too long and got his M18 ahead into the position he never lost. Second in the Formula 5000 section of the

*Here, Jock Russell leads Ulf Norinder. (Courtesy Eric Bryce)*

race was then claimed by Dean, who had come from twenty-seventh on the grid, with Hailwood hanging on to take third. Stewart was the overall winner of the heat, incidentally.

Heat two started in fine style for Pedro Rodriguez as far as Formula 1 was concerned, but it was Redman who led the Formula 5000 runners, as well as Amon, Jean-Pierre Beltoise and a few other Formula 1 drivers. Around one-third distance, though, Redman punctured a tyre on debris left following a blow-up from Beltoise, and he surrendered the class lead to a repaired Surtees TS8 driven by Hailwood. Redman rejoined on lap nine, but he only got as far as Becketts before the engine refused to start and his day's work was over. Hailwood, in sixth overall, was dominating the GKN Trophy class, and the nearest of his rivals was Dean who spun when his car jumped out of gear. Fortunately there was sufficient daylight between him and Gardner for him to recover. Ulf Norinder, making a Formula 5000 comeback, was lying fourth and in the last running car as they finished in that order.

Round six was held at Castle Combe, on 15 May, but without Redman as he was driving a Gulf-Porsche 908 at the Targa Florio the following day. As there was no Grand Prix that weekend, however, Gethin substituted for the Lancastrian. Hailwood was another absentee as a head gasket had blown during unofficial practice, damaging his only engine on the day before the race. Tony Lanfranchi was also listed as a runner in the programme, but when the cars came to the circuit there was no place on the grid for his recently-acquired Surtees TS5. With no sponsor, he decided he couldn't enter the race.

During practice, Gethin showed that he hadn't lost his touch as he recorded the fastest time for the thirty-lap race. Next to him was Gardner, although Ganley recorded an identical time a little later on in qualifying. Allen and Mike Walker also recorded the same times as each other, but they were a little slower than the first two and lined up fourth and fifth respectively, whilst Dean was next, a fraction over two seconds slower than Gethin.

Heavy rain greeted the seventeen-car entry for the single thirty-lap heat, and it was Gardner who saw Quarry first, spraying the following pack which was led by Gethin. Ganley, Allen, Mike Walker and Dean were in close attendance, before first of all Gethin, and then Ganley, detached themselves from the rest. Gethin kept the pressure on Gardner, and managed to put some daylight between himself and his sometime Formula 1 colleague, Ganley. Dean got in front of Mike Walker on lap thirteen, but the Lola driver called it a day three laps later as his car had no oil pressure. On lap twenty Gardner was in charge at the front with the two directly behind seemingly content with their positions, but Allen and Dean were both keen to finish fourth. Dean pushed hard, however, and overdid things on the Dean Straight, spinning across the track and hitting the marshal's post. Dean was knocked unconscious, and the race continued under yellow flags whilst he was extricated from his car and taken to hospital with a suspected broken neck. The positions in the race should have remained unaltered. Norinder was fifth but almost put this in doubt when he spun before the end, almost taking the approaching Ganley out. Luckily, no contact was made between them and they both continued. On the next lap, number twenty-seven, it was Ganley's turn to spin his McLaren on Farm Straight. Fortunately he managed to regain control before Allen came into view, and he proceeded in the right direction to take the flag in the position he had occupied for most of the race. Myerscough was sixth, two laps down.

Going into the next round, the series' second visit to Mallory Park on 31 May, the championship was led by Hailwood on 22 points, 1 ahead of Redman whose crash whilst in Sicily left him suffering first- and second-degree burns to his face, neck, hands and right leg when the car broke on the opening lap. Allen was in third position with 16 points, 1 ahead of Mike Walker. The other points-scorers were all in single figures.

Fred Saunders was back for the second Mallory Park meeting. (Author's collection)

The series leader now had an engine for his car, and it proved to be a very efficient unit as he took pole position, albeit with an identical time to Gethin who was still covering for Redman. Despite doubts as to whether he would compete in the 1971 Rothmans European Formula 5000 Championship at all, the 1971 Tasman series champion, Graham McRae, was back for his first championship race of the year. The car, a McLaren M10B, was the same one that had done so well 'down under', and he managed to put it on the second row alongside fellow countryman, Gardner. Rollinson, back in Formula 5000 kit, recorded the same time as Gardner but lined up behind McRae. Ganley was the next on the grid, after recording a time six-tenths slower than the two on the front row, 44 seconds.

Fourteen cars came to the line to contest the first heat, with John Surtees lowering the Union flag to set them off on the first of the twenty-five laps. Hailwood was first into Gerards, followed by Gethin, McRae and the rest, with David Berry, back in his Brabham BT16, the last one through. Gethin suffered a puncture on lap eight on the way down the Devil's Elbow, and although he managed to make it back to the pits to have a new wheel fitted, he was a lap down when the chequered flag was shown. At the front, though, McRae was gaining on Hailwood, and as they entered the Esses on lap seventeen, the driver known as 'Cassius' overtook the Team Surtees works driver. Four laps later it was Gardner and Rollinson's turn to pass Hailwood. With no other changes to the top four for the remaining laps, Norinder, Prophet and Keith Holland were the only other finishers to complete the full distance. Berry's bad luck continued when his Brabham lost its oil with just three laps remaining.

Another new wheel for Gethin meant that the start of the second heat was delayed. When it did start, Hailwood overcame Gardner and McRae, but McRae was keen to take his second win of the day and took up the fight, equalling the lap record set by Gethin in the previous year's championship. With three laps to go, though, it was the Sid Taylor-prepared McLaren that came into second place to chase Hailwood's Surtees to the flag. The difference between them at the end was a little over two-and-a-half seconds in favour of Hailwood, with McRae over fifteen seconds behind in third.

The aggregate times made McRae the winner for the first time in 1971, and the heroics of the second heat gave Hailwood second place. Gardner extended his lead in the series when he took third place, whilst Rollinson, Norinder and Gethin were the others to take points away from the meeting.

Away from the Rothman's Championship, David Hepworth took his own four-wheel drive Formula 5000 car to Shelsley Walsh for the Shell/RAC-sponsored Hillclimb Championship on 13 June. This was the same car that Bev Bond and Lanfranchi had driven in the 1969 Guards series, and it took the owner up the hill in less than thirty seconds. It was the first time that anyone had done this at this venue, so unsurprisingly it was the best time of the day and a new course record. Also present in Formula 5000 cars were Tony Griffiths, behind the wheel of a Brabham BT35X, and Roy Lane, Richard Thwaites and Bob Rose, who each drove a McLaren M10B.

The Monza Lottery race meeting was also the venue for the next round for the Rothmans European Formula 5000 Championship on 20 June, and although the main event was set for Formula 2 cars, there were fourteen Formula 5000 cars on the grid for the first heat of their own series. The Dutch Grand Prix was held the same weekend, so with Redman still unable to drive, Sid Taylor called on Derek Bell to drive the McLaren in which both Redman and Gethin had been so successful earlier in the season. The previous round's victor, McRae, was missing from the grid as well, having blown the engine on his car during practice. Mike Walker was also unable to start as his engine had a piston fail before any racing for points took place.

Spice was the first to disappear from the first heat after he dropped out on the warm-up lap with engine timing problems. When the flag was waved to set the remaining runners on their way, though, Bell showed why he had been called into the Sid Taylor team. Gardner was followed by Rollinson, Trevor Taylor, Allen, Prophet, Holland, Norinder and Russell before the first of the Formula 2 non-qualifiers from the main event showed. Myerscough's race was over before the end of the opening lap after going in hard at Lesmo. Hailwood also didn't finish the first tour either, when the engine on his car blew up. Bell, though, was pulling away at the front, and he looked to have things sewn up until lap seven when his engine also gave up. This allowed Gardner to assume the lead for the next two laps before Rollinson powered through into first where he remained until the chequered flag was shown. Gardner stayed in second, and Trevor Taylor in Len Terry's latest Leda, finished third.

Rollinson started the second heat in the same manner as he finished the first, and stormed off into a lead he never lost. Gardner's progress wasn't so assured, though, and he became a casualty on the first lap. Trevor Taylor bettered his first heat position by one, whilst Allen came through to finish an untroubled third. So Rollinson recorded a first Formula 5000 haul of maximum points, with Trevor Taylor taking second place and Allen, third.

When the series returned to the UK, Tony Trimmer joined the entry list at Mallory Park on 4 July, in Rollinson's old Surtees TS5A with a Lola-modified Chevrolet engine that had been used by Hailwood in 1970. Redman was also back, after passing a 'fitness test' at Oulton Park the week before. McRae returned, too, with a newly-repaired Morand engine in his McLaren. The rest of the field was made up with the usual runners, each with a point to prove to the Leicestershire crowd.

Gardner took pole position, and then Hailwood repeated the time that the Aussie had set. McRae was next fastest, with Redman showing that he was back in business by qualifying fourth. Hailwood, though, was the first to get his car away from the line, with Redman scorching through to take second place. Gardner was close to Redman, whilst Trevor Taylor and McRae were fourth and fifth respectively. McRae caught and passed the car in front early on, and sought to catch Gardner and Redman, but as the latter was lapping Spice at the Devil's Elbow, Hailwood's Surtees crossed the finishing line. Redman was the next to finish with the pair from the Southern Hemisphere following in tandem. Trevor Taylor's Leda finished fifth, ahead of Allen's McLaren.

The start to heat two was slightly delayed after Prophet's McLaren lost a wheel spinner on the warm-up lap that had to be replaced before the cars could go. Hailwood was unperturbed, and set off at a pace that was matched by Gardner. Ganley came through from his position on the second row to take third at Gerrards, and before the end of the opening lap, McRae also got ahead of Redman. Jock Russell was trying to keep on the track as best as he could but failed to do so, he hit the bank at Gerrards, avoiding Goulding and Myerscough, and fortunately was unhurt. The top four continued in their positions from the opening lap for the remaining twenty-four, and Trevor Taylor repeated his feat of the previous contest. Spice, however, did a lot better and was sixth, his best placing of the season to date.

The aggregation of the two heats saw Hailwood awarded 9 points for his victories, followed by Gardner. Redman was quick enough in the second heat to gain third overall, just over a second in front of McRae. Trevor Taylor and Allen picked up the remaining points.

Whilst the Rothman's Championship runners were battling it out at Mallory Park, Hepworth continued to campaign his car at a hillclimb event at Fintray House in Scotland. He was the hill's record holder when he set a time of 29.9 seconds in a previous visit, but this time he was four-tenths quicker and took another BTD. Willie Forbes was also present in his Lola T142, but could only record a best time of 30.8 seconds. Hillclimbing continued on Saturday 10 July, when a combined Midlands Automobile Club and Vintage and Sports Car Club (VSCC) meeting took place at Shelsley Walsh. Amongst the runners was Tony Griffiths in his Repco-engined BT35X, and the driver of the 5.0-litre-powered car claimed a BTD for the day of 31.81 seconds.

Formula 5000 cars returned to racetracks on 23 and 24 July 1971. John Coulter brought a Lola T142 to the lesser-known tracks in the north, Rufforth and Croft, and took part in a pair of Formula Libre contests. His entry fee proved to be a worthwhile investment when he won in the first of these. It was almost a double win, but when his car momentarily caught fire on the penultimate lap in North Yorkshire, halting his progress, he decided to retire ... just in case!

More hillclimbing was held on the last day of July at Great Auclum, Hampshire, as part of the Shell/RAC Championship. A quartet of Formula 5000 runners took to the hill, but none of them could beat a 3.5-litre Brabham BT35X driven by Sir Nick Williamson to the first prize. His victory by just one-hundredth of a second was also a new course record. Despite this setback, Hepworth, who was the fastest Formula 5000 pilot, maintained a healthy lead in the championship. Tony Griffiths drove a 5.0-litre Repco version of the winner's car, and was third fastest after the first run with Roy Lane, in a McLaren M10B, fourth when the morning came to an end. These positions were reversed after they had completed their day's work, however. The fourth of the Formula 5000 cars was another M10B, driven this time by Richard Thwaites who finished seventh.

On 1 August, the Rothmans European Formula 5000 Championship returned to the home of the British Automobile Racing Club (BARC), Thruxton, for a pair of fifteen-lap heats. Gardner came along with a new Lola T242 to maintain his challenge in the series he led from Hailwood, Redman, Allen and the rest. Making his debut in the series and driving a McLaren M10B was the Belgian Teddy Pilette, although he could little to prevent the new Huntingdon car dominate qualifying. McRae came through to equal the time of 1 minute 12.6 seconds that the Australian had set, and although two-tenths slower, it was Hailwood who made up the front row. Redman was fourth fastest and found Rollinson's Surtees alongside him. The Belgian was on the next row, eighth fastest of the sixteen starters.

*At Thruxton, Brian Redman had a great day. (Courtesy Eric Bryce)*

Redman made the best start as the tyre smoke belched from the cars when they left the line, with Hailwood and then Gardner trying to keep pace with the Sid Taylor-prepared car. McRae was also keen to keep in touch, and managed to pass Gardner before the second tour began. Mike Walker was the first and only car to retire before the fifteen laps had been completed, after a tyre came off the rim as he approached the Chicane. On lap eleven, McRae found a gap at Kimpton and passed Hailwood to move up yet another place. He nearly clinched the top spot on lap twelve at Chicane when Redman was trying to avoid Bob Miller's Dulon, but finally made his move as they reached Allard. He was successful and went on to record another heat win by just over a second. Redman managed to keep the advancing Hailwood at bay and record a time that was exactly one second faster than the Surtees team driver. Gardner kept his position to finish fourth, whilst Rollinson was content to come home in the place he had started from, despite his car suffering a broken shock absorber during qualifying. Allen benefited from Mike Walker's exit to finish sixth.

When heat two came on to the grid, both Redman and Rollinson were absent. Their vehicles had developed problems that couldn't be fixed in time, so just fourteen cars lined up for the race. Gardner made an impressive start but so did Hailwood, and it was the latter who led McRae and the Lola T242 driver as the race got under way. Allen was out to improve on his performance in the previous heat, but found Trevor Taylor also fighting for fourth place. On lap eleven, Hailwood ran wide at Club, allowing McRae to repeat his feat of the opener. Gardner was also keen to pass Hailwood, and achieved this quite soon afterwards. Taylor first managed to shake off Allen and then tried to pass Gardner to record third place, but this proved an impossible task and he finished fourth. 'Monsieur' Pilette had a 'moment' at Seagrave, but managed to finish sixth this time, one place behind Allen.

So with McRae recording his second win of the season, his points total so far jumped to 21. Hailwood's 6 for second brought him closer to the series leader, and Gardner scored 4 more points this time, giving him a total of 50 in his quest for the title, 7 more than Hailwood. Redman didn't score a point but had the satisfaction of setting a new fastest lap in heat one, which was equalled by McRae but then bettered by Gardner in the later contest. Gardner's time of 1 minute 12.2 seconds was two-tenths faster than the earlier times, and a new outright lap record for Thruxton. This was equivalent to an average speed of 117.47mph. Pilette picked up a point for his troubles.

Round eleven of the series was held on 14 August, at Silverstone, with the news that Hailwood had been drafted into the Surtees

Formula 1 team for the Italian Grand Prix on 4 September. This must have given him some confidence as he went out and set the fastest time in qualifying for the twenty-five-lap single heat. Alongside him on the grid was the series leader, after recording a time that was four-tenths slower than Hailwood. The same difference existed between the third- and fourth-placed drivers, McRae and Rollinson. Redman found things more difficult; the best he could do was to start from row four as he had been forced to qualify in the rain that had fallen after the first few had already been out. The conditions also caught out Allen, he crashed at Becketts which bent the rear end of his McLaren and it wasn't able to be repaired in time for the race.

Oulton Park's first ever winner, Don Truman, led the cars on their formation lap in an E-type Jaguar before the rolling start, and as he peeled off, Hailwood was first into Copse. Gardner and McRae stayed in touch with the leader but failed to pass him, whilst Pilette came from the last row of the grid into fourth place on lap three. McRae was determined to add another win to his CV but couldn't find a way to catch and pass Gardner, and on lap ten he himself was overtaken by the Belgian. Spice was another on a charge; after eleven laps he was ahead of Redman and passed McRae two laps later, but shortly after his race ended when a holed piston brought his engine to a stop. McRae was back up to fourth as a result of Spice's misfortune, but Redman had other ideas and McRae was demoted again a lap later when the Lancastrian powered past him and Mike Walker. Fourth place became a poisoned chalice, though, because on lap twenty-two Redman's M18A ran out of petrol at Stowe. Mike Walker was the next to inherit the position, and he managed to keep the Kiwi at bay until the flag fell, thirteen seconds or so behind Pilette but two seconds in front of McRae. Prophet collected the final point for sixth.

One week later, a combined Formula 1 and Formula 5000 race was held for the Oulton Park Gold Cup, promoted by the Mid-Cheshire Motor Club. With the Formula 5000 cars making their first championship appearance in Cheshire in 1971, the contest was held in two twenty-lap parts, with the first getting under way at 2.25pm. Only eight Formula 1 cars were on the grid at the start, with former Formula 5000 driver, Peter Gethin, at the front in a BRM P160, having transferred from McLaren earlier in the season. One of the Formula 1 runners, Jean-Pierre Jarier, suffered electrical problems during practice and started from the back. The best of the Formula 5000 cars was Gardner in another new Lola, a T300 that was on the third row with Rollinson and Redman for company.

The winner of the Formula 5000 class was to be awarded £750 for his efforts on the day, which was the same for all of the races that were between one hundred and one hundred and fifty miles long during the 1971 season. As the race started, Gardner was keen to claim this amount following Henri Pescarolo's March 711, Gethin, Howden Ganley in a Formula 1 BRM P153 and John Surtees' eponymous TS9, the first of his peers, into Old Hall. Redman was keen to get his hands on the first prize as well, and he kept the pressure on the Australian with Rollinson and Hailwood right behind him. Trevor Taylor and Mike Walker were also in contention, and had most of the usual midfield runners behind them. Gardner came into fourth place overall when Gethin pitted on lap five with a badly vibrating front wheel caused by a flat-spotted tyre. Hailwood passed Rollinson ten laps into the race. Redman circulated in fifth but second in his class until lap fifteen, when Hailwood managed to pass him as he pulled up with gear selection problems. The three finished in that order, whilst Pescarolo took the victory overall.

In the second heat it was Hailwood who was the first of the Formula 5000 entrants to see the marshals at Old Hall. Gardner and Rollinson were in close attendance, though, and the pressure told as he spun at Esso, allowing the pair to pass.

Hailwood rejoined but his car was damaged and he retired after a couple of more laps. McRae was now in third place in the Formula 5000 race, but his car was starting to overheat and Mike Walker was closing in. The Lola driver, though, started to suffer similar problems, and the two finished in that order, the only other runners to complete the full forty laps. Surtees finished as winner of his part of the race.

The results were amalgamated and the winner of the 1971 Gold Cup was Surtees, whilst the £750 first prize for Formula 5000 went to Gardner, who was also third overall. Rollinson was fourth in the combined results, giving him the second place prize money and points. Two places behind Rollinson in the full standings was Mike Walker, earning himself 4 points and a few quid into the bargain.

*Left: Graham McRae was another from the Southern Hemisphere who tried to stop Gardner. (Author's collection)*

*Frank Gardner on his way to a win and, hopefully, the championship. (Author's collection)*

*David Prophet on the charge. (Courtesy Norman Hayes)*

*Top left: Derek Bell was a mid-season substitute at Oulton Park. (Author's collection)*

*Top right: John Myerscough wasn't. (Courtesy Norman Hayes)*

*Above: Alan Rollinson leads Chris Craft through Cascades at Oulton Park ... (Courtesy Eric Bryce)*

*... whilst Mike Walker does the same to Graham McRae. (Courtesy Eric Bryce)*

*At Snetterton, Fred Saunders continued in his Irish-built F5000 car. (Author's collection)*

Redman was nearest to him, but a full second slower. Hailwood's and Rollinson's TS8s found themselves side-by-side on the second row, whilst McRae was behind them with Mike Walker. Spice had a good qualifying session and lined up with Saunders on row four.

Tony Trimmer was present in a Surtees TS5A that qualified ninth, but when the cars came to the grid he was placed ahead of Spice, which allowed him to be in front of the McLaren driver at Riches as the race got under way. By then, however, the rest of the cars in front of him on the grid had gone through, with Redman at the head. Gardner led the chasing pack, and McRae managed to get ahead of the drivers from the second row. Halfway through the race, both Hailwood and Rollinson had pulled out; the former pitted with a wheel mounting problem whilst the latter's engine was overheating badly. Up at the front, despite the closeness of Gardner, Redman looked assured of the win that would give him pole for the second heat. McRae had become detached from the leading pair but had Mike Walker close by. On lap nine, though, Redman and Gardner tangled at the Esses and both were out of the race – McRae was now in the lead, and decided to put his foot down to shake off the Lola T192. In the end he finished eighteen seconds in front. Pilette had the race of his life thus far, and came from the very last place on the grid to finish third. Spice managed to pass Trimmer before taking fourth, and Saunders came in sixth. Berry finished eighth in his Brabham BT16/21B.

Over the same weekend a Formula Libre race was held at Snetterton, and the other Taylor, Robert, was present with his Kitchiner K3A. John Jordan and John Coulter were also there in their 4.7-litre McLaren M1C and 5.0-litre Lola T142 respectively. Neither of these two could beat the Kitchiner driver to the chequered flag, though.

Snetterton was also the venue of the next round of the Rothmans series on Bank Holiday Monday, 30 August, and fourteen cars came to the grid for two twelve-lappers. The BARC was the promoter of the meeting that featured five other races, including a Formula F100 event that was won by Tom Pryce in a Royale RP4. The Formula 5000 practice, though, was attended by fourteen cars, with Allen one of the absentees and Trevor Taylor another. Gardner wasn't bothered by this, and went out to see whether he could add to his championship aspirations by taking points from the event. He showed he meant business by taking pole position for the first heat in a time that would have broken the lap record, had it been achieved during a race.

Without Gardner and Redman for the second heat, a dozen cars were sent on their way by the BARC official, Grahame White. Saunders made a tremendous start, and he led them through Riches on the opening lap. The Irishman's lead was short-lived, however, and as the lap came to an end, Mike Walker, Pilette, Spice and McRae had all found a way past the Crosslé-Rover driver. Pilette overtook Mike Walker on the next lap, but then he himself was passed by McRae. The three continued in these positions until the end of the twelve laps, followed by Trimmer, Saunders and then Terry Sanger. Berry finished seventh, a lap down, but Spice's race was over on lap nine when his fuel pump broke.

Once again the results of the two heats were added together, and it was no surprise when it was announced that McRae was the overall winner. Mike Walker and Pilette were the others on the podium, with the Belgian in third. Trimmer took fourth, with Saunders and Berry in the final points-paying places.

The week after the Snetterton event was the Italian Grand Prix, and the entry featured at least six drivers with experience of Formula 5000 racing in the UK. Three of these finished in the points in what was, at the time of writing, the closest ever finish in Formula 1 history. The first four home were separated by less than two-tenths of a second, with the gap between first and second just one one-hundredth. Those top five in success order were: Gethin, Ronnie Peterson, François Cevert (who was nine one-hundredths behind Gethin), Hailwood (another nine one-hundredths back), and Ganley, who crossed the line just over half a second after the winner. Chris Amon was sixth, and two other sometime-Formula 5000 drivers were also classified, Jackie Oliver and Jo Bonnier, in seventh and ninth respectively.

Round fourteen of the Rothmans series was also held on foreign soil, Hockenheim playing host on 11 September. Following their Snetterton shunt, Gardner was present in a new Lola, but Redman's M18 wasn't ready for this meeting. Despite his non-appearance, twenty-one cars were present and listed amongst the entrants was Emerson Fittipaldi driving a Lotus fitted with a Pratt and Whitney 56B turbine engine that had been in Monza the previous week. This car was actually a Formula 1 car, but was allowed to compete in this race.

Gardner took pole even faster than the 'interloper', who sat next to him on the grid. Third fastest, but second of the Formula 5000 drivers, was Mike Walker, sharing row two with Rollinson. Allen was back and he put his car on the fifth grid slot next to Pilette.

Gardner showed his intent by leading into turn one with Fittipaldi behind. Pilette made an impressive start to show in third position by the end of the first circuit. Rollinson hadn't gained or lost a place, but the battle for fifth between Allen, Mike Walker and McRae was well and truly on. Rollinson's car gave up on lap six, and he pitted into retirement. McRae passed Pilette on the next lap, whilst Trevor Taylor was keen to be in the mix as well, and on lap eleven was up to fifth after passing Mike Walker's Doug Hardwick-entered Lola T192. As they entered the first chicane on the next lap, though, the engine gave up and his race was over, allowing Allen and Keith Holland to pass. Fittipaldi wasn't able to get in front of Gardner, and their positions remained unaltered for the rest of the fifteen-lap heat.

The second heat was almost a repeat of the first, but this time Gardner and Fittipaldi had McRae for company until lap nine. As the top two upped their pace so did McRae, until he crashed heavily and set the McLaren alight when the fuel cell ruptured on impact with the barrier. McRae managed to get away from the wreckage before the inferno really took hold, but was taken to hospital with burns to his fingers and shock. Gardner repeated his first heat win six laps later, with Fittipaldi still in second place. Some way back was the next Formula 5000 car, a McLaren M10B driven by Pilette who had

Trevor Taylor for company. Fifth and sixth were Allen and Mike Walker.

The overall result was the same as that of the second heat, but as Fittipaldi didn't qualify for points, the last scorer in the race was Trimmer, who finished seventh.

Whilst the Rothmans European track series was going on, back home in the UK the joint sponsored ShellSPORT/RAC Hillclimb Championship once again attracted Formula 5000 cars. The latest round was at Harewood on the same day as the Hockenheim event. Whilst no Formula 1 drivers were present in Yorkshire, a few competitors from earlier British track races were. Tony Griffiths' Brabham BT35X suffered with gear problems, and the best he could do was to finish fifth, whilst Thwaites had difficulties of his own with the McLaren M10B before he crossed the line in sixth. At the sharp end, though, Lane and Hepworth looked to be the Formula 5000 drivers who would make the biggest impact. Hepworth became the first man to beat the 40-second barrier by almost a second, but that time was eclipsed by Lane, in another M10B, by almost four-tenths of a second when the results were published.

Triumph and tragedy were present at the next round of the Rothmans European Formula 5000 Championship when the series returned to Cheshire on 18 September. Following his success in Germany, Gardner once again planted his Lola on pole position for the planned one-off twenty-eight-lap race. Redman was absent again because of a commitment he had elsewhere, so Derek Bell was drafted in by Sid Taylor to fill the gap, and he was the next quickest qualifier. Rollinson made it on to row two again, and once Mike Walker's times had been ratified, he was there as well. Trevor Taylor was back at the scene where his last Formula 5000 race had ended in an accident, and he was fifth. Hailwood also returned to Oulton and he was next to Trevor. Pilette was in seventh position on the track that he had only previously raced at some nine years before, in a Formula Junior, and that experience had come to an end after two practice laps! At the back was Peter Hawtin in his privately-funded Cooper T86B.

At the start, Bell was left wondering as Gardner and Walker rushed away from the line with Hailwood also pushing ahead as they approached Old Hall. Rollinson demoted Bell further before the end of the opening lap, leaving the sports car driver to fend off Pilette, Trevor Taylor and the rest of the fifteen-car field. With the Belgian closing in on Bell, it looked to be only a matter of time before he was pushed even lower down the list. Hailwood eased past Mike Walker's Lola at Knicker Brook on lap four, and set about the chase to Gardner's similar car. As they exited Esso for the fifth time, however, they were met by flames that came from Hawtin's car which had broken in two and caught fire on the approach to Hill Top. The driver died instantly. With yellow flags being waved for the next ten laps the race was effectively over, meaning Gardner was the winner of the race and with this victory, the championship was his, too. Bell's day came to an end on lap twelve, when gear selection became a problem and he retired. Before that, Trevor Taylor had also brought his car into the pits without any brakes, signalling the end of his day. The flags came in on lap fifteen, but after a pit stop by Pilette, the order settled down into a procession. The drivers that followed Gardner across the line were Hailwood, Rollinson, Mike Walker, Allen and Pilette in that order to score the other points from the race.

On 26 September, the new champion was back in action at the wheel of his Lola, and had Redman to contend with yet again when the series made its next appearance at Brands Hatch. Redman had reason to celebrate after it was disclosed that he had signed to share a sports car seat with Mario Andretti for Ferrari for the 1972 season. Obviously enthused by this, it was Redman who took pole position for the single thirty-lap race, more than half a second quicker than Gardner. Third fastest, and with a similar gap between himself and Gardner, was Rollinson, and then came Allen. Mike Walker and Trevor made up the third row. Hailwood, though, was a non-starter after blowing his engine whilst testing on the Club circuit the day before the meeting.

Redman stole away as the race began, followed hastily by the rest of the field in grid order. Mike Walker altered this at Westfield, as he passed Allen on the opening. On lap three, Spice rearranged things even more when he came from ninth to take seventh place. Redman and Gardner broke away from the chasing pack, and on lap eight the leader set a new lap record of 1 minute 27.6 seconds which he broke five laps later, recording a time four-tenths faster. Gardner equalled the quicker time on lap sixteen, and the battle continued. On the twenty-second tour, Gardner again recorded the same time, but Redman was determined not to let him get ahead and with two laps remaining, he set yet another lap record of 1 minute 27 seconds, equivalent to an average speed of 109.66mph. As the finishing line approached, Gardner got caught up in some back markers and decided to take the sensible option and ease off to finish second. Rollinson finished where he started, thirty-odd seconds after the winner, but eight in front of Mike Walker. Allen and Trevor Taylor did enough to halt the charge of Spice, to pick up the points from fifth and sixth respectively.

Tony Griffiths was present in his Brabham BT35X at Weston-super-Mare on 1 September to do battle in the annual speed trials organised jointly by the Burnham-on-Sea and Weston-super-Mare Motor Clubs. After the run-off of the top ten on the day, first prize went to the Repco-engined car after it shaved almost a second off the existing course record, too. Lane also beat the record, but he had to settle for a class win this time.

One week later the hillclimbers were out at Castle Howard for what was the end to their season, and Hepworth became champion when a 5.0-litre car called a Guyson Sandblast Special recorded the best time of the day. Having decided against using his four-wheel drive vehicle, he set another record time. Richard Thwaites was second, over one second slower in his M10B. A Formula 5000 car, designed by Ron Harris and given a Chevrolet engine, was driven by Malcolm Dungworth and finished fifth; the same car later competed at the HSCC race meeting at Oulton Park in 1991, driven by Malcolm Carter.

A non-championship Formula 5000 race that had been planned at Mallory Park for 10 October was cancelled, meaning that the climax to the season for the 1971 Rothmans runners was held at Brands Hatch, on 24 October. With the majority of the Formula 1 teams joining in, the event was described as the Rothmans World Championship Victory meeting, held in honour of Jackie Stewart winning the 1971 Formula 1 title. The feature race that had both Formulas represented didn't count for points in the Grand Prix series either.

For the Formula 5000 runners, this was a chance to show the Formula 1 team owners what they could do. Thirteen cars showed up from the latter category, one fewer than from the former. Reine Wisell was back behind the wheel of a Formula 5000 car, taking the place of Redman in the McLaren M18, but he couldn't stop Gardner from setting the fastest lap in this class. He went lapping in a time that unofficially equalled the old Formula 1 record, 1 minute 25.8 seconds. Wisell did start as joint second fastest of the Formula 5000 drivers, however, when, along with Rollinson and Mike Walker, he set a time identical to Redman's record from the previous meeting in Kent. The Swede completed row seven of the joint race grid. Holland and Spice formed an all-McLaren M10B row next, and Guy Edwards in a similar car started from the back row, two behind the championship regulars.

With the race under way, Wisell was the first of the Formula 5000 runners to go out, after he and Formula 1 racer, Pescarolo, had a coming together at Druids on lap two which finished both of them. After five laps, Rollinson led the chase for class honours in twelfth place overall, followed by Gardner and Mike Walker. This became eleventh a lap later, when Ganley's Formula 1 BRM P160 retired with engine problems. On lap fourteen, Rollinson advanced to tenth after Oliver was the next to call it a day, braking problems being the cause of his demise. On the very next lap, though, tragedy marred what should have been a joyful occasion, when an ominous pillar of black smoke was seen rising beyond the trees at Druids. Everyone knew something was wrong, and it was John Surtees in a Formula 1 TS9 who explained what he had seen as he was behind Jo Siffert's BRM P160. Apparently, the Swiss driver's car came under the bridge at South Bank, snaked left, right, and left again, demolishing the marker board, then rebounded off the bank and travelled partially over the marshal's post, hitting the bank once more before it burst into flames with Siffert stuck inside unable to get out. The marshals were similarly helpless as three of their fire extinguishers did not work correctly and Siffert was killed by the crash. The race was stopped, and the results declared in the positions the drivers held on lap fourteen, making Rollinson the master of his peers. Gardner was second, Mike Walker third, Spice, Pilette and Holland, fourth, fifth and sixth in that order. The rest of the meeting was abandoned.

With Gardner as champion, the top ten of the 1971 Rothmans European Formula 5000 Championship looked like this:

| Position | Driver | Car | Engine | Points |
|---|---|---|---|---|
| 1 | Frank Gardner | Lola T192<br>Lola T300 | 5.0 Chevrolet<br>5.0 Chevrolet | 95 |
| 2 | Mike Hailwood | Surtees TS8 | 5.0 Chevrolet | 58 |
| 3 | Mike Walker | Lola T192 | 5.0 Chevrolet | 40 |
| 4 | Alan Rollinson | Surtees TS8 | 5.0 Chevrolet | 35 |
| 5 | Brian Redman | McLaren M18A | 5.0 Chevrolet | 34 |
| 6 | Graham McRae | McLaren M10B | 5.0 Chevrolet | 33 |
| 7 | Ray Allen | McLaren M10B | 5.0 Chevrolet | 30 |
| 8 | Teddy Pilette | McLaren M10B | 5.0 Chevrolet | 18 |
| 9 | Trevor Taylor | Leda LT25 | 5.0 Chevrolet | 16 |
| 10 | David Prophet | McLaren M10B | 5.0 Chevrolet | 10 |

# CHAPTER 4

## MORE INTERNATIONAL COMPETITION ARRIVES

As in the previous year, a number of British competitors went 'down under' to take part in the Tasman series, before embarking on the 1972 European season. Frank Gardner took a Lola T300 to Pukekohe for the first of these, the New Zealand Grand Prix, and beat all-comers to win by twenty-seven seconds in front of Mike Hailwood's Team Surtees TS8A. David Hobbs was four seconds off the pace, in a McLaren M22A. Other regulars from the European series included Teddy Pilette in his 1971 car, and Graham McRae, who was back on home soil using a new Leda that he had co-designed and christened the LT27/GM1.

McRae won the round at the Levin circuit, near Wellington, whilst Gardner failed to finish after an uncharacteristic trip off-track when his Lola lost a wheel. Hailwood's title ambitions were high after finishing third. Round three followed one week later, with the drivers competing for the Lady Wigram Trophy at Christchurch. McRae displayed his knowledge of the circuit and led from start to finish. Hailwood was second, whilst one of the locals, Kevin Bartlett, who wasn't known to European crowds, was third. He bettered this at Teretonga, on New Zealand's South Island, when he took the top honours in his McLaren M10B. Pilette was second there, whilst Hailwood and McRae failed to finish. Despite that result, after the four-race New Zealand leg of the series, the championship was led by McRae.

The series moved across the sea to Australia a week later, and at Surfers Paradise McRae added another win to his tally. Gardner was runner-up, with Frank Matich the best of the local drivers. At Warwick Farm, Matich led the field across the finishing line after starting from pole. Gardner followed him, beating Matich's front-row colleague, Bartlett, to second place. McRae recorded another win at Sandown the following week, when Gardner was back in second again, and announced his retirement from single-seater racing immediately afterwards, whilst Hobbs took third place. The win meant that the remaining race wasn't really necessary for McRae to retain the championship, which was just as well as he was forced to retire at Adelaide International Raceway the following week. Hobbs took over in front after that, and recorded his first Tasman victory. Pilette was third.

When the 1972 European Championship race season opened, it started where it had finished in 1971, with Brands Hatch holding the first of fourteen rounds planned for the year. The same points-scoring system was retained, except for the last round when double points were on offer.

F5000 'down under'! Graham McRae shows a clean pair of wheels at Sandown. (Author's collection)

1971 European champion, Frank Gardner, shows Pukehoe some of his style. (Author's collection)

Above, left: 'Mike the Bike' at Pukehoe. (Author's collection)

David Hobbs was also in New Zealand. (Author's collection)

Kevin Bartlett wowed the crowd at Teretonga. (Author's collection)

*Frank Matich did the same at his home track of Sandown. (Author's collection)*

Prize money was increased slightly, but restricted to the first sixteen instead of the twenty who had benefitted in the previous season. Some rounds featured a single Formula 5000 contest, whilst others had one Formula 5000 and one combined race with some Formula 1 entrants, but only the first race would count for points. Rothmans continued as championship sponsor.

With seventeen entrants, the first twelve would qualify for the Race of Champions, a race that would feature fourteen drivers from the 1972 Formula 1 World Championship to be held the following day. When the cars went on to the track, however, just eleven were present on the black stuff. Incidentally, Gardner was also present in Kent that day, but he entered, and won, the Wiggins Teape Paperchase-sponsored Group 2 Touring Car event, rather than defend the title he took in 1971.

Dutchman Gijs van Lennep, a winner at Le Mans in 1970, joined the mainly British and Southern Hemisphere drivers on the grid, driving a TS11. None of them could do anything about McRae's new car in qualifying, although the Dutchman was the nearest to him. French hillclimber Herve Bayard, also driving a TS11, was another who was thwarted by the New Zealander. McRae took pole position just three-tenths slower than Gardner had done at the unfortunate Victory meeting the previous year. Rollinson took Gardner's place as the Lola works man, and lined up on the second row with the new Ferrari sports car driver, Redman. These four got away before the rest of the field and looked to be having their own race, with Keith Holland's McLaren M10B nearest to them and trying to keep the rest at bay. His race was over around half-distance, however, when his clutch gave up. With Redman in the lead, McRae overtook the McLaren driver at Druids on lap fourteen. Van Lennep looked to have secured second place after passing the Lancastrian later in the contest. With the laps running out, though, he started to drop back with handling problems, and Redman and Rollinson demoted him down the order. The top four continued to the finish in that order, but after the flag had swept all the runners by, a protest by Redman's team principal, Sid Taylor, saw McRae disqualified for passing whilst yellow flags were displayed. This promoted everyone up the order, as well as giving additional points to the top three plus Ray Allen, Pilette and Fred Saunders, who were fourth to sixth in that order.

In the Race of Champions, McRae was the fastest of the Formula 5000 qualifiers but he didn't start. This meant that, in fourteenth place, Van Lennep was the first of the Formula 5000 car drivers on the thirty-car grid, and with his race time being quicker than any he managed in qualifying, Redman was the next fastest. After forty laps, though, neither of these could complete the race, and it was Rollinson who upheld the honour of his class. He was tenth, coming in ahead of a couple of Formula 1 runners but a lap or so down on the winner, Emerson Fittipaldi, in a John Player Special Lotus.

Rollinson was keen to improve in the next round when the quest for the title reached Mallory

Park on 26 March, and with no Formula 1 cars in the way, his hopes of seeing the chequered flag first were high. Gordon Spice had other ideas, though, and it was he who put his Kitchmac on pole but only just; he set the time, and Rollinson equalled it. This was the car that was supposed to have been the Kitchiner K8, powered by a Rolls Royce engine. It didn't appear, however, so Tony Kitchiner constructed this car, based on a McLaren M10B, and used a Chevrolet power plant.

Van Lennep was away in Sebring but Sid Taylor chose not to bring in a replacement, meaning that just eleven cars were on the grid at the start. Holland was next fastest in a 1970 car, a McLaren M10B, with Ray Allen in a works-entered Surtees TS11 alongside him. McRae suffered all kinds of problems in qualifying, and decided not to enter the race.

A single fifty-lap race saw Rollinson sprint away, leaving the rest to fight for the other places the entire distance. Allen and Holland had also got in front of Spice on the opening circuit of the fifty, and they were keen to score as many points as they could. Holland and Spice then made contact at Gerrards, damaging the McLaren, but both carried on. Pilette reduced the field by one more when he retired at the end of lap one. Holland took the chase to Allen, but not until eight laps from the end did he get his reward – it turned out that a slow puncture in one of his rear tyres had affected the handling of his car. Allen was sufficiently ahead of Spice to finish third, David Prophet in a M18A was a lap behind the Kitchmac driver, and he took fourth, whilst Fred Saunders' ageing Crosslé took the remaining point although he only completed forty-six laps. Bob Howlings was the only other finisher, three more laps down, yet another McLaren driver in Allen's old M10A.

Five days later, Good Friday saw Rollinson leading the championship with 15 points before the day's activities got under way at Snetterton. Redman was second following his win at Brands Hatch that gave him 9, with Allen next on 7. Once more just eleven cars came to the line, but this time it was van Lennep who dominated the practice sessions. Spice showed that his pace at Mallory Park wasn't a one-off as he repeated his qualifying position. McRae, Redman and Rollinson were the next fastest, but the series leader failed to start because he had broken the gearbox on his Lola T300 during qualifying. McRae's woes from the previous round came back as the race got under way, and he went straight into the pits instead of onto the first lap as the runners prepared for the start. That didn't stop van Lennep from shooting off into the lead. Spice was next, followed by Pilette, Holland, Redman, Allen, newcomers Steve Thompson and Clive Santo, and Saunders in that order. Spice found a way past van Lennep on the second lap, but the others remained unchanged until the fifth of the twenty laps when Holland's race was over with a problematic fuel pump. Van Lennep hadn't given up, though, and with Pilette and Redman he closed on the leader and pulled away from the rest as the race wore on. The Dutchman's pressure paid off on the thirteenth lap when he eased ahead of the Kitchmac at the hairpin, setting off into a lead that he held for rest of the race. Spice, though, had a sick car, and despite trying to nurse it home, he spun into the banking at the Esses on the penultimate lap, promoting Pilette to second place. Redman had a misfire in his M10B but managed to hang on to third place until the flag fell. Thompson marked his debut with fourth place, with Allen and Saunders picking up the final points positions, the former scoring twice the number of the Irishman.

Brands Hatch Club circuit was next for the newer drivers to face a few days later on Easter Monday. Rollinson and McRae had had their cars fixed and joined the grid, and Dave Berry and Ray Calcutt were also there making the numbers up to fifteen for the sixty-lap contest. McRae showed he was back in business by claiming pole position in a time that beat his own lap record by two-tenths of a second.

Redman set the same time, but after the Tasman champion, so lined up alongside him. Rollinson also signalled his return when he was a couple of tenths behind the top two. He shared the time and the second row with Holland. The two from the Benelux countries started from row three, with van Lennep slightly faster than Pilette. Allen and Calcutt were team-mates and row mates on the next line, behind the two overseas pilots.

*At Brands Hatch, Ray Calcutt pulls out all the stops. (Courtesy Richard Bunyan)*

*Alan Rollinson managed a few more. (Courtesy David Lawson)*

*Meanwhile, Steve Thompson showed the Kent crowd a nice car. (Author's collection)*

*Dave Berry travelled from north Wales to enter this Brabham. (Author's collection)*

Despite the programme advertising fifteen runners, this became fourteen before a racing wheel had turned as Prophet's car was pushed off the grid with fuel seeping into the cockpit. When the cars did get to go, McRae and Redman showed why they were at the front and roared into Paddock side-by-side. McRae edged in front, though, and began to pull away from Redman as the first lap came to a close. Rollinson was catching up but had one eye on his mirrors as Holland, van Lennep and Pilette weren't too far behind him. After ten laps, McRae was six seconds ahead of Redman, which became ten seconds on lap thirty-five. There was little change behind Redman in the intervening laps, but on lap thirty-nine Rollinson ran wide at Clearways. That mistake allowed Holland and Holland's finest, van Lennep, to rush through the gap that was created. Pilette wasn't so lucky; having pressured Holland into making a mistake on lap forty-six, van Lennep went after Redman, but couldn't find a way to get past, and finished two-tenths behind as the flag fell. McRae had finished over thirteen seconds before the two of them. Rollinson regained one place after Holland's slip put him into the Armco at Bottom Bend, and finished fourth. Pilette took fifth whilst Calcutt, although two laps down, recorded his first championship point on his 'home' track.

For the first trip into Europe in 1972, Pilette went home to Belgium, when the new circuit at Nivelles was used for the two heats that made up round five of the Rothmans European Formula 5000 Championship. Just six days after the drivers had been in Kent, the 1970 SCCA Champion, John Cannon, was present and brought along a 4840cc Oldsmobile/Rover-powered March 725, which stole everyone's thunder when he planted it on pole. McRae was so keen to keep up that he spun his LT27 in practice, but not before registering the second fastest practice time. Pilette and van Lennep were together again, one row better off than their previous outing, whilst Redman had to settle for fifth position next to Allen.

Although sixteen cars qualified for the first heat, only thirteen actually started the twenty-seven-lapper. Calcutt and Thompson had hoped to take part, but a holed piston for the former, and oil pump problems for the latter put paid to their hopes. The race was delayed when the organisers allowed everyone three warm-up laps as they weren't sure about the weather conditions, and gave teams extra time to decide on tyres. When they did start, some ran on slicks, some on grooved slicks, whilst others used intermediates. The third driver to drop out before racing finally got under way was Max Reinhard, his Kincraft died on the grid with a dead battery. McRae was the first to show at the front of the pack, followed by van Lennep, Pilette, Rollinson and the rest. Cannon and Redman slipped into fifth and sixth respectively as the lap drew to a close. Cannon's fortunes faded on lap two when his engine seized and he spun and stopped on the way into the hairpin. He managed to get the car going again, but retired after completing just one more lap. After five laps in front, McRae felt his tyres going off and the slick-shod car of van Lennep got by. Redman was also on slicks, and it was only another two laps before the Kiwi had to let him pass as well. Redman then took the lead on lap eleven, but wondered why on the next lap as his McLaren came to a sputtering halt as he went past the pits. This allowed the Dutchman to retake the lead, pursued by Pilette, Rollinson and McRae in that order, although Rollinson gave up on lap seventeen after an upright broke on his Lola T300. With the remaining three holding station, the race was over ten laps later. Fourth position was taken by Allen, whilst Santo and John Coulter were fifth and sixth.

Pilette used home advantage to pull away from the field in the second heat, but the joy of his countrymen was short-lived as McRae went past five laps later. Van Lennep was looking to score an outright win, but he, too, was disappointed when the engine on his Surtees started to misfire and he headed for the pits. He rejoined but was six laps down with his chances of victory gone, so used the remainder of the heat as a live testing session. Rollinson added to Pilette's misery when he snapped up second place before the end, but was almost twenty-one seconds behind McRae. Cannon had his car repaired in time for this heat, and earned a fine fourth position behind Santo.

With McRae safely on the top step of the podium, he took the North Sea Trophy home as well, and Pilette restored some Belgian pride when he was second overall. Allen was on the third step and just missing out were Santos in fourth and van Lennep, fifth. With the 2 points he scored, van Lennep joined Redman at the top of the championship table on 19 points. Rollinson and McRae were just a point behind, and Pilette was another 2 adrift.

With all that going abroad, the first of the season's hillclimb contests at Prescott was held over the same weekend, and it was also the first part of the BARC/Castrol Championship for the year. Formula 5000 was represented by Richard Thwaites' McLaren M10B and Richard Shardlow in a similar car that had been used previously by the course record holder, Roy Lane. Lane and the 1971 champion, David Hepworth, though, were both missing from the event as their cars were broken. At the end of all of the runs it was Thwaites who recorded the BTD, with a time of 49.83 seconds, and he repeated his success the following Sunday whilst competing in the same championship at Pontypool.

Silverstone was the next to host a round of the Rothmans series when it returned to the UK on 22 April. Formula 5000 had a two-day event, with Formula 1 cars present for the second on the Sunday. McRae was out to create a hat trick of wins, and did his hopes no damage when he sat in pole position in the first contest. Redman, though, got the best start, and lead going into Copse. McRae held on to his tail with van Lennep next, followed by Cannon, Rollinson and nine others. The number behind the Canadian reduced after seven laps, however, as Rollinson retired with engine problems. Eight laps in and McRae put the power down on the way into Woodcote and Redman was demoted to second. The Lancastrian's tyres were wearing out and van Lennep was closing, but the Dutchman ran wide on the final tour and lost a lot of ground before coming back on to the track, leaving Redman to finish in his starting position. Van Lennep's mistake did not push him any further down the field, and he was third. Cannon was another to finish in the same place as he started, but Allen and Spice benefitted from Rollinson's retirement.

On Sunday 23 April, the previous day's winner sat on row four with Denny Hulme next to him. Redman, van Lennep and Rollinson were just as keen to score more points, and they took the next Formula 5000 places on the grid. In between the first of these two was Graham Hill, the lowest of the Formula 1 runners. As the race got under way, Rollinson made the best start of his class but only just in front of Pilette and McRae. At the end of lap two McRae managed to dispose of Pilette, and on the third lap he also got in front of a slowing Lola, driven by Rollinson, which made it to the pits and had to have a new damper fitted before rejoining. McRae was on full throttle to catch Peter Gethin in the Formula 1 BRM P160, and within a few laps he managed to pass the former double Formula 5000 Champion. With two laps to go, however, his car spun at Becketts, allowing Gethin back in front to take sixth overall, but McRae recovered to finish the class winner. Van Lennep led the chase for second in class from Cannon, Pilette and Allen, although the chances of the latter became dented when he hit the barriers at Abbey. Van Lennep maintained a better line than he had in the previous day's race, and he held on to second place in front of the March driver, who in turn kept Pilette behind. Thompson came through to assume the place vacated by Allen, whilst Santo scored the final Formula 5000 point of the day.

In the BARC/Castrol Hillclimb Championship meeting that was held at Harewood on the same day as the Silverstone track race, Thwaites brought along a 5.7-litre McLaren M14D to compete. Lane was in a similar car that had been used by Andrea de Adamich and Denny Hulme in Formula 1 races, in the class for 1600cc racing cars. Hepworth was present in his usual four-wheel drive car of his own design, whilst for a change, Mike McDowell used a 5.0-litre Brabham BT36X with rear wheels borrowed from Tony Griffiths. These must have been effective as it was his car that was the fastest before the run-off for the top ten contestants. Lane ran up the hill in 40.57 seconds during this period, a little over a couple of tenths faster than Thwaites, to record the quickest time of the day.

Round seven saw sixteen cars and drivers cross the sea again, but this time it was the Irish Sea not the North Sea. Mondello Park held a pair of thirty-lap heats, but this time McRae wasn't present to extend his championship lead as he was preparing to take part in a US series. A few of the local Formula Ireland series joined the rest of the regulars, headed by Brian Nelson in a Crosslé 22F, who was on row two with Rollinson. Both of these drivers set the second fastest qualifying time, but not until Cannon had also travelled round the track in 55.4 seconds. McRae's absence gave Redman the chance to pull back some points on his rival, and he looked to have done so when he was the fastest qualifier for the first heat, two-tenths quicker than the three behind him.

The rain was heavy at the start, and Redman dominated the rest when he took a flag-to-flag victory. Cannon was the next to show, keeping Rollinson, van Lennep and Holland behind, with Nelson, who slipped back a little, pushing to catch up. Holland's enthusiasm was dented slightly, though, on the second lap, when he spun his McLaren at Dunlop, but he managed to recover and set about the chase again. On lap eight, Cannon left the circuit at Shell and took his time to rejoin, and Rollinson moved in front of van Lennep. By lap nine, Holland was back behind van Lennep, and after another five he'd passed both him and Rollinson but he couldn't catch Redman. Rollinson also went missing from the top ten after he'd stalled his Lola around the mid-point of the race, gifting van Lennep third position that he held on to until the end of the heat. Santo, Thompson and Edwards made up the top six, but all were lapped by the winner.

With the weather a little better for the second heat, Redman showed his class once more and powered away into the lead that he never lost. Van Lennep was closer this time, but couldn't find a way to get his Surtees TS11 past and had to settle for second at the flag. Holland had to work hard to keep Cannon and Thompson behind him for the first seven trips around the circuit, and his resistance finally crumbled on lap eight when the March driver got ahead. Thompson's persistence also paid off as his Surtees TS8 passed the McLaren M10B seven laps later.

Redman regained the championship lead after scoring 9 points in Ireland, giving him a 5-point advantage over van Lennep who finished in second place overall. Holland was the final podium dweller, just ahead of Thompson. Cannon and Santo took the other honours, 2 to the Canadian and 1 to the Brit.

Once again, hillclimbers put their cars out over the same weekend, and this time it was the first round of the Shell/RAC Championship. Loton Park was the venue, and six drivers bettered the course record with Hepworth being the fastest of the lot. Lane was the second fastest Formula 5000 runner, but he wasn't the second fastest of the day as Sir Nick Williamson took that title. Thwaites' run was less than effective, and he finished a disappointing ninth.

Almost a month went by before round eight brought Formula 5000 Championship cars back to the place where they had started back in 1969 – Oulton Park – on May Bank Holiday Monday. Eight Formula 1 cars were entered for a joint race, including Emerson Fittipaldi, Denny Hulme, Ronnie Peterson and Tim Schenken. Also driving in this class were the sometime Formula 5000 pilots, Reine Wisell and Vern Scuppan. All were competing for the coveted Gold Cup.

Before the main event, the Formula 5000 racers opened the programme in a twenty-lap race on their own, with the top ten invited to enter the Gold Cup race. After taking fifth place in the Formula 1 McLaren M19A at Monaco, Redman used the first Formula 5000 Chevron car designed by Derek Bennett, the B24, in Cheshire. Also behind the wheel of new machines were Trevor Taylor and Pilette, who were in a Leda LT27 and a McLaren M22 respectively. Leda then provided McRae with another new LT27, known also as the GM1, that he had co-designed. The best he could do in qualifying was to finish seventh, but engine problems ruled him out of the twenty-lap race. Top spot, almost one-and-a-half seconds quicker than the Chevron, went to Rollinson in a Lola T300, who lapped the international field in 1 minute 26.6 seconds.

With a wet track in front of them, sixteen cars came to the grid using tyres that were designed for the rain, the exception was Redman who chose to go on intermediates. It looked to have been a good decision, too, as he

*Back in England, Pierre Soukry has a go. (Courtesy Norman Hayes)*

sprinted away from the rest as the race started, followed by the pole-sitter. Both he and Rollinson were relatively untroubled for the duration, and the race was really to see who could finish third. Trevor Taylor mounted the first serious challenge, but he only lasted four laps before the clutch on his LT27 broke. Pilette took over the mantle and kept Holland at bay to take the place. Completing one lap fewer than the top four, but still able to score a couple of points was Allen, whilst Edwards picked up the final point when he was sixth in front of a frustrated van Lennep.

The Gold Cup race was held over forty laps and started the second event after lunch. Gethin in his Formula 1 BRM took the pole, whilst the fastest Formula 5000 competitor was on row two, Rollinson in his Lola T300 alongside Dave Walker in a John Player Special Lotus. The weather was a little better but there was still rain in the air. The first corner saw Gethin and Hulme jostling for the overall lead, but as far as Formula 5000 was concerned, Redman was the man in charge, hot on the tail of Fittipaldi. Rollinson was next; he was also ahead of a couple of other Formula 1 cars. Gethin retired his car at the end of lap eight, promoting the Formula 5000 men, and Rollinson retired with a broken cross-member. Before the end, Schenken got through to keep Redman off the podium. The overall victor was Hulme, who along with Fittipaldi was the only one to complete the full race distance. Schuppan was fifth, a lap ahead of Allen in sixth and Edwards in seventh place.

The next round of the Shell/RAC Hillclimb on 10 June at Shelsley Walsh saw the renewal of rivalries between Thwaites, Lane, Griffiths, Hepworth and the rest. Lane emerged from the class runs as the fastest of the day when his McLaren M14D managed to scale the hill in 31.52 seconds. Hepworth was the fastest of the top ten run-off entrants. In the championship, Lane led the field with 41 points, 1 more than Williamson. McDowell and Hepworth were joint third on 36. Williamson took over in the lead after the next round at Doune the following week, driving a 2.0-litre March. A future British Touring Car Champion also took part in this event, but in a single-litre Mini Cooper S rather than a Formula 5000 car, and he recorded a class win. Of the Formula 5000 entrants, Hepworth was two-hundredths of a second faster than Thwaites but a bit more than the time recorded by Lane. This time he drove a Guyson Sandblaster with a 5.0-litre engine.

The Rothmans series returned to the tight and twisty Leicestershire track at Mallory Park on 18 June. Redman was absent as he had other work to do in the L & M-sponsored race series in the United States, so a good points score would help all of the drivers eat into his championship lead. McRae was absent for the same reason. Once more Rollinson showed his class when he recorded his second consecutive pole position with a time of 42.2 seconds, and Thompson lined up alongside him with his best qualifying position of the season so far. Redman's nearest rival, van Lennep, took third place on the grid flanked by Allen for the first of the two twenty-five-lap heats. Holland and Trevor Taylor completed the top six. Cyd Williams was also present on the grid for his first Formula 5000 race in a McLaren M10B.

Rollinson showed that his qualifying performance hadn't been a flash in the pan as he led the sixteen-car train on a very wet track into Gerards. Thompson, behind, was working hard to try to catch his cousin, as well as keep van Lennep in third position. Around three-quarters distance however, Rollinson and Thompson swapped places when they came across Santo who was someway behind the rest. Thompson never looked back, crossing the line over seven seconds before the rest. Van Lennep came through to take second place after a spin by Rollinson let him, Holland and Trevor Taylor past before the end. Santo was next and Williams finished tenth. Holland, though, had a mishap of his own on the slowing-down lap which forced him to miss the following heat.

The second heat saw Thompson clearly in the mood to make it an outright victory for the ninth round. This was evident as the flag fell, sending them on the way for the second time that day, and he won comfortably. Rollinson and van Lennep diced for second, but once more fate conspired against the Englishman and he spun on the nineteenth lap. This dropped him not only behind van Lennep, but Pilette as well, although he recovered in time to finish in fourth place behind this pair. Williams came home in fifth this time, whilst Ashley was sixth.

Despite his spinning antics, Rollinson recorded third place overall behind a joyous Thompson and van Lennep. The 6 points for the Dutchman brought him within 8 points of the missing Englishman, Redman, and 7 points in front of Rollinson. McRae was now back in fourth place, 1 point behind the Lola driver. Frenchman Pierre Soukry did enough over the two legs to record fifth place in his McLaren M10B, whilst Williams' efforts were rewarded with sixth position.

The Golden Jubilee of the Yorkshire region of the BARC was celebrated with a round of the club's Hillclimb Championship, jointly sponsored with Castrol at Harewood. As well as points, the drivers were competing for the Montague Burton Trophy. The recipient of this and the top points haul was Lane, who was behind the wheel of the McLaren M17D that he had campaigned so well throughout the season. Thwaites and Hepworth came close to Lane's time but were unable to go faster before the day came to an end.

The 1972 British Grand Prix commemorating the seventy-fifth anniversary of the RAC was held at Brands Hatch, and one of its supporting races was round ten of the Rothmans European Formula 5000 Championship. Rival tobacco company, John Player, was the title sponsor of the meeting, however, so this round was renamed the Charles Heidsieck Challenge Trophy race. With the race being staged on 13 July in beautiful sunshine, it made a change not to have rain spoiling the twenty-five-lap contest. Redman was missing, working in the United States. Rollinson recorded the fastest practice time yet again, but this time he had a TS11 driver next to him, van Lennep. Only fourteen cars were on the grid at the start, including McRae, the new owner of Leda Cars Ltd, although he was at the back after missing the practice session. He qualified during the Formula 1 qualification process. Ian Ashley started from fourth in an old Lola T190.

Although Rollinson got away cleanly, the best of the opening laps was driven by McRae who crossed the line in sixth as the second lap began. His charge took him to the front on lap five, and as the laps ran out, he took an unexpected victory. Rollinson's misery continued as van Lennep also got past him on lap seven, but he managed to hang on to third place as the flag was waved to signal the end of the race. Holland came through in his McLaren M10B to take a lonely fourth from Allen. Ashley was close to fifth, but the McLaren M18 driver passed him and crossed the line just one-tenth of a second before the Lola did.

The next round of the BARC/Castrol Hillclimb Championship was held on 22 July at Gurston Down. With glorious weather and a resurfaced track, hopes were high for a new record run. Most of the usual drivers of Formula 5000 cars of this discipline were present. Thwaites and Lane were joined by Jonty Williamson behind the wheels of McLarens, but in the end the BTD of 32.85 seconds was recorded by the first of these men.

Bouley Bay, Jersey was the next venue for the hillclimbers, and it was the Shell/RAC series that took them to the Channel Island the week after Gurston Down. Hepworth's car was stuck in Portsmouth as a result of a strike by dockers at the port. In the Formula 5000 cars, Lane had problems throughout the day, whilst Thwaites finished in the best position, second, followed by McDowell and Griffiths. Thwaites was in his usual M10B but the other two used Repco-powered Brabhams.

Two of the regular track racers warmed up for the next round of the Rothmans Championship by entering the Silverstone Formula Libre race on 29 July, and used their time to great effect. Thompson took along his Surtees TS8, with Prophet in a McLaren M10B with a new wing. The latter took pole position, and when proceedings got under way they gave a display that wouldn't have gone amiss in the European Championship. Thompson made the best start but Prophet wasn't about to let him have an easy ride, and on lap seven he took over. That wasn't the final act, though, and on the last of the ten laps, the Surtees driver shot back in front and saw the flag inches before his rival. Thompson also had the joy of setting a new outright lap record of 52.6 seconds, equivalent to an average speed of 110.05mph!

On 6 August, Silverstone was also the venue for the next round of the championship, giving van Lennep the chance to take the lead as Redman's American duties kept him away from this meeting as well. The Dutchman didn't shake the world in qualifying, however, making the second row, over a second behind McRae but a little bit less behind Rollinson who, after damaging his usual Lola at Becketts, forfeited his place when he drove the Kitchmac that Saunders had acquired in place of his usual Crosslé. Van Lennep did have the satisfaction of knowing that the other eight cars were behind him, though, including his team-mate Allen. Amongst those the pair found themselves in front of were Cannon and Thompson.

Qualifying places didn't count for anything, however, when the twenty-five-lap race got under way, and van Lennep showed he was hungry enough to take the lead as the pack shuffled into Stowe. Cannon was another to show his keenness for victory and he, too, demoted McRae before the lap unfolded. As lap eight started without McRae, who had decided that the wet track was no place for his GM1, obviously the previous week's run had proved advantageous and Thompson came through into third place. Ashley was keen to get on to the podium but Thompson was just as keen to stop him. After spinning at Chapel Allen on lap seven, he had dropped to last place but recovered to seventh as the race wore on. Russell then got ahead of him three laps later. With the rain still persistently falling the organisers decided to cut eight laps from the race distance. This gave van Lennep the chance to pull away from all his pursuers although Cannon caught him up on the last lap but failed to find a way past. Despite the pressure from the Canadian, the Surtees driver crossed the line just four-tenths in front of the Oldsmobile-powered March. Thompson maintained his position, as did Ashley, whilst Russell and Santo were the other two points scorers on the day.

This win meant that the chase for the title was now led by 7 points in favour of the former Le Mans driver, van Lennep. He was the only one to make any significant ground on Redman, as McRae's non-finish meant he still only had 36 points compared to Redman's 43. Rollinson also failed to score; he finished just out of the points in seventh place, leaving him 4 shy of the Kiwi.

Santo went to Brands with his McLaren on 12 August, and won a Formula Libre contest that was part of the Lombard Formula 3 Championship race day, although he didn't record the fastest lap.

Loton Park was the venue for the tenth round of the BARC/Castrol Hillclimb Championship on 13 August, but none of the big car runners was able to make an impression for the BTD. Thwaites, however, did record a class win. The Shell/RAC Championship continued at Shelsley Walsh a week later, and this time Formula 5000 drivers filled the first three places, with McDowell the fastest of them all. Lane was second quickest followed by Thwaites. Further down the results, but in the top ten, were Hepworth and Griffiths.

Another joint race with Formula 1 cars took

place in Kent, over the August Bank Holiday weekend, in what was billed as the Rothmans 50,000. Redman was back in the UK for the race, using a Formula 1 McLaren M19A bearing number 1. Tony Lanfranchi took part in qualifying using an M18 for his first Formula 5000 drive of the year, but he failed to meet the standard and drove in the supporting race. Fittipaldi took pole position for the joint grid, but McRae was the fastest of the bigger-engined machines.

Behind the first seven Formula 1 runners, the New Zealander was the first of his peers to be seen by the crowd going into Paddock Hill Bend, and he kept them at bay until he had to pit after ten laps with fuel leaking into his cockpit. This meant that Rollinson became leader of his class well ahead of van Lennep and Thompson, but refuelling stops would be necessary so they could run for the one hundred and eighteen planned laps, and they would change things. Van Lennep became the first to pit for fuel on lap thirty, giving Thompson the chance to circulate second of the Formula 5000 runners. Rollinson stopped seven laps later, pushing his cousin further up the order. All this time Prophet was another climbing through the ranks, although when Rollinson rejoined, he came under close scrutiny from the now fully-fuelled Lola driver. On lap fifty-seven that pressure paid off, as Rollinson reclaimed one placing, finally passing Prophet. Van Lennep needed a marshal to push-start him after his pit stop, so he was promptly disqualified. Thompson fell back behind Rollinson following his first stop, and there was more drama five laps from the end when Rollinson's car collided with John Watson's Chevron B20, although they both managed to continue without losing a place. Thompson's car then ran out of fuel with just two laps to go, and Prophet inherited the place he vacated, taking the second Formula 5000 position, but ninth overall, two places behind Rollinson. The third Formula 5000 car classified was that of Thompson, even though he failed to finish, but his one hundred and seven laps completed was more than the rest had done when the chequered was shown to the winner, Fittipaldi.

The supporting race on the day was for the drivers and cars that had failed to qualify for the main event. After one hundred kilometres – twenty-four laps – Ian Ashley was the leading Formula 5000 driver, finishing second to David Morgan's Formula 2 Brabham BT38A. Tony Dean was third in another Formula 2 car, with Lanfranchi crossing the line behind him.

More hillclimbing from the Shell/RAC Championship occurred at Prescott, on 2 September. On a bright sunny day it looked like McDowell was the man to beat, as he broke Lane's course record early on. Williamson then beat McDowell's time in his non-Formula 5000 entry, but that wasn't the end of the matter; Lane came out to win the record back before the finish and claim top spot. Hepworth was another record breaker, but the best he could do was to finish third, demoting McDowell a place down the standings. Thwaites was fifth. The series moved on to Harewood the following weekend, and this time McDowell was the name that was seen at the top of the time sheets with a new course record. Hepworth improved to second place, but Lane dropped to third. Thwaites was another who improved his previous week's position by one, and Griffiths came through in fifth.

With three rounds remaining and Redman back Stateside, the thirty-lap race on Brands Hatch Grand Prix circuit on 24 September gave van Lennep a chance to extend his lead in the championship. McRae and Cannon were also away, which meant that Rollinson could also make up some ground. The New Zealander's trips to the 'other side of the pond' proved fruitful, and he added the L & M-backed SCCA Formula 5000 title to his Tasman success, the same weekend as the race in Kent. Redman was joint third in the American series.

With his Lola in full working order, Rollinson showed his intentions with a blistering lap that took him on to pole position, whilst a car similar to the one he drove in the previous round now had Spice as its driver, and he started next. The Surtees team-mates, van Lennep and Allen, were together again on the next row, whilst Prophet was a bit further back in fifth grid position. Thompson completed the top six qualifiers, whilst Ashley was the only other driver to beat one-and-a-half minutes for the lap.

Rollinson led the entry round on the warm-up lap, and as soon as he got the signal to start racing he led them into Paddock Hill Bend as well. Spice became the first retirement when the car's electrics failed after four laps. Van Lennep assumed the place vacated by Spice, with his team-mate behind fending off the attentions of Prophet. Prophet in turn was coming under close scrutiny by Thompson, who managed to pass the McLaren on lap fourteen. His race came to an end six laps later, though, when a shock absorber broke on the TS8, leaving Prophet virtually untroubled for the remaining ten laps. Ahead of Prophet, Allen never bothered his colleague, and it seemed that van Lennep had decided not to trouble Rollinson either, who set a new lap record. Ashley added another 2 points to his season's total, whilst Edwards added just 1 when they were fifth and sixth respectively. Chris Baker was present for his first outing in a Formula

*Backed by Donington supremo Tom Wheatcroft, Roger Williamson tried his hand at F5000. (Courtesy Norman Hayes)*

*Defending his championship in style, Frank Gardner at Oulton Park. (Courtesy Norman Hayes)*

*Ray Allen in Cheshire. (Courtesy Norman Hayes)*

*Gijs van Lennep was in northwest England, too. (Courtesy Norman Hayes)*

5000 car, a Lola T190 that had been driven by Frank Gardner, but unfortunately he finished out of the points in seventh. Lanfranchi was eighth.

The final round of the BARC/Castrol Hillclimb was held 'up north' at Harewood, whilst the Rothmans race was going on 'down south' at Brands Hatch. Thwaites recorded the best time again whilst Hepworth, back in his four-wheel drive motor, was second. Lane had a problem going up the hill, but still managed to set the third fastest time. Sadly it wasn't enough to allow a Formula 5000 runner being champion; that honour went to Chris Seaman who drove an MG Midget for most of the season. On 1 October Dewsbury's Thwaites made sure that he was the first ever victor at a Scammonden Hillclimb, and this was made worthwhile when he repeated his success. In the other major championship of the year, the Shell/RAC series, the title was won by Sir Nick Williamson.

*Jock Russell in a McRae. (Courtesy Graham Petch)*

On 13 October, Oulton Park welcomed Formula 5000 cars for their second appearance in 1972 for the penultimate round of the championship. McRae was back after his very successful American duties, as were Redman and Cannon, and it was the second of these three who had the best of the times after practice. McRae was alongside Redman, and Rollinson was on the next row of the grid with the new British Formula 3 Champion, Roger Williamson, given an opportunity to impress in his first ever Formula 5000 contest in the Kitchmac usually driven by Spice. Thompson, and Cannon on his first visit to the Cheshire circuit, made up the top six, with Redman's title nemesis, van Lennep, some way down on the grid in tenth. Allen missed the race after giving up the seat in his Surtees to his team-mate because the Dutchman had damaged his TS11 during testing the day before. Berry was back with his old Brabham, and he started three places from the back of the grid.

When the cars were set free, it was a close thing between the top two to see who led entering Old Hall, but on the Avenue it became clear that it was Redman who was just in front. Rollinson maintained his grid placing, whilst Thompson and Cannon exceeded their positions by passing Williamson. The new man, though, soon caught and passed them both to get back to where he started. On lap thirteen the top four were close together, and approached Hill Top with Redman still in front. Coming up to the super fast Knicker Brook they came across a spinning Russell. Redman had to take to the grass to avoid him, and in doing so he damaged the radiator of his Chevron and with it his chances of victory and title hopes. McRae was more fortunate and carried on into a lead that he never lost. Rollinson was promoted to second place, and he finished over seventeen seconds behind the winner. Cannon showed why he had been the SCCA Champion a couple of years previously, especially after contact between himself and Williamson. All of this bumping saw the newcomer run off the track into the barriers, fortunately he was unhurt, and the Canadian took third place in his stead. Van Lennep made up six places to finish fourth which extended his lead in the standings, and Pilette and Prophet completed the top six. Williamson did enough to be classified seventh finisher, whilst Wrexham's Berry was three laps down but placed eighth.

With double points available in the last round, the top four overall were able to win the title. Van Lennep was out in front with 59 points, Rollinson had 47 and McRae was on 45 and looking to claim a third championship title of the season. Redman was fourth and possibly an outside bet, still on 43 points. It was the outsider who led the way in practice when he took pole position on Brands Hatch Club circuit a week after his Oulton debacle. Despite his comments pre-season, Gardner made an appearance in a new Lola, a T330, and placed it next to Redman's Chevron for the fifty-lap contest. McRae was immediately behind Redman, whilst Gardner's shadow was filled by Rollinson. Van Lennep and Cannon made up row three. After his spin the previous week, Russell gave the keys to his Leda to Brett Lunger, an American that had raced against Redman, McRae and Cannon in the American series earlier in the season.

Redman was in determined mood as the flag fell to signal racing could start, and he roared off the line. McRae made light of Gardner's challenge as he went past the new car on the way to the first corner. Redman was in no mood to make any mistakes this time, but McRae was keen to have a piece of the action as well and the two circulated closely for each of the fifty laps. Lapping backmarkers became a formality for the pair, and everyone except Gardner was a lap behind them when the chequered flag was shown, the advantage going the way of the Chevron, two-tenths ahead of McRae. Van Lennep once more recorded fourth place, with Rollinson and Williamson in fifth and sixth respectively, despite the latter having troubles with a lack of brakes. Lunger retired a couple of laps after half-distance with electrical troubles. He was joined in the 'retirement home' by Edwards, whose McLaren M10B had a burst water hose on lap thirty-four.

A joint race with Formula 1 cars brought the curtain down on the European season the following day. Redman switched cars, and Formulae, and used a McLaren M19C on the day. Holland used some of his savings to buy the Chevron B24 that was Redman's usual car during 1972, and entered it the race. Fastest of the Formula 5000 drivers invited to take part, though, was McRae. Gardner was second fastest but decided against taking part, meaning that van Lennep lined up next. Cannon shared the same time as the new champion, but only after the Dutchman had set it. Rollinson was next. In the front of everyone, though, was the new Formula 1 World Champion, Fittipaldi.

Ronnie Peterson out-dragged his 1973 Lotus team-mate at the start, but as far as Formula 5000 was concerned, it was the new owner of the B24 who showed everyone that he could be the best amongst his peers. He continued in this position for the full forty laps, and took eleventh place overall. Over ten seconds later McRae was twelfth on the road, with Ashley edging out Rollinson for third step on the Formula 5000 podium.

Despite victory in the Formula 5000 race and his double points haul, Redman had not done enough to prevent van Lennep becoming champion at his first attempt, and the points at the end of the season are shown in the table.

| Position | Driver | Car | Engine | Points |
|---|---|---|---|---|
| 1 | Gijs van Lennep | Surtees TS11<br>McLaren M18 | 5.0 Chevrolet<br>5.0 Chevrolet | 65 |
| 2 | Brian Redman | McLaren M10B<br>Chevron B24 | 5.0 Chevrolet<br>5.0 Chevrolet | 61 |
| 3 | Graham McRae | Leda/McRae LT27/GM1 | 5.0 Chevrolet | 57 |
| 4 | Alan Rollinson | Lola T300<br>Kitchmac | 5.0 Chevrolet<br>5.0 Chevrolet | 51 |
| 5 | Teddy Pilette | McLaren M18<br>McLaren M22 | 5.0 Chevrolet<br>5.0 Chevrolet | 25 |
| 6 | Ray Allen | McLaren M18<br>Surtees TS11 | 5.0 Chevrolet<br>5.0 Chevrolet | 23 |
| 7 | Steve Thompson | Surtees TS8 | 5.0 Chevrolet | 19 |
| 8 | Keith Holland | McLaren M10B | 5.0 Chevrolet | 16 |
| 9 | John Cannon | March 725 | 5.0 Oldsmobile | 15 |
| 10 | Frank Gardner | Lola T330 | 5.0 Chevrolet | 8 |

# CHAPTER 5

## FEWER HORSES, MORE POWER?

When the championship regulations were announced for 1973, it was stated that cars could run with engines of 2750cc up to 5000cc, and that turbochargers were allowed for cars with engines of up to four litres in capacity. Minimum weight limits were also introduced, with smaller machines needing to achieve at least 1210lb, and bigger-engined cars requiring a further 40lb.

Fifteen points-scoring rounds were also announced, with the final race again a double points event. The points were awarded to the top ten finishers as follows: 20-15-12-10-8-6-4-3-2-1. To quell any arguments with the teams, Rothmans, which continued as series sponsor, increased prize money as well. In races of over fifty but fewer than seventy miles long, the pot was increased to £3450. The winner received £750, with cash prizes going all the way down to £100 awarded for sixteenth place. The longer races also had an increased prize fund of £7080. For those, the victor won £1500, whilst the last cheque was for £200, again paid to the sixteenth finisher. An additional £1000 went to the champion at the end of the year.

The European Championship season began where it had finished in 1973, at Brands Hatch, but on the Grand Prix circuit instead of the Club version, and 17 March saw the opening round. Twenty cars faced the starter for a twenty-five lap contest, but without Brian Redman who had been drafted, with Reine Wisell, into Carl Haas' team of Lola T330s in the L & M-backed series in the USA. Cars bearing the manufacturer's name of Trojan appeared on the grid for the first time. Former Brabham director and designer Ron Tauranac came on board to help develop the T101, which had both Keith Holland and Bob Evans behind the wheel. Graham McRae returned from 'down under', having retained the Tasman Championship over the winter break, and carried on with his GM1. A personally-owned GM1 was driven by Alan Rollinson, who was fifth in the Tasman series. Steve Thompson, using a Chevron B24, was also back to see what he could do in Europe, having finished fourth in the overseas series. Another returning old face was Peter Gethin, and this time he used a B24 as well.

As if he had never been away – and despite the fact that his car was ready only a few hours before qualifying began – Gethin clocked a time of 1 minute 23.9 seconds to claim pole position. Holland was the next fastest but almost a second slower. With the same time as Holland,

American Lola T330 driver Brett Lunger was joined on row two by Edwards in a similar car, with half a second being the difference between them. Lunger's Hogan Racing team-mate, David Hobbs, was directly behind on row three, with McRae to his left. Making a first appearance in Formula 5000 but some way down the grid was a South African who would one day become Formula 1 World Champion, Jody Scheckter, in another T101, in preparation for an assault on the American L & M series.

Gethin raced into the lead after the rolling start got the green light, and showed he meant business as he pulled away from the other nineteen runners. Lunger dropped to sixth on the opener but the rest kept their starting order, just one place up. At the end of the lap, though, four cars were no longer running, including that of Ian Ashley, Evans, Clive Santo and Ray Allen who became entangled when Scheckter spun at Dingle Dell. The South African was luckier than this quartet. He rejoined the throng and by lap seven had made up a lot of ground, but he went no further as a faulty tyre valve forced him to pit before the lap was complete. Edwards retired at the same time promoting McRae to third place, but neither he nor Holland nor any of the remainder could catch Gethin. Lunger was now fourth being chased down by Tony Dean. After starting from eleventh on the grid, another newcomer, the Dane Tom Belso, was keen to make his mark, but after getting up to fifth, he was passed by Thompson on lap ten. He was further reduced in the order when the reigning champion, Gijs van Lennep, passed as well. McRae lost his way four laps before the end when his car overheated following a cracked cylinder head. After the twenty-five laps were completed by Gethin in a time of 35 minutes 54.7 seconds, it was Lunger who followed, twenty-three seconds later. Dean hung on to third despite some hard charging from Thompson, and Hobbs and van Lennep completed the top six, although the latter had been lapped by the winner. Teddy Pilette demoted Belso to eighth although they, too, were a lap down.

Twenty-four hours later Gethin repeated his victory in the non-championship Race of Champions that also featured eleven Formula 1 cars. Reliability, or rather a lack of it, was evident for all but four of them as they failed to finish the forty-lap race. Denny Hulme, James Hunt and Tony Trimmer were the best three, and they were second to fourth respectively. Dean was fifth whilst the final Formula 1 peddler, Jean-Pierre Beltoise, was next.

Mallory Park was the venue for round two on 1 April. Trimmer came into the race as a deputy for van Lennep who was competing in a Sports Car event at the Nürburgring. Although he had previously competed in England in Formula Ford, making his way from New Zealand for his European Formula 5000 debut was David Oxton. He brought a new maker's name along, too, when he used a Begg FM5.

Trimmer found the Armco on Stebbe Straight as practice opened on a wet day, and a 'DNS' was posted against his name. After the mess had been cleared up, Ray Allen looked to have set the fastest time but as the session progressed, the weather improved, and McRae snatched the pole from the Surtees TS8A driver. Gethin and Scheckter also got faster as the track dried out, and they were the nearest to McRae when qualifying was over. Lunger, Hobbs and Rollinson further demoted Allen to complete the top six. Begg's debut was ruined when a timing chain snapped and no replacement could be found.

The rain looked likely to return in time for the fifty-lapper, so everyone except McRae and Edwards decided to use wet tyres and eyebrows were raised. The rain started to fall as the cars went onto their warm-up lap, but by the time the race had started it was dry again. Lunger was clipped by Belso as the cars were waved away, but that spelled the end for Belso as he had broken a drive shaft. Lunger was pushed into the pits where he decided to change his wet tyres to become slick-shod. All the drama on the grid was of no consequence to Gethin, who went into the lead pursued by Scheckter. Holland, Hobbs, Thompson and McRae in that order followed at a distance. McRae's gamble looked to have backfired when he dropped to eighth, behind Rollinson and Dean, a little later on lap three. Thompson first moved ahead of Hobbs and then disposed of Holland on lap five, before Edwards fell off on the next lap after sliding into the barriers at the hairpin. Scheckter was the next to have gremlins; the gear linkage on his Trojan came away and he retired at the end of lap seven. On lap ten the order of the top four was Gethin, Thompson, Holland and Hobbs, and that was maintained for another ten until Gethin thought his wet tyres were going off and decided to go into the pits to ask his crew to check. That gave Thompson a chance to record a win on his home track, but Holland got in front and gave the local man some work to do. Gethin was passed fit to carry on and came back out behind Thompson to see about regaining the lead. Holland also thought that he had a tyre problem, and he also sought reassurance from his team, but like Gethin he was given the okay. He rejoined but was someway behind the front runners. On lap thirty-five, Hobbs found himself the focal point of the attentions of the chasing McRae and Allen, and the pair passed him. Three laps later he came in for a change of rubber. With only eight laps remaining, McRae and Allen got ahead of Gethin whose tyres were losing grip. McRae managed to wrest the lead from Thompson four laps later, and despite the chequered flag taking another five laps to be shown, and being shown to Thompson before the New Zealander, it was the latter who was awarded the win after the timekeepers had checked their facts. Allen was third, Gethin fourth, Dean came through to take fifth, and Holland was sixth.

Despite his disappointment at the Mallory Park meeting, after the race it was announced that Trimmer would be present in the series for the rest of the year with a McLaren M18 that Tony Lanfranchi and Ray Calcutt had used previously. His first test after the announcement was at Brands Hatch at the Easter Monday Championship meeting. Before that, over the weekend of 6-7 April, Silverstone hosted a combined race for the Daily Express International Trophy; seventeen Formula 1 cars racing over forty laps with just the sixteen fastest Formula 5000 drivers qualifying. The day before that contest, the bigger boys also had their own race in competition for the GKN Vanwall Trophy, as well as championship points, with fifteen tours fewer to complete. Hobbs and team-mate, Lunger, were the fastest qualifiers in their respective Lola T330s. The first pair behind them was Dean and Holland, who recorded identical times to one another, but the Yorkshire-based Chevron B24 driver was slightly ahead of his rival's Trojan T101. John Gunn put his March 73A into fifth grid slot, but its engine blew up after setting the time and he failed to start. This left Thompson alone as a member of the row three club.

*International Trophy time again for David Hobbs ... (Courtesy Stuart Dent)*

*Top left: ... Keith Holland ... (Courtesy Stuart Dent)*

*Top right: ... and Steve Thompson. (Courtesy Stuart Dent)*

*Bottom left: Teddy Pilette added some international flavour to proceedings ... (Courtesy Stuart Dent)*

*Bottom right: ... whilst Tony Dean brought Yorkshire relish to the race. (Courtesy Stuart Dent)*

During the race it was the same two at the front, with the Englishman having the advantage over his colleague until lap thirteen when the American came through at Stowe. Lunger lasted about half a lap at the front before spinning at Becketts, giving Hobbs the opportunity to get back in front. Lunger composed himself and restarted his campaign for first place. Both drivers were lapping quicker than the previous lap record held by 'Cassius', and when the flag was shown it was Hobbs that saw it first. Twenty-five seconds or so after this pair had crossed the line, Dean came over it. The ShellSPORT and Radio Luxembourg jointly-sponsored Lola T330 driven by Belso was a lap down, but he was fourth. Begg-driver Oxton had a magnificent baptism to the series when he was rewarded with fifth place, Pilette was sixth.

Although Sunday's race was a non-championship contest, everyone was keen to do well. Fittipaldi made an outstanding impact in qualifying when he put his JPS Lotus on pole, two-tenths faster than team-mate Peterson. Jackie Stewart was also on the front row in the brand new Tyrell 006, after recording a time three-tenths slower than the second JPS driver. Gethin had won the previous joint race but he wasn't present for this one, so fastest of the Formula 5000 men was Hobbs, on the third row, flanked by Carlos Pace and Clay Regazzoni from the other class. His team-mate was on the next row, accompanied by Niki Lauda.

As the Union flag set the twenty-nine cars on their way it was mayhem after Fittipaldi stalled, which allowed Peterson to lead into Copse followed by Stewart, Denny Hulme, Regazzoni and the rest. The first Formula 5000 car seen by the assembled crowd was Lunger's Lola, which had Hobbs' similar car in its wake. Dean's was the next of the larger machines to show. These three maintained their positions until the twenty-fourth tour when the Chevrolet-engine of Hobbs' car let go and he managed to make it to the end of the lap where he retired. Lunger lasted another six laps before he, too, called it a day. Dean then took over in front and looked set to take a rewarding win, but his luck ran out on the penultimate lap when a bolt fell out of the rear suspension of his Chevron. With van Lennep back, his Lola T330 was now in front and he finished seventh overall but at the head of the Formula 5000 time sheets. Belso was directly behind him, both on the track and on the papers, in a Surtees TS11. Third position went the way of Holland, who was next but one across the line. The overall winner was Stewart, having completed the 117.08 miles in a time of 52 minutes 55.2 seconds, exactly twenty-three seconds before van Lennep.

Snetterton in Lincolnshire became the next circuit to host a round of the championship when sixteen cars came to the line on Good Friday, 20 April. Twenty-five laps was the set distance, and after van Lennep had set the fastest qualifying time, it was Lunger who came next. The American had switched cars and teams after the previous round, and was now behind the wheel of a Trojan T101 that was entered by Sid Taylor. In addition to starting from pole, the Dutchman earned himself a case of Charles Heidsieck champagne whilst his mechanics were awarded a bottle of the fizzy stuff as well. Thompson, Oxton, Dean and another newcomer, American Bob Brown, completed the top six. McRae did not start the race.

Van Lennep led the charge into Riches as the racers were given the signal to go. Lunger and Thompson maintained their grid places, but Oxton was deposed by Brown, Dean and Holland. The Begg driver led the next group and had Pilette, Edwards, Russell and Rollinson behind him. Two of the runners who were a bit farther back, Ashley and Santo, left the track at the hairpin after Belso pushed them wide and they spun. All three continued, but the Henley Ford-backed Lola T330 driven by Ashley was forced to retire at the end of the lap. On lap five, Holland moved ahead of Dean and set off after Brown, and Pilette came through in sixth place after shaking off his colleagues in the second group of chasers. The Belgian then got ahead of both Dean and Holland on lap seven. Thompson was dropped by the leading duo around the same lap when the tyres of his Chevron started to lose grip. The next twelve laps saw the top four circulate in the same order, but then the fan belt came off Pilette's engine and his race was over. This left Dean untroubled in fourth place where he finished the race. Brown was similarly lonely in fifth. Two great battles, though, continued before the flag dropped, the main one being for the win, and it was the nose of Lunger's Trojan that passed over the line just over half a second before van Lennep's Lola. Edwards and Oxton were also having a tussle, for sixth place, until the top two caught them up before the finish. Edwards remained strong enough, though, to reach the line ahead of the New Zealander.

After finishing fifth at Snetterton, Brown had to be helped from his car and he was later found to be suffering from pleurisy so he was missing from the Kent track. Despite his absence, nineteen cars still came to race on Easter Monday. With Trimmer, the additional entries came from McRae, John Bowtell, Chris Oates and Colin Hyams. Topping the practice time sheets after a seventy-five minute qualifying period was the same driver as had been on pole a few days earlier at Snetterton, van Lennep. Next to him was the same shadow as well, Lunger, but they had a trio of drivers behind them who had all qualified with a lap of 49 seconds. These were headed by Russell who was followed by Belso and the returning McRae. Thompson was a little slower, but was alongside the fifth-placed driver.

When the race started, Oates was missing from the grid, making it eighteen Formula 5000 cars that set off on the first of sixty-five laps on a wet track. Out of the spray it was Lunger who emerged first, with van Lennep, Belso who had shifted in front of Russell, and the rest following.

Russell wasn't to be outdone, though, and before the end of the lap he bravely charged into second place. Thompson had also found a way to get in front of everyone except Lunger, Russell and van Lennep. On lap two Russell led a Formula 5000 race for the first time in his career, and started to pull away. His confidence was slightly dented when he spun at Druids, but he had sufficient in hand to remain in front. Thompson, meanwhile, was ahead of van Lennep before the end of the second tour, with his mind set on winning. This became increasingly evident by the end of lap four when he came through to second place, and a lap later overtook Russell for the lead. Van Lennep looked vulnerable in fourth, and this proved to be the case when Belso passed the reigning champion, and Russell started to drop down the order after succumbing to worn out tyres. Lunger and Belso swapped places on lap thirty-eight when the American was forced on to the grass at Clearways to avoid a spinning Edwards. Lunger lost out again at the same place seven laps later when Dean forced his way past, and then things got worse when he spun at Druids, allowing Pilette to pass as well. Santo came up to sixth when he passed Holland eight laps later, and the top six carried on in that order to the finish. Only two drivers failed to finish, Rollinson and Oxton.

On leaving Kent, the championship was led by the day's winner, Thompson, with 60 points, 2 ahead of Lunger and 6 in front of Dean. Belso had earned 31 so far and was in fourth place.

Round six on 13 May was Oulton Park's first Sunday meeting, and it attracted seventeen cars, including Gethin taking over Brown's B24. Van Lennep was away on GT-driving duty with the works Porsche team, winning the Targa Florio with Herbert Muller. Santo took over the drive in the Dutchman's Lola T330, in place of his usual Surtees TS11. McRae was preparing to drive in the Indianapolis 500 and was another missing from the grid in Cheshire. Lunger reduced the entry further when he put his Trojan into the wall during qualifying. Chris Craft and Clive Baker joined the field using the McLaren that Pilette controlled in 1972, and a March 73A, respectively, whilst Kaye Griffiths was entered for a comeback in the Kitchmac.

*Bob Evans, in an early season attempt to become champion, in 1973. (Courtesy Norman Hayes)*

*Above, left: Colin Hyams shows his credentials. (Courtesy Norman Hayes)*

*Above: David Oxton was also out to impress ... (Courtesy Norman Hayes)*

*... as was Tony Trimmer. (Courtesy Norman Hayes)*

As far as qualifying was concerned, it was Dean who was the sensation on the day, lapping in his Chevron in 1 minute 24 seconds to take pole position. Holland lined up next to him, whilst Evans' T101 and Gethin were on the row behind. Fifth and sixth fastest were Pilette and Edwards, but the field was further condensed after the nose cone of the Lola driven by the latter became damaged during the warm-up, and no replacement could be found in time for the start. The series leader, Thompson, was immediately behind Pilette. Griffiths was unlucky, though, as the cylinder head cracked after just six laps and he posted a 'DNS'.

Twenty-seven laps of the full circuit needed to be completed before a winner could be found, and showing his intentions to be that winner was the Yorkshire man, Dean. Holland was next to show, with Evans lighting up his tyres before moving off the line before the rest. By the end of the lap, however, Pilette had pushed Evans and Gethin down the order, making it a Chevron one-two on the second tour following a spin at Esso by Holland, who did manage to continue albeit a long way down the order. Dean's car started to sound a little out-of-tune before he started on lap seven, and his problems increased when he spun at Old Hall. Pilette didn't need to be asked a second time, and seized the opportunity to take the lead that he never lost. Dean continued in second place but he started to suffer similar tyre trouble that Russell had encountered at Brands Hatch, which allowed Gethin to come through. He was then also passed by Thompson, Evans and Belso, although the Dane had a misfiring Lola to deal with and Dean repassed him with three laps to go. Holland was coming back and he, too, caught and passed the ailing Belso as well as, on the final lap, the leader, Pilette, to record sixth place in the race. After the flag fell on Chevron taking a clean sweep on the podium, however, the Belgian ran out of petrol, and needed a recovery vehicle to bring him back for the prize giving.

On Bank Holiday Monday, 28 May, Willie Green was due to make his Formula 5000 debut at the wheel of a Trojan T101 at the next round at Mallory Park, but he failed to appear. Thompson was another who didn't show, but his absence was due to an accident he had whilst testing at Silverstone the previous Thursday which left him with severe bruising and a terminally damaged car. Russell, Hyams and Griffiths were also non-runners, although the McRae of Russell was at the track but a fire had slightly damaged his car the night before the race. Van Lennep had been competing at the Nürburgring on the day before the meeting began, and after a complicated journey back to the UK, he made it in time to qualify sixth. Ahead of him in ascending order were Edwards, Brown who had recovered from his illness, Oxton, Dean, and faster than them all, Holland. Rollinson started from the back with a ten-second penalty as his car, a GM1, hadn't been able to practice.

*At Mallory Park many cars were yellow, including this one with Ian Ashley at the wheel. (Courtesy Stuart Dent)*

The race started with Holland showing why he had managed to take the pole, followed by Dean and a very fast-starting van Lennep, but soon afterwards the drive shaft of the Chevron let go and that was the end of Dean's hopes. The Dutchman followed Holland closely, and the pair started to pull away from the rest led by Oxton. Rollinson was on a charge and after two laps was up to eleventh place but after three more, with steam pouring out of his car, retirement was his only option. Brown got in front of Oxton on the same lap, who then lost out to Pilette two laps later. On the fourteenth trip around the Leicestershire track, the Belgian tried to overtake Brown at the hairpin but overdid things and spun. He managed to continue, but not until Belso, Oxton, Lunger and Evans had all passed. Belso's race came to an end on lap nineteen when he came to a halt at the hairpin, and he walked back to the pits a very frustrated driver. Van Lennep had pitted three laps earlier with tyre troubles, and rejoined some way down the field. Pilette started to regain some of the places he had lost after his earlier off-track excursion, and was fourth by lap thirty-one. That became third after a deflating rear tyre on Oxton's Begg meant he needed to take things easier, and the B24 passed. His quest to achieve second almost became a reality when Brown missed a gear at the Devil's Elbow on the last lap, but the American recovered in time to finish by half a car's length. Holland, though, had already crossed the line over forty seconds earlier. Evans also got past Oxton, recording fourth whilst Lunger displaced a recovered van Lennep to finish sixth. Only two more cars were running as the race came to an end, Chris Featherstone's older Lola T190X, and a T330 with Edwards in the driving seat.

Misano was scheduled to be round eight of the championship, but it had to be cancelled when the local council refused to give the circuit permission to hold the meeting. All the teams and drivers had already practiced for the race, with Pilette registering the fastest lap time before the cancellation. Zandvoort was the venue for the next round, and it, too, was cancelled.

McRae's appearance at the Indianapolis 500 had earned him the 'Rookie of the Year' award after running as high as fifth. He was eventually classified as sixteenth, despite only driving ninety of the one hundred and thirty-three laps that were completed before the race was stopped due to rain. On 8 July he was back in Europe at Mallory Park for the next British round of the Rothman's series. This proved to be a wasted journey, however, when he crashed his car in practice. The following week the New Zealander made his Formula 1 debut at the British Grand Prix at Silverstone, behind the wheel of Frank Williams' Marlboro-backed Iso, but sadly a sticky throttle ended his race after just one lap.

Meanwhile, at Mallory Park, Thompson returned having bought a new B24 from Chevron to replace his Silverstone-wrecked version, and he started from row six. Craft was also the driver of a new motor from Bolton when he appeared on the same row of the grid for the fifty-lap contest. Green was present this time, in a Trojan T101, on the row behind this pair. Up at the front and beating all the qualifying times was Ian Ashley, in the Doug Hardwick team-entered Lola T330. Lunger was next fastest, followed by McRae, but McRae's accident meant the space was vacant, so the slot on the front row gave Belso a clear track in front of him. Evans was fifth with Holland sixth, but he found his car had gear problems in the warm-up and he did a deal to drive Featherstone's ex-Frank Gardner car in the race instead, so started from the back.

When the flag waved the race away, Lunger got in front of Ashley and the open road in front of Belso allowed him to pass the pole man as well. Holland's penalty seemed to have done him no harm as he bustled his way through to ninth position at the back of the first of the chasing packs. Green was some way behind, but led the second group. Holland's race ended, though, on lap four, when a stub axle broke on his replacement car. On lap twelve, Lunger came to a halt at the hairpin when he found a lot of backmarkers in front of him and he was unable to pass them. This gave Belso the chance to get in front, pursued by Ashley and Lunger who managed to restart. Pilette was fifth after passing van Lennep and began chasing down Edwards. Seven laps after Lunger's aberration, he came back to the front; Ashley's earlier attempt to pass Belso had seen the Englishman go off into the scenery whilst the Dane's defence wasn't good enough to prevent the American passing him. A lap earlier Pilette passed Edwards to take third place, and with the top three retaining their positions, the rest of the race up front became a bit of a procession. Edwards came under attack from van Lennep but he, too, managed to maintain his composure, crossing the line in fourth almost a second before the reigning champion. Thompson was hardly ever in contention but finished sixth, one lap down. Craft's Chevron debut was marked by seventh with Santo next. Green scored a pair of first championship points when he finished ninth, three laps behind the winner.

*Willie Green's Trojan wasn't yellow, however. (Courtesy Stuart Dent)*

*The great Dane, Tom Belso, in action. (Author's collection)*

Two weeks later the Irish were the next to see sixteen Formula 5000 cars when they visited Mondello Park for a pair of thirty-lap heats that was termed the 'Rothmans Dublin Grand Prix'. Sadly, Rollinson was not amongst them as he announced that financial difficulties had curtailed his season. McRae was back in his repaired GM1, one of four who shared the fastest qualifying time after Holland. The other two were Lunger and van Lennep. Fifth on the grid was Dean, flanked by Ashley, who had also set identical times to one another, two-tenths slower than the previous four with a time of 53.4 seconds. Gethin was present in the works B24, but his time of 54 seconds could only register as the tenth fastest practice time. In fact, fourteen of the cars were under the previous lap record.

A standing start on the first heat saw McRae pull away first followed by Holland, van Lennep, the series leader Lunger, Dean, Edwards and a strong-showing Gethin. These positions remained largely unchanged until the ninth circuit when McRae spun at Dunlop and got stuck on the grass until the field passed by. His race lasted just two more laps when he pitted to change a deflating rear tyre that his team was unable to find a replacement for. Holland grabbed the chance and was never headed for the remainder of the session. Van Lennep was second and Dean third.

With a wet race looking likely, the second heat was delayed whilst the teams changed tyres, and as they set off Holland made the best start, seemingly unaffected by the rain that began to fall. Van Lennep settled into second followed by Edwards and Dean, both of whom overtook the Dutchman on lap eight, and he then fell back two more places three laps later when Evans and Gethin passed by. After another three laps Edwards and Dean were in front of Holland, although the latter dropped back to sixth after an audacious attempt to take the lead on lap sixteen backfired. Holland retook first place on lap nineteen and started to pull away from Edwards. At the end of the thirty laps he'd done sufficient to win, crossing the line two seconds in front. Van Lennep was third.

Aggregated results made Holland the overall victor with Edwards next, and van Lennep's second and third places in the heats were enough to give him the third podium place overall. Dean, Evans, Oxton, Pilette, Belso, Ashley and Lunger, in that order, made up the top ten. Thompson and Craft were the only other classified runners.

On 5 August, the 1973 Formula Atlantic driver, Brian Robinson, made his Formula 5000 debut at the Silverstone meeting that was set as round ten, using an ex-McLaren M19. Thompson took pole position following a wet practice session, but the race became a victim of the weather when, after a few racing laps, relentless rain flooded the track, leaving it too dangerous to race.

Following the cancellation of the Silverstone race, Brands Hatch became round ten of the series on 27 August. Twenty-four cars came to the Kent track to see if they could take away the first prize money, though only the fastest twenty qualified for the race. When the start came, only eighteen of them came to the grid for sixty-five laps. A trio of runners recorded the same time after qualifying, although two of them, Trojan drivers Evans and Lunger, failed to start, Evans having a leaking fuel cell that was detected as he approached the grid. The other, Gethin, was on pole in his Chevron B24. Lining up on row two, but with no one in front or alongside him, was Holland, one-tenth slower than Gethin. Edwards was joined on row three by Pilette, and these two had Dean and Ashley behind them respectively.

Gethin showed no mercy as he took off from the line with Edwards, Holland and the rest in his wake. Ashley charged through to take fourth that became third as the second lap began and he slipped past Holland to put pressure on Edwards. Pilette was behind Holland, with van Lennep behind him, but on lap six he spun on some oil at Clearways and dropped down to fifteenth. With Gethin pulling away, the second- and third-placed men were soon caught by those in fourth and fifth, and the battle was on for the runner-up spot. Edwards, though, spun on more oil at Paddock on lap twenty-five, allowing Ashley to get closer. Sensing a chance to pass both of them at Druids, Holland got too close to Ashley and they made contact. Both pitted, and the extra time taken by Ashley's crew dropped him out of contention, but Holland managed to rejoin in ninth place. In the interim, Pilette had got ahead of Edwards and although he was starting to catch Gethin, never looked likely to threaten the leader. Belso had come through into fourth position whilst the pit crews were working on Holland and Ashley's cars. His progress was further enhanced when he got ahead of Edwards on lap thirty-seven after Edwards made contact with Robinson. With the race seemingly in the bag, Gethin suddenly slowed with eight laps left, a piston having broken on the engine of his car. This gave the lead to Pilette who went on to record his second win in the series for 1973. Belso's persistence paid him second place points, whilst third on the track was Dean. Santo was fourth, and sporting a new nose cone on his Trojan in fifth place was Holland. Edwards was another to have a new nose, and he followed Holland across the line. Craft and Green were seventh and eighth respectively.

*Setting an example, Guy Edwards drove well at Brands Hatch. (Courtesy Rob Ryder)*

This win gave Pilette the lead in the championship with 88 points to Lunger's 85. Dean was a point worse off than his American rival but still in contention for the title.

Apart from championship points, the Oulton Park Gold Cup was the prize for the Formula 5000 runners on 9 September who had the competition to themselves this year. This was the first time the race had not been run for Formula 1, Formula 2 or Sports Cars. Seventy-five miles over twenty-seven laps was the distance, and showing his intention to be the winner was Gethin when he set a time of 1 minute 24 seconds to take pole position. Dean was eight-tenths slower but made it on to the front row next to the works Chevron driver, and Ashley's recent good form continued when he added the final front row position to his CV with an identical time to Dean. Holland and Evans made it an all-Lola second row, with a couple of tenths of a second difference between Holland and Ashley, and the same difference between each other. Two-tenths after Evans the next trio recorded the same time as each other, with Pilette first, followed by Belso and then Lunger. Ray Allen was in the seat normally occupied by van Lennep as he was away on sports car duty, whilst Green was also present to see what he could do at his favourite UK track.

Ashley made an inspired start and his Lola T330 led going into Old Hall for the first time. Dean also put his Chevron B24 ahead of Gethin's similar car, whilst a little further back, Lunger had got in front of Holland to appear in fifth. Looking determined to make his mark on the race, Pilette pushed Holland further back as they approached Cascades. This approach gained him fourth place soon afterwards when he passed Evans at Knicker Brook on the second lap, making it look like a Chevron train behind Ashley. The leader started to have trouble with gear selection, and after seven laps he had no response when Dean challenged. Ashley started to fall back and Gethin did the same as the eighth tour began, and the former champion picked out Dean as his next target. The pace of the works car was beginning to tell, and on lap nine a mistake by Dean at the first corner allowed Gethin to slip by. After entering the same corner side-by-side, Pilette found a gap five laps later and he squeezed into second place. Holland dropped out at the end of the same lap. That didn't bother the leading trio, and Gethin looked to have an unassailable lead for the second race in a row. Just like at Brands Hatch, however, he was determined to hold on and make the moment his. Pilette looked unlikely to catch Gethin just as Dean looked unlikely to take second place back from the Belgian, and on the line there was an eight-second gap between the top pairing. Ten seconds after Pilette it was Dean's turn to see the chequered flag. Evans relieved Ashley of fourth place two laps from the end and that was as far back as the early leader fell. Lunger made up the top six, but Green failed to finish.

Denmark became the latest country to host a round of the Rothmans series when two forty-two-lap heats were held at Jyllands Ring on the weekend of 22-23 September. The first heat was held on the afternoon of the first day, whilst Sunday afternoon was the time allotted for the second. Ashley booked his place on the front row for the first day's events when he set the fastest qualifying time of the eighteen entrants. Belso joined him on the front row, and behind them were Pilette and Thompson. Dean was on the third row with van Lennep, back from sports car duty in Italy, next to him. Jac Nelleman made it a second Dane in the race when he took over the McLaren M18 more usually seen with Trimmer behind the wheel, but he had broken a wrist in the previous round, in Cheshire, when he and Holland clashed prior to the latter's retirement.

Ashley used his position to good effect when he shot into the lead as the race started. Belso followed with Thompson, van Lennep, Pilette and Dean keeping a close eye on the local man. Pilette got in front of van Lennep on lap four, and two laps later he was ahead of Thompson as well. With a ten-second lead it looked like it was a foregone conclusion for Ashley, but Pilette was continuing his charge and he came through to take yet another place on lap thirteen. Belso had a flat tyre and started to drop back into the clutches of Thompson, who then passed the Lola driver, and his agony was doubled when van Lennep also got through. These five finished in that order, whilst into sixth place came Nelleman who inherited the slot when Holland spun in unison with Edwards. Ashley's margin of victory was over twenty-two seconds.

On day two, the grid for the second heat was almost a carbon copy of the first, but this time it was Pilette who made the best start knowing that he had to make up a lot of time if he was to win overall. Although he set a new fastest lap for the circuit, the Belgian was no more than ten seconds in front all the time the race went on, and when the chequered flag was shown this had been reduced by a further six-tenths. Belso borrowed the Kitchmac and it was he who finished directly behind Ashley. Lunger, Holland and Nelleman made up the top six.

Ashley, therefore, left the circuit the winner, with Pilette and van Lennep picking up the points for second and third respectively. Holland was the meat in a Danish championship in fourth, with Belso on the top of him and Nelleman beneath.

Making up for the previous cancellation, a race was booked at Zandvoort the week after the Danish outing. John Watson came in to take over from Green who had had a disagreement with his team. Also making an appearance on home ground was future double-Indy 500 winner, Arie Luyendijk Senior (though he was called Luyendyk by then). He replaced Trimmer this time. Lunger and Gethin were notable absentees, both being needed more at the final round of the L & M series in the USA. In atrocious conditions it was Watson who set the fastest time in practice, and he had Pilette for company on the front row despite him running out of petrol during the latter stages of qualifying. Evans was third fastest with an identical time to Pilette.

The weather didn't improve for the race although Watson wouldn't allow the threat of rain to bother him and he set off like a rocket, leaving the rest seemingly standing. Pilette collected his thoughts and was the next to show, with Edwards and Holland behind him. On lap five, however, the Irishman at the front locked up his brakes, spun, and ended up losing the nose of his T101 as well as first place. Pilette assumed the lead but Edwards was closing in on him, and he took over in front on lap nineteen when the Belgian spun at the same place as the now-retired Watson. With assistance from Evans who had gone off a few laps earlier, and a local policeman, he managed to get going again two places worse off than he had been before the incident, but after the race he was disqualified for receiving outside assistance. Holland was behind the new leader, Edwards, but was soon caught and passed by Dean. Thompson, Belso, Craft and McRae also overtook Holland with four laps to go as he had to pit to replace a damaged left front tyre, and the top six held station until the end. Holland rejoined to finish seventh, with Luyendijk taking the final point.

After crossing the North Sea, Snetterton was the venue for the penultimate championship meeting of the season on 7 October. Dean broke the lap record during practice and put his Lola on pole position on the grid. McRae was next, having required an engine rebuild to start the race after a valve broke towards the end of the qualifying session. Ashley took the third spot on the front row, whilst Pilette and Evans propelled their cars to fourth and fifth respectively. Substituting for Trimmer this time was Bernard Bird, in what was his first ever single-seater race!

Holland had a spin on the warm-up but was allowed to start the thirty-lap event. Dean made a blistering start, with Pilette, Ashley and Evans falling in behind him. McRae's car was clearly not right as, at the end of the opening lap, he'd slipped back to eighth place. Dean was being shadowed closely by Pilette and Ashley, with Evans and Gethin a bit further back. Gethin got in front of Evans on lap five and was looking to catch Ashley, who in turn was closing in on Pilette, but he was given instructions from the Clerk of the Course to pit before starting lap nine which he did at the end of the lap. His problem was a cracked oil pipe that was causing it to leak onto the track. McRae was another to call it a day after nine laps. Having pitted two laps earlier to change a rear wheel, Gethin's race was over on lap twelve when he complained of a strange vibration. Dean spun around the same time as Gethin was retiring, giving Pilette the lead who was strongly pursued by Evans and Thompson. Evans' persistence paid off on lap seventeen when he got his nose in front at the hairpin. Pilette, though, wasn't about to throw in the towel, and he stuck to the back of the new leader's T101. Despite trying everything he knew, the Belgian finished a tenth over one-and-a-half seconds behind the man from Gloucestershire. Thompson started to drop back but did enough to record third place. Holland was fourth, Belso fifth and Santo sixth. Bird was still running at the end but was nine laps down and unclassified.

On 21 October, Brands Hatch Grand Prix circuit was used for the final championship contest of 1973, and the championship race was still very much in the balance. The leader going into the double points-scoring race was Pilette with 136 points – Dean was 23 points behind. The longest race of the season, forty-five laps were given to the competitors of the BARC-organised meeting.

Making its first appearance at the last round was the new McRae competition car, the GM2. This came the week after the driver/designer sold his factory to Roger Penske. Formula 1 driver Clay Regazzoni was present for his second-ever Formula 5000 race driving a Lola T330 that had been used previously in the American series. Brendan McInerney drove another Lola that he had been sharing throughout the season, albeit somewhat unspectacularly, with Trevor Twaites. Watson was also present to take part in his next Formula 5000 contest and looking to better his non-finish at Snetterton. Lunger was another hoping to make an impact, having returned from America to take part. Before the race Russell announced that this would be his last.

Two one-hour sessions were allocated to practice and qualifying, and it was a wet track that greeted twenty-six drivers and their cars for the first of these. The marshals were kept busy with several spinners during the session, but fortunately no one made contact with the barriers although a number of cars suffered punctures. The weather for the second was initially improved but soon deteriorated. After both sessions were over it was the title leader, Pilette, who had set the fastest time. Holland was second, whilst Santo recorded his best qualifying position of the season, third. Dean suffered a torrid time and was eleventh, whilst Regazzoni was further down and occupied the fifteenth bay on the grid.

When the cars came to face the crowd on race day the weather was dry but cold, and the rolling start saw twenty-six thunderous machines rolled forward as one onto Paddock Hill Bend. At the front Pilette started slowly, which gave Holland the opportunity to lead followed by Ashley, Lunger, Watson, Evans, Gethin and Belso. Pilette finally got up to speed and slotted in behind the Dane. Ashley was keen to record a winning end to the season and pushed Holland hard, whilst behind them, Watson was making great strides of his own. By lap five it was this trio who were the top three, with the second- and third-placed drivers swapping places on the next lap. Watson was catching Holland, whilst Edwards was catching Ashley. On lap thirteen the Irishman made an a attempt to pass at Druids but his Trojan didn't have enough grunt to pass Holland's similar car and he had to back off. With all that going on, Dean was making progress and was up to fifth by lap eighteen with Pilette behind him. McRae's new car wasn't performing too badly, and he got ahead of Evans' motor just before half-distance to feature in seventh place. Santo and Thompson made up the top ten. As the second half of the race began to take shape, Edwards found himself lapping quicker than anyone else, which meant that he was able to pass Ashley on the entry to Hawthorn. Three laps later and the speed allowed him to pass Watson at Clearways. Now with Holland in his sights he was travelling quicker than ever before but was struggling to find a way past. On lap thirty-one the orange Trojan driver made a mistake at South Bank, and Edwards' blue Lola didn't need a second request to take the lead. Watson saw this happening and thought he had a chance to catch Holland, but oil pressure problems made him tread carefully. Ashley's race was over on lap thirty-two when he spun off a lap after having to pit for a new tyre, and thereby promoted everyone up one place, including Dean to fourth. Pilette was the next to have a disappointing end to the season when the engine on his Chevron blew up, shortly after Ashley's demise. The remaining laps didn't see any changes in the top six, and Edwards won. Second place was taken by Holland, and Watson had earned the last podium place. In fourth, Dean scored 20 points, meaning he missed out on the title by just 3 points. Santo was fifth.

With Evans named the BP Man of Steel, the Rothmans Formula 5000 Championship table looked like this at the end of the season:

| Position | Driver | Car | Engine | Points |
|---|---|---|---|---|
| 1 | Teddy Pilette | McLaren M18<br>Chevron B24 | 5.0 Chevrolet<br>5.0 Chevrolet | 136 |
| 2 | Tony Dean | Chevron B24 | 5.0 Chevrolet | 133 |
| 3 | Keith Holland | Trojan T101<br>Lola T190 | 5.0 Chevrolet<br>5.0 Chevrolet | 116 |
| 4 | Steve Thompson | Chevron B24 | 5.0 Chevrolet | 114 |
| 5 | Guy Edwards | Lola T330 | 5.0 Chevrolet | 102 |
| 6 | Tom Belso | Lola T330 | 5.0 Chevrolet | 97 |
| 7 | Brett Lunger | Lola T330<br>Trojan T101 | 5.0 Chevrolet<br>5.0 Chevrolet | 95 |
| 8 | Peter Gethin | Chevron B24 | 5.0 Chevrolet | 65 |
| 9 | Bob Evans | Trojan T101 | 5.0 Chevrolet | 64 |
| 10 | Gijs van Lennep | Lola T330 | 5.0 Chevrolet | 59 |

# CHAPTER 6

## AN EXTENDED TOUR OF EUROPE

Before the end of 1973, Trojan unveiled the T102, its new car for the next season and the first of Trojan's cars designed entirely by Jack Brabham's former business partner, Ron Tauranac. The pictures were released before the works team drivers were announced, but it was widely expected that either Keith Holland or Steve Thompson would be behind the wheel. In the end the single chassis was shared by both men, with Holland driving in the first half of the season whilst Thompson took over for the latter half. Although Guy Edwards was announced as number two to Graham Hill in Hill's own Formula 1 team using the T370, the first new Lola Formula 1 chassis since 1962, he was still present for some of the Formula 5000 season.

On 16 March 1974, the first event of the eighteen-race championship that was still being backed by Rothmans took place at the same circuit, and on the same layout as that of the last round of the previous season; Brands Hatch Grand Prix. Both Teddy Pilette and Peter Gethin, who returned from the Tasman series as champion, used a new Chevron, a B28. As part of the Race of Champions bill, and despite no testing for either car, it was Gethin who took pole position for the first race of the season, with Pilette a disappointing ninth. Before returning to the American series, Brian Redman was in the next car to Gethin on the grid, with Edwards alongside him. Redman and Edwards had another new Lola apiece, the T332. Gijs van Lennep was more involved with sports car racing this year, so was replaced in the ShellSPORT team by the Italian driver Lella Lombardi. She was joined in the team by Ian Ashley, who qualified a second behind the pole man, in fourth position, whilst his team-mate was nine places behind him. Vern Schuppan was in an older Trojan, the T101, but managed to be that maker's leading pilot in fifth place, whilst the next fastest motor was another older car, a Chevron B24, driven by Thompson.

Making their debut in the series at this meeting were Mike Wilds and Patrick Sumner. The first of this pair drove a March 74A, whilst the latter had a T101. Holland was found at the wheel of a T102 provided by Ian Ward Racing during qualifying, but after just four laps he hit the brakes and collided with the sleepers, spelling the end of his weekend before it really got going. Before the season started it was suggested that Dan Gurney's Eagle Formula 5000 car would compete in the first three rounds of the European series. Brett Lunger was entered to drive, but was nowhere to be seen at this meeting. Alan

Rollinson was also an absentee due to a fall at home that broke a bone in his ankle, rather than problems with his car.

Gethin made a lot of smoke spinning his wheels as the cars started the thirty-two lapper, allowing Redman to overtake momentarily, but the Chevron soon retook the lead before the first corner unwound. Edwards was third. Ian Ashley was a short distance behind these three leading a group that included Thompson, Dean and Pilette. Schuppan and Wilds were a long way back, but both had had some gearing problems as their race began. This magnified for the Australian as the second lap began when he lost third gear. Edwards, too, had problems, and as lap three started he spun at Paddock taking Thompson on to the grass which led to an early retirement for the Chevron driver. Tony Dean, in a similar car to Thompson, was pushing Ashley for third, with Wilds catching the pair of them. Redman was the next to lose his place when he was black-flagged as a rear tyre was going down. Sumner's car developed an oil leak and Dean found its attraction when he spun at Stirlings, stalling the car which then refused to restart, ending his hopes. With Ashley now in second place and Wilds in third, theirs was the dice of the day which went the way of the newcomer by lap fourteen. Redman rejoined after replacing his flat tyre and set about unlapping himself, but he looked unlikely to catch Gethin or Wilds and these three finished in that order. Proving that she wasn't driving for ShellSPORT as a result of her looks, Lombardi had brought her Lola through the field to take fourth place. Damien Magee, in another T330, was fifth, whilst following a mid-race pit-stop, Ashley rejoined to take sixth.

A number of Formula 5000 cars also featured with fourteen of their Formula 1 colleagues in the very wet, forty-lap Race of Champions the following day, although after the events of the previous day, four of them failed to start. No points were awarded for this contest but in the end that didn't matter to Ashley, who was the first of his class home, finishing eighth overall to Jacky Ickx. Thompson was next, followed by Gethin.

Round two of the championship came a week later at Mallory Park. David Hobbs made a season debut when he brought along his American series-entered Lola T330, whilst also in his first of the season came BP's Driver of the Year for 1973, Bob Evans, in a T332. Eighteen cars faced the starter with Ashley carrying on where he left off after the second race in Kent, at the front. Pilette made up for his previous non-finish by taking second place on the grid, followed by Redman, Holland, Gethin, Edwards, Evans, Hobbs, Brian Robinson, Dean, Wilds and Thompson in the top ten. Ashley's team-mate endured a poor qualifying session and once more started thirteenth. Sumner's car had been relubricated, and started at the back of the grid.

*In Leicestershire, Chris Craft was present to challenge for honours. (Courtesy Stuart Dent)*

Top: Bob Evans was also at Mallory Park. (Courtesy Alan Cox)

David Morgan came out of the pits to have a go. (Courtesy Stuart Dent)

A red flag flew on the second racing lap when contact between the pole man and Redman occurred as they were about to complete lap one, sending the Lola across the track into the banking. Gethin also hit Redman's car and was hit himself. Edwards, in the meantime, was rapidly approaching the marshals' post at the end of the start-finish straight, and after hitting it he ended up with a bruised ankle and left the Observer with a broken leg. Something happened to Thompson as well, as his car was badly damaged, and Magee's Lola had a broken nose section.

Ashley's car was another with a disjointed nose, and whilst it was repairable, his joy at being on pole turned to despair at being unable to race as no spare was available. Magee's crew taped up the car's nose. Redman, Edwards and Thompson were non-starters as well, but their machines looked well past redemption. The field was further reduced during the warm-up laps for the new race when Holland pitted and retired with mechanical problems, leaving just twelve healthy cars to start. Pilette took advantage of his colleagues' absences and set off into the lead followed by Evans. Behind them though it looked like another red flag might be needed, as Hobbs, Wilds, Dean and Magee approached the opening corner almost as one very wide Formula 5000 car. For the first four laps it looked as if the defending champion would take his first win of the new season, but before starting lap five he retired into the pits with transmission failure. Magee followed him after it was decided that the tape-up job wasn't safe and he was shown the black flag. A lap later he, too, retired. Back on the track, Evans and Hobbs were providing the entertainment the Leicestershire crowd had paid to see, with Hobbs asserting himself on lap six to pass at the Esses. Wilds then pursued the T332 driver but it took another ten laps before he, too, demoted him. Hobbs, though, was in control of things up at the sharp end and whenever Wilds looked like closing, he put a little more pressure on the gas pedal and pulled away. In the end, four seconds was the margin of Hobbs' victory. Evans suffered handling problems throughout the fifty laps, but despite the two in front having a lap on him, did enough to finish third. Dean was fourth for a while but with an oil warning light advising him to pit, he failed to finish, giving the points for that position to Clive Santo. Robinson was the only other driver to score on the day – Nick Wattiez was classified sixth, but he failed to complete ninety per cent of the race distance and wasn't awarded the 6 points that he would have achieved had he completed three more laps.

Before round three of the series, it was announced that Redman would not only be driving in America, but that he had also been drafted into the Shadow Formula 1 team for the season. This appointment, to replace the unfortunate Peter Revson who died at the South African Grand Prix a few weeks earlier, meant that he was only able to compete in a couple more rounds of the Rothmans-backed championship. To show that he wasn't going to go quietly, however, he gave Gethin a run for his money before finishing practice just one-tenth shy of the former champion's qualifying time. Hobbs was the third fastest driver, and he made up the three-car front row. Wilds was next, and he was to have had Holland for company but oil surge problems ruled him out of the race yet again. Gethin's old Chevron B24 was driven by Dean and he used it to good effect, lining up fifth on the grid. His line was completed by Ashley and Pilette. The Belgian, though, wasn't happy, and his team managed to fit a new engine on the morning before the race. Evans' qualifying time hadn't been too good, with his car having handling problems again, and his race started from the grid slot next to Lombardi, on row four. Tom Belso came out for the first time in 1974 and put his Lola T330 in ninth position. Completing the top ten was Edwards, who raced despite the fact that the bruised foot he thought he had turned out to be a broken metatarsal! Colin Andrews was another newcomer, in a Surtees TS8 previously used by Thompson, and he started nineteenth of the twenty-one entrants.

Gethin and Redman made a clean getaway as the flag dropped, with Wilds who had to start his car in second gear, able to pass Hobbs before they exited Copse corner. Gethin and Redman ran close to one another and, as they approached Bridge, they were side-by-side. As the pair entered Luffield, Redman made a determined effort and managed to take the lead. Ashley also demoted the US-bound Hobbs and so at the end of the first lap the order of the top six was Redman, Gethin, Wilds, Ashley, Hobbs and Pilette. At the end of the second, Ashley and Wilds had swapped places, and Hobbs regained a place at the end of the next one as Wilds' gearbox started to give him problems. Pilette dropped the March driver a place further down as the race progressed. Hobbs regained third place on lap eight when the Hogan Lola driver outbraked the ShellSPORT equivalent car going into Becketts. No major changes appeared likely to alter the top three for the second half of the twenty-lap race, with the race leader seemingly comfortable in front of Gethin. As the chequered flag was waved all three had retained their positions, with Redman's advantage over Gethin being almost one-and-a-half seconds. Hobbs was another couple down. The main battle seemed to be for fourth place, with Ashley and Pilette being the protagonists. This went the way of Ashley, four-tenths of a second quicker than the reigning champion. Wilds bravely finished sixth despite not having any gears at all as he crossed the line. Picking up the lower points was Dean, followed by Evans, Belso and Lombardi.

Easter weekend saw two rounds of the series being held over a four-day period, with the first of them falling on Good Friday, April 12, at Oulton Park in Cheshire. Using the 2.76-mile International circuit for thirty laps and making his penultimate Formula 5000 appearance in the UK for 1974 following the announcement about his future, Redman was present at this Oulton Park round and was just as keen as he had been in his first appearance in the series. His determination was underlined when he lapped the circuit in a time of 1 minute 33.2 seconds to take the outside spot on the front row. Pilette, though, saw this as a chance to repeat his success of the previous season on what Chevron saw as its test track. He went out and set a time almost one-and-a-half seconds quicker than the Lancastrian. Sandwiched between these two, and a second slower than his team-mate, was Gethin. Evans' car was handling better than last time out and he qualified fourth. Ashley was next to him, one place ahead of Schuppan who had Hobbs and the series leader, Wilds, with him on row three. On row four, Brian McGuire and Chris Craft were over ten seconds slower than the pole man, and more than six behind those directly in front of them. When the racers came to line up for the thirty-lapper, though, McGuire's T101 was missing. Dean started right at the back as he was given a ten-second penalty following an engine change after qualifying.

*Clive Santo joined the fray in 1974 ... (Courtesy Norman Hayes)*

*... and so did Trevor Twaites. (Courtesy Norman Hayes)*

*Italian lady driver Lella Lombardi was sponsored by Radio Luxembourg, and used its frequency as her race number. (Courtesy Norman Hayes)*

*Belgian Teddy Pilette was in a Chevron bearing the reigning champion's number, though. (Courtesy Norman Hayes)*

*Brian Redman got so wet in Cheshire. (Courtesy Norman Hayes)*

When the flag fell to signal that the race was on, it was Redman who wasted no time waiting for the rest of the field and led the way. Gethin fell in ahead of his team-mate, with both Chevrons a little way ahead of the rest. Wilds led Ashley up Deer Leap at the end of the opening lap, followed by Evans, Hobbs and Lombardi. Schuppan retired with a flat engine. The top three circulated in the same formation for the first seven laps, until Gethin allowed Pilette to pass to see if he could catch Redman. The lower order runners, though, were keen to make an impression, and with more gear trouble Wilds began to get caught. First of all it was Ashley who passed, but then Hobbs got ahead of them both to take fourth place. Pilette saw a gap at Knicker Brook on lap ten and shot past the leader, but ran wide on his exit going up Clay Hill; Redman didn't need a second chance to resume the position he thought he had lost. When he rejoined the track, Pilette found himself alongside Gethin, but the two made unavoidable contact that sent the Englishman sideways into the Armco and out of the race. Pilette was keen to get back at Redman and, in going for it, equalled the outright track record that Redman had set earlier in the race. This pace propelled him back in front as the cars finished the thirteenth lap, passing at Old Hall. Seemingly in control at the front, Pilette's vehicle began to appear twitchy, and, after just a further four laps, started to slide up Deer Leap in an erratic fashion; he retired into the pits without starting lap eighteen. This meant that the former Chevron test driver, Redman, was back in front with Hobbs the best of the rest. Hobbs believed he could take the fight to Redman and began to chip away at his lead. With nine laps to go, the difference was twenty seconds, and with only a couple to go there were less than four between them. Hobbs was within touching distance of the lead, approaching Knicker Brook on the final tour, and decided to try to give Redman a shock at Druids, but the red Lola driver was able to stay ahead. A momentary lack of concentration saw Redman almost lose control as he put the hammer down going up Deer Leap for the final time, but Hobbs was unable to profit. The winning margin in the end was just two-tenths of a second. Behind them, Ashley kept in front of the others but sixteen seconds behind Hobbs to take the final podium berth. Magee was six-tenths behind Ashley, and the same gap was extended to the fifth-placed finisher, Lombardi. Evans was a lot further back but he still took sixth place. Wilds failed to finish.

Brands Hatch provided the tarmac for the Easter Monday contest and this time the grid positions were laid out on a two-by-two formation. Wilds made up for his disappointment in Cheshire and it was he that occupied the number one slot. Pilette was another keen to make amends, and he was just one-tenth slower than the March driver after qualifying. Evans' Lola lined up directly behind Wilds' car, and he was just three-tenths slower than the pole-sitter. Gethin recorded an identical time to Evans which placed him behind his team-mate. The next four grid positions were taken by Lola drivers, with Belso and Redman on row three and Ashley and Hobbs behind them. Holland's Trojan T102 was in ninth place with another Lola driver, Santo, completing the top ten. Wattiez took part in qualifying but his best time of 54.7 seconds was outside the 'pole plus ten per cent' time and he wasn't allowed to compete in the race.

Evans relegated Pilette to third as the race began, but his demon start wasn't enough to get in front of Wilds. Belso was another to get in front of a Chevron driver when he passed Gethin going into Paddock. Redman joined the group that quickly detached themselves from the rest, and on lap three, this group had a new leader when Evans made a purposeful move on Wilds along the Bottom Straight. Six laps later the top six became a top five because Pilette needed to pit to change a wheel. A few laps later the leading batch became six again when a determined drive from Holland brought him into the leading group. He, too, had to pit, with electrical troubles. On lap seventeen, Redman put more pressure on the accelerator and moved ahead of Belso, whose car was beginning to falter. Two laps later the new Shadow Formula 1 driver took third when he overcame Gethin. The race was set for sixty laps and at half-distance, Redman was four seconds behind the front pair, and five laps later he was right behind Wilds. After another five, he edged past the March and went after Evans' T332. The battle intensified with ten laps to go because the pair was separated by a hair's breadth. Redman signalled his intention on more than one occasion, but he was unable to press hard enough to pass and Evans' car had enough to stay in front for the remaining distance. Wilds seemed to be alone in third but with two laps to go, Ashley, Gethin and Schuppan caught him up and passed him, pushing him back into sixth place. These four continued in these places for the rest of the race.

So after the first five rounds of the Rothmans European Formula 5000 Championship, the front runner of the series was the soon-to-be-departing Redman, with 67 points. Hobbs was second, 20 points behind, with Gethin and Wilds on 45 and 42 respectively. Evans and Ashley, in that order, were the only other drivers in the 40s, with 1 and 2 fewer than Wilds.

The first excursion across the seas for 1974 was to Zolder in Belgium, which was the venue for round six of the series over the weekend of 27-28 April. Working on home ground, Pilette was keen to impress his fellow countrymen, and looked likely to do so after setting the fastest qualifying time for the first of the two-part fifty-lap race that took place on the Saturday. Second to the Belgian was his Team VDS partner, Gethin, in a similar Chevron B28.

*Across the waves, Damien Magee tried to show Zolder fans what he could do. (Author's collection)*

Sixteen cars came on to the track for the first race, but that became fifteen after Twaites' over-enthusiasm saw him blow an oil filter on the warm-up lap that meant his race was over before it had even begun. Eventually, when the race did get under way, it was the former champion who led ahead of his colleague. Schuppan's Lola was the next to show, with Evans in a similar motor the closest of the rest. Hobbs was following the top four but was passed by Holland and Wilds before the end of the first lap. With the two Chevrons pulling away and the two Lolas doing likewise, the next dice for fifth became a four-car struggle, with Holland's Trojan, Wilds' March and Hobbs' Lola joined by Ashley in a similar car to the present-day US television race commentator. The first of these to go, though, was the Trojan, when oil leaked onto the rear tyres and it spun out of contention on the sixth lap. Hobbs came through to fifth on lap eight after Wilds began to have gear trouble, and Ashley demoted Wilds further two laps later. Then Hobbs pitted to have a tyre replaced, putting him down the order and promoting Ashley and Wilds to fifth and sixth. Fourth-placed man, Schuppan, also began to have trouble with gears, and on lap eighteen his race was over, when no fourth gear spelled the end of his involvement. This meant Ashley was now fourth, and, with the top three remaining unchanged when the chequered flag fell, that was the best he could do. Wilds' car had no third gear but he soldiered on, with Craft's B28 closing in. With the laps running out, though, the best Chris could do was finish just over a second behind the ailing March driver.

Heat two was held on Sunday 28 April, and with Twaites' Lola joined at the back of the grid by Lombardi in a similar T330, there were seventeen cars on the grid. At the head of them all was the previous day's heat winner, Gethin, with Pilette alongside him but with positions reversed from the earlier session. The Belgian was the first away this time, with Gethin followed by Wilds, Evans and Craft ahead of the rest. Hobbs caught these three and once again a quartet contested the placings after the top two. There was disappointment for the home fans, though, after Pilette's engine blew up on lap four. Gethin went on to take victory, relatively untroubled for the remainder of the twenty-five laps. Wilds' race came to an end on lap ten, allowing Evans to finish one place better than on the previous day. Craft was next after he detached himself from the rest. Holland's repaired Trojan came home fourth, with Magee and Lombardi coming through to make up the top six.

The overall winner wasn't in doubt with Gethin at the head of the placings. Evans and Craft joined him on the podium with Evans slightly higher than his rival. Wilds, Clive Santo and Patrick Sumner made up the top half-dozen overall. Pilette's consolation was the fastest lap of the day that was also a new lap record. Gethin's win brought him to within 2 points of the overall series leader, Redman, with 65 points. Evans was 9 points adrift of Gethin in third, whilst Wilds' 52 points gave him fourth at the end of the first overseas event of the year.

On 27 May, round seven of the 1974 championship brought the field back to the United Kingdom, and to Thruxton in particular, for a thirty-lap contest that saw nineteen cars venture on to the grid. Hobbs was busy finishing fifth in the Indy 500 the same weekend so he missed this race. His seat in the Hogan Racing Lola was kept warm by Derek Bell in his first Formula 5000 outing for 1974, and his experience showed through when he added pole position for this round to his racing CV after qualifying had taken place. Next up, in his best grid position of the season, was Ashley. Directly behind Bell was the Chevron B28 driver, Gethin, whilst his team-mate, Pilette, lined up behind Ashley's car which was similar to the pole-sitter's. Redman was another absentee, giving a number of the drivers a chance to take the overall lead, with Schuppan being his substitute in Sid Taylor's Lola T332. He qualified eighth. Making his debut in a Formula 5000 car was future Renault and Ferrari Formula 1 pilot, Rene Arnoux, in a modified McLaren M19 Formula 1 car. The Frenchman qualified in a low grid position.

As the first lap started to unfold it was Hobbs' replacement, Bell, who was found at the front of eighteen other loud cars, with Pilette and Ashley in close attendance. Wilds managed to push Gethin down the order, but the former champion was ahead of Evans, Holland, Belso, Dean, Edwards and the rest. Bell and Pilette dropped Ashley, with the leader showing the crowd some fantastic driving, setting a new lap record early on that Pilette equalled later in the contest. Shortly after setting the new record the top two came across back marker, Nick Wattiez, and they decided to overtake on either side of the T330 driver. Unfortunately for Bell, Pilette emerged in the lead and Bell tried to get back on terms for the next dozen or so laps. With eleven tours to go the Englishman was back in front, but the wheels on his car made contact with those of the Belgian's Chevron and sent him running wide onto the gravel, causing a slow puncture and meaning that once again he was momentarily in second place. Pilette looked to be in control at the front but with just one hundred yards before the line his car came to a stop, no fuel! The tyre problems of Bell, though, meant that he was too far behind to take advantage of his rival's misfortune, he had already been passed by the Radio Luxembourg-backed T330 car of Ashley, Gethin's B28 and Evans' T332. This meant he missed out on a podium place by a couple of tenths shy of seven seconds. Belso was fifth, Holland was sixth and Pilette classified one place further back. Sumner took his best finish so far in the UK season when he was a place behind the Belgian.

The Whitsun weekend of 2-3 June was the series' second trip across the English Channel, with Holland's Zandvoort being the venue for the first time since September 1973. Bell wasn't available to fill in for Hobbs this time and so it was a regular from the Dutch Formula Ford Championship, Leen Verhoeven, who was found in the Hogan Lola. Another three of his countrymen, Roelof Wunderink, Arie Luyendijk and 'Boy' Hayje, filled seats in the cars as well. None of these, however, could match the pace of another Benelux driver, the Belgian Pilette, and his team-mate Gethin, who were the fastest of the runners. Evans' Lola T332 was the next fastest just a tenth down on the two Chevron drivers, with Ashley's T330 version a further tenth of a second slower. Ashley, though, had a wheel collapse later in the day, meaning that he wasn't able to improve on that. Fastest of the Dutchmen was Wunderink who recorded a time of one-and-a-half seconds down on that of Pilette, sixth on the grid. Verhoeven started eleventh despite having a moment at Panorama with Lombardi alongside him.

On the second day, bright skies welcomed the cars as they came to the grid. After a seemingly long wait as they formed on the tarmac, it was Gethin who stole a march on his Team VDS colleague, but Pilette soon found his way through at Tarzan before the first lap was completed. Evans made an attempt to split the two Chevrons but was unable to do so, whilst his second-row colleague, Ashley, became an easy target for the three behind him. This meant that Edwards, Craft and Wunderink were now fourth, fifth and sixth respectively before lap two had even started! Pilette started to look dominant yet again, an easy winner. After him Gethin was just as comfortable in second place, and Evans and Edwards were competing for third. By lap five though, Evans was catching Gethin with his superior cornering ability, but the two-time ex-champion had the better straight-line speed and there seemed little the former could do to overtake. After nine laps Ashley had to stop to change a flat tyre, which dropped him well down the order. Shortly before half-distance Pilette's lap times were beginning to lengthen, and it appeared that he had a problem with a tyre and he had to pit. This handed the lead to Gethin and he was followed across the line by Evans, Edwards, Craft, Holland, Wunderink and Lombardi before the Belgian could do anything to get back into the race. Over the next five laps, Evans found some extra power to keep Gethin in check and set a new fastest lap into the bargain, but was still unable to find a way to pass. Holland's Trojan found that it didn't want to complete the full thirty laps, and after twenty-one it came to a smoky end. With the laps running out, Evans' challenge began to fade and the win was taken by Gethin by four seconds. Edwards maintained a steady pace to record third place, whilst Craft crossed the line next. Pilette had found a new lease of life and passed both Wunderink and Lombardi during the last ten laps on his way to fifth place. Ashley's re-shod Lola took eighth, Veerhoeven ninth and Brian Robinson took the last championship point for the tenth placing. The other two from the host country were eleventh and twelfth, with Luyendijk being one in front of Hayje.

A pair of Italian circuits was next to host the Rothmans European Formula 5000 Championship, with Mugello on 23 June being the first. The race was meant to be two twenty-five lap affairs that was also the inaugural event on the Florentine circuit, with the first used to decide the grid placings for the second. Torrential rain reduced the first of these to just seven laps, however. The opening heat was headed by Ashley at first, but he was passed by Gethin when the race started with Evans slotting in behind the top two. Hobbs marked his return by coming through to pass all three of them on what turned out to be the penultimate lap. Evans also overtook the two in front and he was credited with second place.

The organisers announced that the second heat would be started at 8.00pm in the hope that the weather would improve. This didn't happen, though, and the race didn't last as long as the first as the rain was just as hard. This time it was Pilette who was in front when the red flags signalled the end after just four laps. Hobbs, Evans and Robinson led the chasing group and they were awarded those places. Overall, the podium places were given to Hobbs, Evans and Pilette. That meant that in Monza the week following their wet adventures, it was Gethin who led the title charge with 100 points. Evans was 2 adrift, whilst Hobbs' third place was a distance of 30 points behind the leader.

Monza was the venue of the Gran Premio della Lotteria, and it was the winner of the two twenty-lap heats that would claim that title for the 1974 season. The weather was a little better than in Florence and once again it was Chevron drivers who dominated qualifying. Gethin led the trio followed this time, not by his team-mate Pilette, but by Wunderink and Craft. Pilette was down in fourteenth place for the first of the heats. Marking a first outing for Brabham BT43 was Martin Birrane, one place behind the Belgian. Gethin was the first winner of the heats with Pilette taking an amazing second place after both Wunderink and Craft had to retire with an over-warm engine apiece and the rest of the field fell to Pilette's aggression. Evans came back to pass Schuppan, but with Hobbs hot on his heels as well he couldn't afford to rest until the end. These two came up to lap Patrick Sumner and ended up with damaged nose cones each; Evans hit the back of the Trojan whilst Hobbs made contact with the exhaust of Evans' car. Schuppan's woes continued when he had a slow puncture. As the flag came out it was Gethin, Pilette and Evans who made up the top three with Hobbs slipping back to eighth, another victim of a slow puncture.

Heat two saw sixteen cars face the starter with Gethin once again at the front. Pilette was better placed this time and he fell in behind his team-mate, with Edwards taking third place ahead of Evans. Brian McGuire led Lombardi and Hobbs in the next group for a couple of laps, with Schuppan a bit further back. Birrane's weekend was over by the beginning of lap three, though, when his Brabham's gear linkage broke. Evans came through to take third place, with Schuppan also making rapid and effective progress to make fourth place his own. The Aussie then got ahead of Evans' overheating Lola and set after Pilette, with Hobbs also passing the ailing motor. Schuppan passed Pilette on lap twelve and then he had Gethin in his sights. His quest was looking good until the rear wing stay broke at 180mph on entering the Curva Grande, and the car spun across the track detaching its nose cone. He managed to continue but in a lowly position. Pilette resumed second place but then had the attentions of Hobbs to contend with that he couldn't resist, and he finished behind the two Englishmen.

The overall winner wasn't in doubt, but Pilette's finish gave him the 15 points for second place, whilst Evans had done enough to add 12 to his championship chase. Lombardi was fourth in her home country, one place in front of Hobbs and a couple above Schuppan.

The next Formula 5000 Championship event was at Mallory Park on 14 July, and Hobbs was back in the USA. A new replacement in the shape of Dave Morgan proved to be more than capable when he took pole position, and the Charles Heidsieck Champagne Award, for doing so. His time of 41.2 seconds was two-tenths faster than Pilette's, who came closest to him. Several other drivers recorded 41.6 seconds, but Gethin was the first so he was third with Evans alongside him. Holland – in a Lola T332 provided by Embassy Racing in place of the Trojan he had used previously – and Ashley recorded the same time as the second-row men, and they were on row three. Edwards was meant to be in Holland's car, but after he broke his wrist when colliding with Birrane in a private practice session, his season came to a temporary halt. Schuppan and Belso shared row four, and Wunderink and Lombardi were on the fifth to complete the top ten.

*Top: Out on the track, Keith Holland was keen. (Courtesy Alan Cox)*

*Whilst Teddy Pilette wasn't about to give up. (Courtesy Alan Cox)*

Morgan made a great start and led into Gerrards as the flag fell. Evans got ahead of Pilette whilst Belso got the jump on Gethin and the others in front of him and fell in behind Pilette. Ashley squeezed past Holland whilst Dean managed to enter the top ten after passing Wunderink and Wilds. Holland was the first to drop out of the top ten when the nose cone fell off his car, necessitating a pit stop to reattach it that dropped him to nineteenth. An altercation with a backmarker, Colin Andrews' Surtees TS8, though brought an end to Morgan's race on lap six when he went into the bank and his front suspension bent. That gave the lead to Evans with Pilette just behind, but it was a short-lived lead as it was the Chevron driver who was in front on the next lap. Belso had a charging Gethin behind him but his pace only saw the top four close up to one another. On lap thirteen Evans went back in front at The Esses, and on lap fourteen Gethin made a positive move on Belso. A couple of laps later Gethin was up with his team-mate, and after the Belgian pitted with a mysterious handling problem, he was in front. Evans, though, hadn't given up, and as they came up against more backmarkers he and Gethin chose to go either side of Nick Wattiez' Lola T330 on Stebbe Straight and it was the T332 that came out slightly in front. The pair continued to circulate very close together, and despite everything Gethin threw at his rival he was unable to retake the lead and finished two-tenths behind. Ashley suffered a puncture but got ahead of Belso whose car was losing gears, and the two of them managed to keep their cars on the road to finish third and fourth respectively. Schuppan was fifth. After Pilette rejoined he unlapped himself and, along with Gethin, set a new official circuit lap record, a time of 41.6 seconds being the same as Gethin's qualifying time. This earned him sixth place, with Lombardi, Craft, McGuire and Clive Santo completing the points scorers.

With suitcases and passports needed again, only a few of the teams travelled across the Irish Sea to Mondello Park in the Irish Republic for the two thirty-lap contests on 28 July. Twelve cars entered the twisty, bumpy circuit, and after qualifying it was the current second-placed driver, Evans, who completed a lap quicker than the record that Graham McRae had set in the race in 1973. Second fastest was Schuppan, followed by Craft and Gethin. Damien Magee came to join the party in a Trojan T101, but he was found on row six over two seconds slower than Evans.

Good weather greeted the small grid on race day but the first heat was delayed; not only was the weather dry, so were the circuit's fuel tanks and there needed to be petrol there to refuel the cars for the second heat. This problem was overcome when a tanker was rushed from Dublin to fill them up. When the grid came to be formed, it was Evans who made sure he was first in line to fill up. Behind Evans, though, mayhem occurred when Ashley, Belso, Wunderink and Lombardi had a coming together at the Shell hairpin. Ashley and Lombardi managed to recover but the others were out on the spot. Schuppan was Evans' biggest threat in qualifying, and his hopes were raised when he took over in front before the first lap was over. Evans, though, was equally determined, but it took another fourteen laps before he could wrest the lead back, and then he only managed it because the Australian missed a gear. Gethin was keen to maintain his championship lead and it was he that led the remaining chasers. Craft and Pilette made it a trio of Chevrons and they weren't too far behind Gethin either. Ashley was the next to fall by the wayside when a broken drive shaft on lap twenty-four brought about his demise. At the flag, Evans' advantage was 5.8 seconds over Schuppan and Gethin was a further 1.6 seconds back in third. Craft thought he had got away from Pilette during the latter half of the race but as the laps ran out, the efforts of the second member of Team VDS brought him within two-tenths. Lombardi was in sixth, Magee seventh and Sumner next, one lap down when the flag came out. Wattiez was four laps behind but he completed the finishers.

With the field reduced to ten cars and refuelled with the help of the Shell tanker, the second heat became a bit of a procession. Schuppan led the way with Evans in close attendance, and these two finished within a second of one another after the thirty-lap distance. Gethin failed to finish after a broken diff' on lap fourteen spelled the end of his day's work. Craft recorded third after getting ahead of Pilette who had only third gear for most of the race but hung on to be the sixth man to cross the line. Wunderink's repaired Chevron made fourth place, whilst Magee was the only other finisher. With overall victory in the Dublin Grand Prix, Evans went home to England very happy as he was now in front of the championship standings as well. Gethin's failure to score left him 5 points behind the new leader.

Following the cancellation of Silverstone's meeting on 4 August, a couple of weeks went by before the next round of the series took place and it was Thruxton's turn to be the venue for the big single-seaters. Six more cars were out this time on 18 August, and thirty-five laps were given over to them to see if Evans could increase his lead in the championship or whether Gethin could put his bid for a third title back on track. Following his shunt at Mallory Park, South African Formula 1 Championship front runner, Eddie Keizan, replaced Holland in Edwards' Lola T332. This was also the last meeting for the Kitchener team's McLaren M19 car after an engine broke whilst Spice was back behind the wheel in practice. Three of the other regulars, Hobbs, Ashley and Wilds were also missing; their absence due to them being drafted into the McLaren, Token and Ensign Formula 1 teams respectively for the Austrian Grand Prix. Hobbs placed the best of them at the Oesterreichring in seventh, Ashley failed to finish the whole distance of fifty-four laps, whilst Wilds failed to qualify.

Whilst that was going on abroad, Evans was usurped for pole by Schuppan and then demoted even further down the order when Gethin went quicker still in qualifying. Evans, though, completed the front row that had three cars on it. On a two-car second row, McGuire was fourth fastest, accompanied by Keizan. Row three was another three-car line, this time it was spearheaded by Craft who had Belso and Pilette for company. Tony Trimmer was deputising for Ashley and he was joined by Magee on the fourth row. Trimmer's team-mate, Lombardi and Robinson completed the top ten.

As the teams were preparing to race it started to rain, and they were faced with making a decision over tyres; none of the front runners chose anything other than slicks. Schuppan made his pole position count as he set off from the line with Evans managing to get the jump on Gethin. Belso made a fantastic start and he fell in behind Gethin with McGuire, keen to regain his starting position, snapping at the rear of the Dane's Lola T330. The top five continued in formation on lap two, but Schuppan was pulling away from the chasing group and Pilette was trying as hard as he could to make it a closer fight for the points. This became more of a possibility when the leader suddenly disappeared from the lap charts as they started lap seven – Schuppan's car had come to a halt with a lack of oil pressure.

That meant that the series leader, Evans, was in a great position to make it three wins in a row, although Gethin was equally determined to stop it happening. Belso had lost his shadow after McGuire was forced to pit with handling problems and Magee came to a stop with a punctured water hose, promoting Pilette to fourth. Keizan was therefore back in fifth, followed by Craft. As lap twelve came to a close the gap between the top two was wider than before as Gethin had a moment that saw him run a little wider than he should have. With Belso alone in third, South Africa's man caught up Belgium's hope on the same lap with Craft soon on the tail of them both. After another seven laps, Craft found that he could pass Keizan and then they both overtook Pilette. The remainder of the race saw these five hold station, with Lombardi coming through to take sixth place. Pilette hung on to seventh and was the only other driver not to have been lapped. Sumner was eighth to add 3 more points to his season's haul.

Imola and Casale were scheduled to hold a round of the series apiece in September, but they suffered the same fate as Silverstone. The reason given for the cancellation of Imola was due to the condition of the track, which had broken up during a 1000 kilometre race a few weeks earlier and had not been repaired. Casale, however, had been cancelled because the circuit owners could not meet the high costs, imposed by the Italian government, of taking the cars into the country. This meant that from eighteen rounds, the driver's best fourteen scores would count towards the title.

On 26 August, Bank Holiday Monday saw nineteen cars come to the Brands Hatch circuit for what was now round fourteen. Evans took pole position with almost a second in hand before Schuppan and the rest. The best of them was Wilds; he was followed by Hobbs, who returned to the seat of the Hogan Racing Lola once more. Brett Lunger was also back in a Formula 5000 car in England although the he could only qualify seventh in a Brabham BT43. In fifth and sixth places respectively was another returnee, Ashley, and Brian McGuire. Chevron drivers Gethin and Pilette struggled a bit, and had their worst qualification of the series starting just inside the top ten, eighth and ninth in that order, but the second of the pairing then crashed his car before the end of practice and failed to make the race. Tenth fastest was Dean. The starting grid was depleted further when McGuire and Hobbs collided on the warm-up lap and the pair had to pit, Hobbs did manage to get back out into the race after replacing a tyre but McGuire's car wasn't able to be repaired, ending his weekend. Lombardi was present but well down on the grid, just before jetting off across the Atlantic Ocean for her preparations to race an Eagle Lola T332 at the Ontario Motor Speedway as team-mate to Formula 5000 debutant, James Hunt, the following weekend.

The sixty-lap race began in good weather, and Evans was the first away with Schuppan making a similarly good start by heading off any other potential passers. Gethin scorched through the others that were in his way and by the time they reached Bottom Straight he was up to third. Keizan was another who found those in front lacking his pace, and he was behind Gethin, whilst Ashley, Dean, Wilds and Lunger fought over fifth position. On lap four Ashley gained a place over Keizan, and that feat was matched by Dean on the next trip around the Kentish track. In passing the South African though, the pair had made contact, and it was enough to make Keizan visit the pits to retire after just eight laps. Two laps earlier Gethin had had problems with a spark plug lead, and his visit to his team had allowed Ashley to move into third and drop him down the order. A few laps later, Magee was up into fourth place after his terrible start and pressing the man now in front, Ashley. With the weather looking rather different from how it had looked at the start, however, the drivers had another possibility to consider, rain! That didn't seem to bother Dean, though, as on lap ten he got back into fourth spot as he passed Magee. Belso's engine blew on lap fifteen, leaving oil on the track that was found by Schuppan at the top of Paddock Hill. This sent the Australian's car careering into the barriers. Fortunately, although the car was damaged, the driver wasn't. Dean soon moved into third as Ashley suffered a puncture. Shortly afterwards, the threatened precipitation came and heavy rain fell. The chequered flag was produced and shown to anyone who was still on track. Gethin spun down the pit straight after he'd seen it, and hit the barrier opposite the control tower. Evans had a similar accident but he hit the opposite wall. Both were alright although the same couldn't be said for their cars; Gethin had twisted the chassis of his Chevron and Evans' Lola suffered a bent nose and a damaged wheel.

After the cars came to a halt one way or another, the Clerk of the Course advised that the positions at twenty laps would be used to create a new grid for a forty-lap race, and the results of both contests amalgamated to decide the points places. Effectively, a two-heat race was the decision. That meant that although Evans' car was slightly damaged, if it could be repaired in time, he would sit on pole position. Gethin's car wasn't able to restart so Dean was alongside the series leader, and a newly-shod T330 driven by Ashley was on row two, with Magee as company. The track was still wet as they came to the line, and it was Dean this time who made the best getaway, leaving Evans unable to do anything about it or the advances of Magee as the race started again. On lap three, though, the Irishman was overhauled by Evans, leaving him to concentrate on catching Dean. Magee was then passed by Ashley. Lunger was climbing through the order as well and doing a good job of it as on lap six he was right behind Ashley. Five laps later he was through and set about trying to catch Evans, whilst Ashley now had Hobbs on his tail. With the surface starting to dry out, though, tyres were going to be a deciding factor, and as everyone had started on wets, the question was; would they last? Lunger's were the first to show signs of going off, and after braking a little too late going into Druids, he found them incompatible with the track and slid off into the barrier before coming to rest at Bottom Straight. A couple of the cars went past him on either side before the marshals could tidy things up. Then Evans started to have a problem with grip and he lost ground, first of all to Ashley and Hobbs, and then Craft. A rejuvenated Magee also found a way to pass and unlapped himself from Dean, and then sought out the others to see if he could do the same again. With six laps remaining the Irishman was in second place and catching Dean, but it proved too great a challenge and when the chequered flag came out for the second time for the Formula 5000 runners, it was the Yorkshireman who saw it first. Ashley hung on to record third.

When the two parts were added together, Dean's courage and tenacity had worn Evans' advantage from the first 'heat' down, and it was he who was adjudged to have taken the overall victory. Magee was second, with Evans a place farther back. Ashley, Wilds and Craft were the next three, followed by Robinson, Hobbs, Wattiez and Sumner. Evans' lead in the championship was now 32 points more than those of Gethin, who in reality was his only threat. Ashley was third, 95 points adrift of Evans.

The Oulton Park Gold Cup was the prize for the next round of the championship that was held on 8 September. The two drivers at the top of the overall standings showed why they were there by setting the pace in qualifying. Both set a time of 1 minute 24.6 seconds so shared the front row with Evans' Lola which was the first to do it, therefore he was on pole. Schuppan's car had been repaired following his moment at Brands Hatch, and he was next fastest but the quickest on the second row. This was the car that Redman had used when he won the Good Friday meeting at this venue earlier in the year. Joining him was Ashley, who had also driven his best qualifying lap in the same time as his grid mate. Pilette was on the row behind these two although he, too, had set the same time as them. Keith Holland was back, for only his second race of the year, as a replacement for Keizan and he joined the Belgian on row three. Keizan, who himself was a replacement for Edwards, had to go back to South Africa for personal reasons. Lombardi, though was back from Canada, and was seventh, with Dean next to her. McGuire qualified ninth but failed to start as he wasn't happy with any of the tyres the team had with them. Holland's old Trojan T102 completed the top ten of a thirteen-car grid, with Thompson at the wheel this time.

*Nick Wattiez tries to prove his might ... (Courtesy Norman Hayes)*

*... and Patrick Sumner does something similar. (Courtesy Norman Hayes)*

*Back in 'Blighty', Tony Dean excited fans wherever he went ... (Courtesy Norman Hayes)*

*... Australian Vern Schuppan was good to see as well. (Courtesy Norman Hayes)*

Schuppan tried to prove his worth as the cars entered Old Hall for the first time, but was unable to separate himself from the two in front of him. At Island his efforts saw him run wide onto the grass, damaging his engine in the process and dashing his hopes of taking the Gold Cup home at the end of the day. Evans and Gethin then opened up a gap between themselves and the rest, with Ashley maintaining what was now third position. Pilette was immediately behind Ashley, with Holland and Lombardi fighting over fifth place. Dean retired after just three laps, and Gethin's race lasted just a couple of tours more as his Chevron developed gearbox problems and he stopped. Ashley saw this as a chance to win the race and he went about hunting Evans down. With twenty-two laps to go the gap between them was over 2.5 seconds, but by lap fifteen this had reduced by almost a second. On lap twenty-five, out of what was meant to be a thirty-lap contest, the pair were nose-to-tail, and on the next trip Ashley got in front when they went round Knicker Brook. Evans' problems intensified when Pilette, Holland, Lombardi and Thompson all got in front on lap twenty-seven. The chequered flag came out at the end of lap twenty-eight because of heavy rain, but it was shown first to Evans before it was realised that he wasn't the leader. As it was, it was shown to Ashley after he had completed twenty-nine laps and he was declared the winner of the 1974 Gold Cup. Pilette was second with Holland recording his first podium place in over a year. Lombardi was fourth, Thompson fifth and a limping Lola, driven by Evans, sixth. The top ten (and the only others to finish) was completed by Sumner, Robinson, Twaites and Wattiez, in that order.

A new-look Snetterton was the venue for round sixteen of the Rothmans European Formula 5000 Championship and, once again, only thirteen cars faced the starter when the race got under way on 6 October. Following some particularly nasty accidents in other formulae, a new corner had been laid at the entry to the straight and sharp hairpin that brought the cars under the bridge. With the new layout not being completed until a couple of days before the race, many concerns were raised by the Formula 5000 teams before sending their drivers out to qualify. Despite such concerns however, Evans took up what was becoming his customary grid place, pole position. This time it was Holland who was closest to him, two-tenths of a second slower in a time of 59.6 seconds. Pilette was the leading Chevron qualifier in the third bay, two places in front of his team-mate Gethin, and sandwiched between the two of them was Lombardi. Tom Walkinshaw started in eighth, behind the wheel of a 3.4-litre Ford Cosworth V6-powered Modus M5 that he had tested at Brands Hatch and got to within a second of the outright Club Circuit lap record. Alan Jones was supposed to be driving a Chevron B24, but both the driver and the car failed to appear.

Forty-five minutes after qualifying, proceedings started with a reduction in the number of laps expected of each driver from fifty to thirty, due to the issues raised over the new surface by the competitors. With the tyres of his Lola screaming, the first driver into Riches was Holland followed by Evans, then Gethin who had swapped places with Pilette, and Lombardi close to him. Lap three had more adventure as Gethin passed Evans. Walkinshaw climbed to sixth but disappeared from the timing screens before lap four started – the oil pump on his Modus having seized at Sear, bringing an abrupt halt to his race. As the new lap started the rain began to fall, and Gethin went sideways coming out of Russell and stalled. With this, the race was stopped, and the teams were given a chance to change their car's 'footwear' into something more suited to the conditions.

When the cars were readied for the restarted race they lined up in the finishing order of the previous session, but with just two cars on each row instead of the 3x2x3 configuration used earlier. The first of these was Holland, but he lost out when he and Lombardi had a coming together as they were released onto part two of the proposed thirty-lap race. This gave Pilette the chance to hit the front for the first time in a long while. Belso came up to second, whilst Holland recovered to finish the opener in third place. Belso took the lead as the second lap of the second part unfolded, and McGuire and Thompson came through into fourth and fifth respectively. After another seven had been completed, Thompson and Robinson both found a way past McGuire. Having only changed from slicks to intermediate tyres, Gethin and Evans found they had made a wrong choice as they slithered around at the back of the field in eighth and ninth places. Thompson now had Pilette in his sights, and a passing move on lap fourteen proved to be successful as was the chase to Belso. By the end of lap twenty-one Thompson was in the lead, and he wasn't passed on his way to the flag. Belso and Pilette, in the meantime, had both had tyre trouble, and although the Dane carried on to cross the line after Thompson, the Belgian had to pit to change a puncture before rejoining somewhat lower down the order. Robinson was the next to finish.

After results from the two halves were added together the winner was Belso. Robinson achieved his best placing of the season by being on the next step of the podium, whilst McGuire's day was brightened by being awarded third position. Pilette was fourth, Lombardi fifth, Clive Baker sixth, Verhoeven seventh, Thompson was eighth overall and ninth place was shared by Holland and the driver who still had the championship lead, Evans.

The penultimate round of the 1974 series was held at Mallory Park on 13 October, with even fewer vehicles on the grid than the previous two rounds. Although twenty-one cars were entered, just twelve cars made it on to the track for the contest that saw the return of Edwards to the venue where he broke his wrist earlier in the season. His determination to return in style was underlined when he pulled up alongside the pole-sitter, Ashley, for the fifty-lap race, although they had both set identical times. Belso's win at Snetterton brought him renewed confidence, and this was evident when he was third on the grid only two-tenths behind the front two. He had the dubious pleasure of sharing the time, and the second row, with the Italian driver, Lombardi. Fifth fastest was Pilette, but he failed to start when he crumpled the chassis of his car at Gerards whilst trying for a quicker time than the drivers in front of him. This left Evans as the only occupant of row three. Gethin was alone on the next row, too, after his colleague from row four, McGuire, lost control at the hairpin and left the car in need of serious attention that couldn't be completed before the race was due to begin. Thompson and Wunderink made up the top ten in that order. Walkinshaw was at the circuit as well but he failed to start the race – a broken wishbone spun the car several times on the Stebbe Straight before it landed heavily against a grass bank at the Esses, rendering it unrepairable in time for the race.

The cars were given a couple of warm-up laps before being released into the cauldron of the race, and after the signal to go was given it was Ashley who started the brightest. His lead lasted for only a short while, though, as a too-heavy foot on the accelerator sent him spinning coming out of the Esses. This was the signal for Edwards to take the lead and show the rest what they had missed whilst he was away. Ashley managed to correct his mistake, however, and rejoined at the back of the pack as they started their second tour. Belso was the first to go altogether, though, when a drive shaft failed on his car at the hairpin. This promoted Lombardi up to second place and Evans and Gethin a place nearer to the front as well. Ashley was also keen to make up ground, and by the end of the sixth lap he was up to sixth place and one place higher at the end of the next one. Evans was gaining on the Italian lady driver, and despite numerous attempts to pass, he only managed to achieve it on lap twenty-one. Meanwhile, Ashley's charge continued, and on the lap after Evans had acquired second, Ashley managed to grab fourth spot from Gethin at the Devil's Elbow. With Evans needing to win to clinch the championship with a race in hand, his mind was set on catching Edwards as the yellow Lola of Lombardi flashed past, two laps after he had performed a similar manoeuvre on her. A lap later a second yellow Lola passed him, this time with Ashley in the cockpit. Gear selection trouble was dashing Evans' hopes. The two yellow Lolas changed places on lap twenty-seven, whilst Evans slipped back even further after falling prey to Gethin's Chevron. Ashley was keen to regain his qualifying position and the gap between himself and Edwards slowly closed, but Edwards put his painful wrist aside and clung on to record the win by a couple of seconds. Lombardi failed to get on to the podium as her car suffered two punctured tyres, which meant that Gethin was able to squeeze in front ten laps from the end. That was as low as she went, though, and she recorded her best result of the season by far. Evans picked up 8 more points for fifth, albeit a lap down on the top four. Thompson completed the same number of laps as the provisional champion and scored 6 more points in doing so. The next three points scorers in descending order, Sumner, Verhoeven and Brendan McInerney, all completed two laps fewer than the required distance, whilst Robinson picked up the final point after driving only forty-seven of the fifty.

Once again the last round of the championship was held at the venue where the season began, on the Grand Prix circuit of Brands Hatch. This was also the last of the races sponsored by Rothmans, ending its involvement of the past five years. This time Alan Jones did make an appearance behind the wheel of a Chevron B24, and he managed to put it on to the grid in ninth place. Eighteen other cars started the race and the top two of the championship were at the head of the field, with Evans slightly in front of Gethin. Ashley and Schuppan made up the second row whilst Lombardi was fifth with Dean next to her. Pilette, Santo and Belso were the mon directly in front of the Australian debutant and made up the top ten. Holland and another newcomer, Bill Wood, shared a Trojan T101 in qualifying which was clearly off the pace, with the former qualifying last-but-one, with Wood being the one! In the end Holland gave the car to Wood to race, but on the warm-up lap he discovered that he had no brakes, reducing the entry from the intended twenty to nineteen.

With the race set for thirty-five laps it was hard to see who was in front as the first two climbed the hill that lead into the opening corner, but then Evans edged in front as they swooped down towards Druids. Schuppan was alongside Gethin by then and, in a brave move, decided he wasn't content to be third and found a way to pass both men that were ahead of him. As all of the cars emerged from the Grand Prix loop, three were missing. Sumner and Robinson had tangled and Walkinshaw was left with nowhere to go. That reduced the field to sixteen with Schuppan at its sharp end pulling away from Evans, Gethin, Ashley, Jones and Belso in that order, as well as the rest. Edwards was well back but led a group that included Craft and McGuire. On lap five, Evans' luck ran out when he broke a camshaft at Hawthorns, whilst just behind, Gethin had to brake sharply to avoid hitting him. This allowed Ashley, Belso who had passed Jones on the previous lap, and Jones to jump up a couple of places. Gethin was back to third within a few laps, though, after first passing Jones and then managing to avoid a spinning Belso. Gethin needed to win the race to stand a chance of regaining a crown he had last held in 1970, but Ashley was having nothing of it and then Gethin's rear tyres started to go off and his chase to gain second place, let alone the win, became an impossible one. With Gethin becoming a distant view, Ashley decided to have a go at Schuppan and closed to within a couple of seconds of the Australian, but back markers got in the way and the challenge subsided for a while. Five laps to go, however, and Ashley got back in the groove, but despite setting the fastest lap of the race, he was unable to catch his rival. At the end the margin of victory was just one second in Schuppan's favour. Gethin hung on to third place with Belso recovering to finish fourth. Santo was fifth, Pilette sixth, Craft seventh, McGuire eighth, Twaites ninth and Chris Featherstone, in a McRae GM1, picked up the last Rothmans Formula 5000 point. Jones was unlucky not to finish after his engine died a little over half-distance, but it was announced that he would be present to do a full season in 1975. Gethin's failure to win gave the title to Evans.

Following his win, Evans was invited to test an Embassy Formula 1 Lola at Goodwood, but problems with the pedals left him unable to set any meaningful times. Meanwhile, his winning Lola T332 was also being tested by a potential newcomer to the 1975 championship, Keke Rosberg. In contrast to Evans, he quickly settled into the car and set some quick lap times in the Silverstone test. A few weeks later Evans was invited to test drive a BRM P160, and along with Wilds – who drove a P201 – he circulated around Snetterton in times of around 59 seconds.

With Redman competing mainly in the USA and eventually becoming the champion there, the top ten from the Rothmans European Formula 5000 Championship looked like this at the end of the season:

| Position | Driver | Car | Engine | Points |
|---|---|---|---|---|
| 1 | Bob Evans | Lola T332 | 5.0 Chevrolet | 193 |
| 2 | Peter Gethin | Chevron B28 | 5.0 Chevrolet | 186 |
| 3 | Ian Ashley | Lola T330 | 5.0 Chevrolet | 152 |
| 4 | Teddy Pilette | Chevron B28 | 5.0 Chevrolet | 108 |
| 5 | Lella Lombardi | Lola T330 | 5.0 Chevrolet | 88 |
| 6 | David Hobbs | Lola T330 | 5.0 Chevrolet | 81 |
| 7 | Vern Schuppan | Trojan T101<br>Lola T332<br>Chevron B24/B28 | 5.0 Chevrolet<br>5.0 Chevrolet<br>5.0 Chevrolet | 77 |
| 8 | Tom Belso | Lola T330 | 5.0 Chevrolet | 72 |
| 9 | Brian Redman | Lola T330 | 5.0 Chevrolet | 67 |
| 9 | Chris Craft | Chevron B24/B28<br>Brabham BT43 | 5.0 Chevrolet<br>5.0 Chevrolet | 67 |

# CHAPTER 7

## A FEW WORDS IN YOUR SHELL-LIKE

A new sponsor came to the Formula 5000 party in 1975; the petroleum giant Shell took over from Rothmans under the banner of ShellSPORT. The points-scoring system was maintained but the prize money was substantially increased; longer events paid out £9000, whilst the shorter ones saw £5000 shared between the top ten finishers. This was also the last season to include European events in the title race.

The Formula 5000 season started on 15 March in a cold and wet Kent. Missing from the grid was Lella Lombardi who had taken up an option to race in the USAC series, although she was at the circuit to take part in the following day's Race of Champions, driving a Formula 1 March 751. Reigning champion Bob Evans missed both races after being signed to drive a BRM P201 in the South African Grand Prix at Kyalami. Despite impressing in post-season testing, Keke Rosberg failed to secure a drive for the season due to lack of sponsorship, leaving twenty-one drivers on the Grand Prix circuit for the opening round. Tom Belso turned up in his car from 1974 to take pole position. Gordon Spice returned to single-seater racing behind the wheel of a Lola T332, but was unable to make an impression on the top ten in qualifying. That was left to David Purley, a new driver making his first racing start in a Formula 5000 machine, who must have found things to his liking as he was second quickest. Vern Schuppan was another in a new Lola, but he did rather better than Spice and started from third. Ian Ashley was another in the previous season's car and he, too, felt few ill effects, securing fourth place on the grid. With Chevron deciding against building a new Formula 5000 car for 1975, Teddy Pilette and Peter Gethin were found driving the new Lola T400. Pilette put his to better use than his colleague at this meeting by qualifying fifth. Brian Redman and Brett Lunger came over from the other side of the Atlantic, and the American reigning champion used Tony Dean's old Chevron B28 to qualify sixth. Australian Brian McGuire, Brian Robinson, Guy Edwards and Tony Dean made up the top ten starters in that order. Dave Walker announced his return to the genre a few weeks before the meeting, driving a modified Chevron B28 that had been driven by Peter Gethin in the previous season, and he was far from happy to start outside the top ten. Another new entrant, who started thirteenth, was Saloon-car specialist Mick Hill in a March 74A that Mike Wilds had used in 1974. Lunger drove a Brabham BT43, but the best position he could manage was sixteenth.

The flag signalled the start of the race and Belso lit up his tyres that slowed his start and allowed Ashley to find a way to pass both him and Purley going into Paddock Hill for the first time. Belso soon got things under control, though, and set off in pursuit of his usurper, closely followed by Purley, Schuppan, Redman and the rest with the exception of Lunger. The American failed to start after a collision on the warm-up lap with one of the drivers at the back of the field. Three laps into the race, though, the crowd saw Purley overtake an ailing Danish-driven Lola T330 with clutch troubles that put him into second place. Redman moved into fourth on the same lap, which became third three laps later after he, too, got past Belso. Purley narrowed the gap to Ashley as the laps were ticked off, and around one-third of the way through he was less than four seconds down. That, though, was as close as he was to get as brake failure soon meant his only way of slowing down was to keep his foot off the gas pedal. Not that this was going to stop his charge for as many points as he could gather, but with Redman his nearest pursuer, it looked unlikely that these would be the 15 that second place would bring. Around half-distance, though, all was not well with Redman's motor and he was forced to bring it into the pits to retire. Gethin slipped in behind Purley in place of the most recent retiree, with Magee nearest to him and Hill, Dave Walker and McGuire lurking in the background. Belso's car came to a stop on lap twenty at Clearways with a broken gearbox. Dave Walker was the next to fall off the lap chart when he hit the wall on the way up to Druids on lap twenty-three. Gethin was struggling to see after losing the visor from his helmet, this made him spin near to Belso and left his car stranded further down the track looking somewhat battered after hitting the bank. Fortunately the driver was unhurt. Magee took on the third place, one lap down with little hope of catching the two in front in the distance left to run. The flag was shown at the end of lap thirty-five to the three who had been in front since the twenty-fourth, Ashley, Purley and Magee. Three laps behind the first two, in fourth, fifth and sixth places were Hill, Leen Verhoeven and Chris Featherstone in an 'old' McRae GM1. Completing the top ten were Edwards, McGuire, Pilette and Gerry Amato, in that order.

The following day's Race of Champions had five more laps than the Formula 5000 race. Once again it was Belso who headed his compatriots, but this time he had eight Formula 1 cars in front of him as well as a few behind. One of those behind was the reigning Formula 5000 Champion, Bob Evans, in a troublesome Stanley-BRM P201. The next quickest in a Formula 5000 car was Purley again. In the end, though, none of them could make an impression on the Formula 1 drivers, as Tom Pryce in a V8 Ford Cosworth-powered Shadow DN5 took the win. Belso failed to finish and Purley trailed home in eleventh place. Ashley was also present on the grid and he had the satisfaction of setting the fastest lap of the Formula 5000 runners, but he, too, recorded a 'DNF'.

From Kent the series moved on to Cheshire, with Oulton Park playing host on Good Friday, 28 March. While the competitors practiced at the track the day before, a heavy snowstorm left the circuit covered in snow. With the help of a lot of locally-produced salt, the marshals and the circuit staff, however, a racetrack was uncovered and the meeting, the first on the new Foster's layout, went ahead. The run-off areas, though, were still white when the cars came out to qualify. Setting the first unofficial lap record for this calibre of cars was Dave Walker, who lapped in 1 minute 6.6 seconds. Four-tenths of a second behind, but still quicker than the rest, was Belso. These two were joined on the front row by Purley. Row two was populated by Ashley and Schuppan, who were meant to have had Spice, Magee and Redman behind them, but after setting his starting time Magee had a moment at Druids that destroyed one-quarter of his car and he was unable to start. Tom Walkinshaw was present in his Modus M5 but his ill-luck continued when broke a half-shaft and could only qualify on row five. The meeting was the first for Richard Scott in a Lola T400 that carried sponsorship from the London Rubber Company's contraceptive brand, Durex. Scott was on row six with Trevor Twaites. Former big American saloon-car driver, Dennis Leech, also entered this event, swapping his Ford Falcon for the ex-Steve Thompson Chevron B24 and qualifying alongside Scott and Twaites.

*Above, left: After the snow had been cleared at Oulton Park, Brian Redman was out to win. (Courtesy Graham Petch)*

*Above, right: Gordon Spice was determined as well. (Courtesy Alan Cox)*

*Tom Belso wasn't deterred by the conditions in Cheshire, either! (Courtesy Graham Petch)*

Eighteen cars came to the grid for the start of a fifty-lap race, and it was Purley who was the first into Old Hall, with Belso and Ashley the two nearest to him, as they accelerated down The Avenue. Dave Walker got in front of Ashley before they exited Fosters on their way into Knicker Brook.

Pilette had started on the fifth row of the grid but by the end of the first lap his experience shone through and he was up to fifth place. This became fourth before they went into Old Hall for the second time as Ashley met the barrier at the end of the pit straight before the corner, and the resulting damage ended his day's work. Leech and Scott, though, hadn't been quite so fortunate with the former spinning, but managing to continue, at Fosters, and Scott held up by someone in front of him as the cars left the start line. Spice was having similar success to Pilette, and by the end of the second lap he had even passed the Belgian to lie in fourth place. Two laps later he was in front of them all but he, too, was then passed by Pilette on lap nine. Spice had Purley in his wheel tracks and with Dave Walker and Walkinshaw also close, he wasn't able to relax for a second. Redman retired after complaining of a lack of vision thanks to spray that was being generated on the cleared, but still very wet, track. Walkinshaw also called it a day when the fuel pressure in his car dropped and he was unable to go any further than Cascades at the tenth time of asking. This brought Edwards up the order and by lap sixteen he was right behind Purley in the hunt for third place, which became his four laps later. With half the race completed the order of the top six was Pilette, Spice, Edwards, Purley, Dave Walker and Robinson. Robinson took fifth when the man in front pitted to change tyres soon afterwards. With twenty laps remaining, Pilette's Lola started to misfire and a few laps later a rather disconsolate Belgian headed for the pits. With his mechanics wondering what to do, he rejoined in front of Robinson but was passed again by the Geordie and Twaites before the end, finishing behind them in sixth. In front of them, Spice still led, and he controlled the rest of the race to take the chequered flag almost twenty-four seconds before Edwards and then Purley. Dave Walker was seventh, Leech eighth, Belso ninth and Scott picked up the last point in his maiden Formula 5000 race.

Easter Monday saw the field return to Brands Hatch, but using the shorter Club circuit for sixty laps this time. Setting the pace in qualifying, and on a circuit without snow to hinder things, was Magee in a Trojan T101. Following his woes at Oulton Park, this time the Irishman saw fit to hit the bank at Clearways before the end of practice, but with a team like his, he managed to have his car repaired in time for the race. Evan's old Lola T332 was next on the grid, driven this time by McGuire. Tony Dean made it on to the second row with an identical time to McGuire, whilst two-tenths slower than both of them was Pilette who still lined up fourth on the grid. Edwards and Dave Walker were on row three with Schuppan and Purley behind them. Walkinshaw and Belso, in that order, completed the top ten out of twenty starters.

Magee made his best start of the season so far whilst behind him, McGuire stalled the Chevrolet engine on his T332, allowing Dean and Schuppan to go ahead with relative ease. Before the end of the lap, Schuppan also edged in front of Dean to take second place. Sadly, that was as far as Schuppan got; an engine problem brought his Huntingdon-built car to a halt at the bottom of Paddock Hill at the start of his second trip around the circuit. Dave Walker then passed Dean to see if he could catch Magee, with a refreshed McGuire looking to get ahead of the Yorkshireman as well. Purley and Belso followed behind the Aussie. With Magee and Dave Walker out in front, two laps later it became the turn of Purley to turn up the wick and pass those in front, taking third place away from Dean. Five laps after that he found some more power, and he passed Dave Walker at Bottom Bend to take the fight to Magee. Lap thirteen became unlucky for the Irishman when he could do little to prevent Purley sweeping into the lead as they rounded Druids, although he did manage to keep in touch initially. Dave Walker wasn't too far behind them, either, and the three of them circulated in close proximity to one another for the remainder of the lap. Magee's hopes ended on the next lap, though, when he came to a halt at the bottom of the exit of Druids with a broken upright on his car. This left Purley and Dave Walker to circulate closely with their nearest pursuer now Dean again, who was a reasonable distance in front of Belso, Pilette and McGuire as well as the rest. These three swapped places a few times as Edwards and Walkinshaw were enjoying a great dice for seventh, but they were never going to bother the top two at this rate. Walkinshaw took the position part-way through the race when Edwards spun his Lola and was forced to pit to change his tyres. Looking like he had more power, the Modus driver proceeded to catch first of all McGuire on lap thirty-eight, to take sixth place away from him. Pilette became his next target, and he passed him on lap forty-six, and four laps later he eventually took Belso's fourth placing. For the remainder of the race the top five never altered, and the only change in the top six came when Belso was forced to pit with a puncture although he did register in the results as ninth. Ashley and Hill were the other two in front of the Dane, and Twaites collected a point for being the one immediately behind him.

A protest after the race about the tyres used by Dave Walker and Dean that went to an RAC Tribunal, however, took away their points but did not change the finishing order, meaning that the drivers who finished after them did not see an increase in their scores. Incidentally, Purley's win was the first by a Formula 5000 car not powered by a Chevrolet engine. The leader board, therefore, had Purley at its head with 47 points followed by Ashley on 24 and Spice, who was a further 4 points adrift. Edwards' total of 19 points so far had him one place in front of Pilette who had 14 points, in fourth and fifth respectively.

The twelfth of April saw Silverstone as the next venue for a round of the ShellSPORT Formula 5000 Championship circus. The race was being televised by the BBC who decided that showing Scott's car with its sponsors' name on was not suitable family viewing, meaning that he had to run in a car with the decals covered up. Not that any of that seemed to bother the driver, he qualified third in an equal time to that which Ashley had set earlier on his way to the second grid position – maybe the extra weight slowed him down! Up at the front was Dean in a car that was new to him, a Chevron B28 that Redman had used in the first two rounds before heading back across the Atlantic to compete in the US series again. Alongside Scott's 'newly-decorated' Lola T400 was Dave Walker's B28. Purley was the fastest man on the third row after completing the qualifying session in a time of 1 minute 20 seconds that looked good enough for pole position, until the four in front of him went out with only a few minutes to spare and bettered it. Schuppan lined up next to the series leader. Lunger was also present – he and David Hobbs jointly held the current lap record of 1 minute 18 seconds, but this time his Brabham BT44 could only lap over four seconds slower than that.

With twenty-five laps to complete, the race started under blue skies. Scott pushed his way between the two on the front row and sped off into the distance. Ashley reacted quicker than Dean and took second place on the way out of Stowe, although the pole man recovered enough to put him behind as they exited Copse. Dave Walker got going eventually and slotted into fourth place, and then he joined the battle for second and third. He achieved the first of these before the first lap ended but was back in fourth as the second lap came to a close. Scott was safely in the lead with Dean apparently similarly secure in second place, but Dave Walker's third place was looking somewhat tenuous with Schuppan on a charge climbing through to fourth after falling back to tenth earlier on in the race. The Australian got the better of Ashley on lap thirteen and set about the chase to Dean, catching him up on lap fifteen. Catching is one thing but passing is another, and Dean made his Chevron as wide as possible in an attempt to thwart the Lola man. It was another five laps before Schuppan was finally able to pass as the pair went round Stowe. With Schuppan the fastest man on the track and Scott coming across back markers, the battle was on. Schuppan's engine then developed a problem with only seven of the eight cylinders firing, although as the flag came out he was just two and a half seconds behind the winner, Scott. Dean followed closely behind in third with Gethin next, making his best finish of the season thus far. Ashley had oil pressure problems but managed to come home fifth, ahead of Belso, Edwards, Walkinshaw, McGuire and Verhoeven who completed the top ten. Lunger retired before the end, but was still joint lap record holder as Schuppan, who set the fastest lap of the day, was almost two seconds slower than the time that he and Hobbs had set in April 1973.

Round five of the championship was also the first trip into continental Europe for 1975, and it was to Zolder in Belgium that fifteen cars travelled to race on 27 April. Two twenty-five-lap heats were amalgamated to find the winner and other points scorers. The Dutch driver, 'Boy' Hayje, came back to the series to debut the Hezemans team's March-Ford V6, but he failed to make an impact on the top ten in qualifying. Saloon-car driver, Alain Peltier from Belgium, also used one of Dean's Chevron cars in qualifying, but his challenge failed when he had brake problems and there were no more to be had from the car's owner, so he didn't take part in the race. Leading the qualifiers, though, was the winner from Silverstone, Scott, who had Gethin for company on the front row. Schuppan's season went from good to worse when he was due to line up third on the grid, with Pilette next to him, but his car suffered a blow-up during unofficial practice before the first heat. Ashley brought out a Lola T400 for the first time after originally practicing in his usual T330, and he shared the third row with Purley. Dave Walker and Walkinshaw were the next closest to the sharp end, whilst Spice and McGuire sat on ninth and tenth places on the start line.

As the cars approached the grid for the first heat, Purley found himself on just three wheels after losing one of them at a point on the track just behind the pits. His crew managed to fit another, but he was five laps behind the rest as he rejoined. Before that, though, Scott and Gethin were away as the flag fell to set them off on the twenty-five lapper. Gethin managed to get his nose in front and as Ashley missed a gear, Scott was also passed by Pilette. The Lola driver kept Ashley and Dave Walker behind for just the one lap, but when the cars came round at the end of the second, it was Ashley who was in second place. Edwards and Hayje were up to sixth and seventh respectively. The first retiree was Walkinshaw whose car spun into the barrier, and he was quickly followed by Pilette when his engine blew-up after just four laps. Four laps later and Gethin was well in front, but Ashley was coming under attack from a rapidly recovering Scott and an advancing Edwards. The latter's challenge fell foul of a broken rocker stud that caused him to retire on lap twelve, bringing the 'Boy' into fourth place, but then he was the next casualty when his engine got stuck in third gear. Ashley was consumed by Scott on lap twenty-one when his T400 missed a gear yet again, and the top three retained their formation until the chequered flag was shown at the end of the twenty-fifth tour.

Heat two saw the rapidly repaired cars of Schuppan and Hayje out on the track along with those of Edwards and Dave Walker, but the latter's luck ran out after the warm-up lap, another victim of a rocker stud having worked loose, dropping his oil pressure and dropping him out of the race. Gethin was again the first to be seen at the opening corner, with Scott once more in his slip stream. Ashley avoided the tangle that dropped Purley and Pilette down the order, and Dean, Edwards and Schuppan followed him through. Scott's challenge only lasted for the first two laps when he, too, had to pit with gearbox problems which brought an end to his involvement in the proceedings. Dean and Edwards were then the nearest to Gethin, although they were some distance behind. Edwards overhauled Dean on lap five but he then lost oil pressure and his day was over. Pilette passed Schuppan to take third on lap eight and then overtook Dean two laps later, but he couldn't make any impression on Gethin and the pair recorded a 1-2 for their team at the flag. Dean failed to finish after spinning at the chicane which allowed Schuppan into second place, but he, too, wasn't meant to go the end – his water pump developed problems. As a result of the retirements, Ashley was promoted to third in the heat.

With the results combined, top points were awarded to Gethin. The winner was followed by Ashley, Robinson and Featherstone. Dean, Purley, Spice, Verhoeven, Scott and Pilette in that order completed the top ten, but weren't awarded points following their failure to finish both heats. That meant that the series was now led jointly by Purley and Ashley on 47 points, Gethin was third with 30 points, whilst Edwards and Robinson were a point apart on 23 and 22 respectively, directly below Gethin.

*On home ground, Dutchman 'Boy' Hayje has fun at Zandvoort. (Author's collection)*

From Belgium the series moved to Holland after a three-week gap. Ashley decided to return to his Lola T332 and the change proved beneficial as he took pole position for the thirty-lap race on the Monday. Sharing the front row with him was his co-championship leader, Purley. Behind these two were Edwards and Pilette, and directly behind them was Alan Jones in the Chevron B28 that Dave Walker had vacated in favour of a seat at the Japanese Maki Formula 1 team, at Zolder and Hayje. Belso and Gethin were fourth row occupants in a pair of Lolas, a T332 for Belso and a T400 for the victor of the previous round.

Ashley made a good start and led the field on the first of the thirty laps followed closely by Pilette, Purley and Edwards, with Hayje coming through to take fifth by the end of the second. On the fourth lap, the Dutchman came up to Edwards at Tarzan but over-cooked his attempt and spun himself well down the order. That brought Gethin into fifth place and into contention for his second successive time in the 1975 championship series. His position strengthened after first of all Ashley's race ended, due to a blown big end, and then Purley dropped down the order with the back of his car hanging loose. Pilette led Gethin, who'd got in front of Edwards earlier, but this lead only lasted until lap twenty-five when the Belgian took the wrong line through Hunzrug, and his team-mate didn't. Scott was up to third and with the flag imminent, the top three made it a Lola T400 1-2-3 that was a confirmed result when it was finally waved. Spice was fourth whilst a rejuvenated Hayje was fifth. Another Dutchman, Verhoeven, was a place further back than his compatriot, and was followed by Robinson, Featherstone and the only other finisher, Edwards.

The Bank Holiday at the end of May saw the championship return to the British Isles and a second Monday meeting was held, at Thruxton, on 26 May. Derek Bell returned to the seat of a Formula 5000 car for the first time since a meeting at the Hampshire circuit where he had driven the Chevron B28 car that Jones had used in Holland. Another ex-Formula 1 driver who took part in the weekend's proceedings was Chris Amon, but after a torrid practice session he decided against taking part in the thirty-five lap race. The best of the seventeen cars that actually made it on to the grid was driven by Ashley, who continued with the tried and tested T332 rather than his newer T400. A familiar car that had a 'new' driver lined up alongside him; McGuire, who used last season's champion's car, another T332, made it an all-Lola front row. Purley was the third fastest, with Belso keeping him company on row three. Scott was in a T400 and he was found on the next row with Spice. Alan Rollinson made a comeback in a McLaren M18/22 but was unable to make any impression on the top ten.

As the race got under way Ashley used his qualifying performance to show how good he was, and that was underlined when he pulled away from the line leaving everyone in his wake. Purley muscled his way in front of McGuire to take second place away from the Aussie who almost lost out to Belso as well, but managed to maintain his place as the lap came to a close. Up at the front, though, Ashley and Purley were pulling clear of the rest of the field. Behind McGuire, Belso had his mirrors full of Scott's Lola who in turn could see Spice and Pilette in his. On lap six, Purley got closer to Ashley than he had done in any of the previous tours, but was unable to take his chance and he was wiped out two laps later when he spun out of the race. McGuire was having problems of his own and Scott soon pounced – through into second place quickly followed by Spice. Belso and Pilette were the next to pass McGuire, and they also went after the cars in front of them. Just after the race was seventeen laps old, Scott had Spice on his tail until the engine failed on his Lola, but then Spice suffered a similar fate with seven laps to go. These mishaps allowed Pilette to come through into second, followed by Edwards who managed to pass Belso. With the remaining distance showing no changes, the top three crossed the line in that order but not before Ashley had a bit of a shock – his engine blew-up about one hundred yards before the end but fortunately the car had sufficient momentum to cross the line ahead of the chasing pack. Belso registered fourth place, Dean was fifth and Gethin sixth. The other points-scoring finishers were McGuire, Robinson, John Turner (in a Lola T330) and Featherstone. Bell failed to finish after his car only managed to complete ten laps.

A couple of weeks later, Bell partnered Jacky Ickx at Le Mans in a Gulf-sponsored Ford DFV-powered GR8, whilst also in the team in a similar car was another Formula 5000 pilot, Schuppan, who shared the vehicle with Jean Pierre Jaussaud. In the two-litre class, Lombardi and Marie-Claude Beaumont had joint possession of a Renault A440 provided by Elf Switzerland. Although these two were not in the top fifteen at the end, Bell and Ickx were on the top step of the podium whilst their team-mates were two steps below. Also during the break in the ShellSPORT series, the British Grand Prix featured a few drivers who had appeared in the current and former seasons behind the wheel of a Formula 5000 car. These included Alan Jones and Rolf Wunderink. At the end of it all the best of these was Jones, who finished tenth.

Formula 5000 racing resumed on 27 July at Snetterton. Eighteen cars came to the circuit but only fifteen came to the grid for the race. Evans returned in a Lola T332 that Sid Taylor had provided for him in place of Schuppan who was away in America – he clearly hadn't lost the knack of driving a Formula 5000 car as he had only one other ahead of him when the qualifying session was over, another Lola, a T400 driven by Pilette. On the second row the fastest was Scott, despite spinning off at the Esses during the session used to determine the grid placings. The T330 of Ashley copied the time Scott had set, but after the T400 driver had done it, so was classified fourth. Purley had some difficulties with engines blowing up before he went out for the timed session, but still managed to start from the fifth grid slot. Spice and Gethin shared Purley's time but they were in the places directly behind the V6 Ford. Belso, Edwards and Hayje completed the top ten. Jones came out to see what he could do, but a succession of problems ruled him out of the race before it started.

Forty laps was the distance expected of the drivers, and it was Evans who led the pack on the first of them as Hayje's engine died on the grid. Pilette tucked in behind the 1974 champion, but at the end of the lap Ashley was ahead of him. Spice and Gethin had found a way to pass Scott, and it was this pair who were fourth and fifth after Purley had pulled off at Riches with a broken water pipe. Pilette got his own back on Ashley on the second tour, although the Englishman wasn't about to give up and had to ensure that the advancing Spice was kept behind him as well. Evans maintained the gap as the laps wore on, with Pilette in second place until lap thirty-one, at which point Gethin displaced his team-mate after he and Ashley had probably had the dice of the race. That had ended when Gethin pressured Ashley into a mistake on lap twenty-five, compounded two laps later when the latter spun the car, although he continued, leaving the inaugural champion to chase after Pilette. Pilette's race was over when his car was damaged and the rear suspension collapsed, promoting Scott into third place. Spice failed to finish after he'd passed Ashley because a stone that had been 'kicked-up' by his rival holed the radiator on his car. With the laps running down, however, Evans was maintaining a solid lead, and finished the race almost eleven seconds in front of Gethin as well as setting a new outright lap record. Scott was third, Edwards fourth and Ashley recovered to take fifth place. Only three more cars finished the race, and in descending order these were McGuire, two laps down, and Hill and Featherstone, who both only completed thirty-three racing laps before the flag came out.

Ashley was meant to be driving a Formula 1 Williams at the German Grand Prix the week after the Snetterton race, but during practice at the Nürburgring he broke his ankle. This ruled him out of not only the Grand Prix, but also the ninth round of the ShellSPORT European series at Mallory Park on 10 August. Ashley's absence gave Gethin the chance to lead the championship going into round ten. After qualifying, though, the fastest was Gethin's colleague at Team VDS Pilette, who had Jones for company at the top of the pile. Edwards and Gethin made it an all-Lola second row with Evans and Scott directly behind, despite the latter trio setting an equal time. Purley and McGuire were slower still and were the fourth row occupants, whilst the ninth man on the grid was Dean and tenth was Twaites. Spice suffered a terrible crash at the Esses during pre-qualifying that left him with two broken ankles, a broken knee and severe facial wounds, bringing his promising season to an abrupt end.

As the cars lined up to start it was Jones who appeared to be in front of everybody else, but he couldn't make the slight advantage tell as it was Pilette who led as the cars approached Gerards on the first trip around the Leicestershire circuit. Gethin showed up in third place with Edwards and Evans closest to him, followed by the second group led by Purley a little way back. McGuire was the first casualty when he crashed his car into the banking at the Esses on lap two, and he was shortly followed into retirement by Twaites who brought his car to a halt on the Stebbe Straight. Purley was the next to call it a day when a water hose burst on the car that had promised so much earlier in the season. Evans' race came to an end at the hairpin on lap four when he appeared to lose control and he hit the barrier. As the contest reached the tenth lap, Pilette was coming under pressure from Jones and they had Featherstone as a mobile chicane as they came to the hairpin. Pilette went to pass on one side, Jones the other, but the Australian hadn't realised that Evans' car was still parked there and the two made contact. With the run-off area now blocked, the race was stopped four laps later meaning that the points would be decided on the aggregate of this and a thirty-lap second 'heat' that followed when the wreckage had been shifted.

Only eight cars survived from the first session, although after some quick repair work, two more cars, driven by Twaites and Purley, joined them, but they lasted barely a lap apiece. Once more it was Pilette who showed the rest how things should be done as he set off into the lead again. Gethin lined up behind his team-mate, whilst Scott found a way to pass the others in front of him to follow the top two. The Belgian then had the Durex-backed driver directly behind him for a while after he managed to pass Gethin at the hairpin. Edwards was another to pass Gethin, and he looked to put Scott under pressure. These three circulated in formation for the remainder of the race meaning that after the aggregation of the two parts, the winner was Pilette. Edwards' two finishes netted him second place as the gap between him and Scott in the second part was so minimal, he didn't drop any further down the order. Scott took the final podium place. Despite being lapped by the top three in the second heat, Gethin was fourth overall, and the 10 points he earned meant that he did indeed lead the championship as he left the meeting.

Ashley had a pin placed in his ankle before the tenth race of the 1975 season, and was passed fit to take part at Thruxton a week after the Mallory Park outing that he had missed. Most of the previous week's damaged cars were repaired in time, but one that hadn't needed any repairs and made the front row this time was Pilette. Gethin was also there, with the previous week's winner slightly in front. Edwards made it into third place with Scott next to him, and the 'patched-up' Ashley sat behind Gethin with Jones alongside him. Schuppan was back in a

UK Formula 5000 race and he was seventh on the grid with another rebuilt Mallory casualty next to him, fellow Australian, McGuire. Completing the top ten qualifiers were Belso and Purley. Walkinshaw was back but driving a March 752 instead of the Modus he had campaigned earlier in the season.

As the thirty-lap, seventy-two mile contest thundered away, it was Pilette at the head of the field who was never to see a faster car in front of him for the whole duration, recording a second successive victory. Gethin and Edwards had a moment on the opener that saw them both leave the race early on, although they did manage to continue for a few laps. This allowed an increasingly confident Jones to challenge for the lead, but he failed to get in front of the Belgian. The Australian himself came under attack from Scott, but he looked safe in second place until the rear wing of his March snapped off, sending the car off the track at high speed. Scott sailed through to record second position and Jones managed to get going again to finish a fraction over twenty-five seconds behind Scott, but in front of the rest. Ashley gained one place more than his grid slot but a lap down. Purley was fifth, Walkinshaw's return gave him sixth place. The rest of the top ten in descending order were McGuire, Turner, and former saloon-car drivers Dennis Leech and finally Hill.

The points position overall going into the teams' next visit to Brands Hatch on August Bank Holiday Monday was as follows: Ashley back at the top with 85 points, followed now by Pilette a point behind. Gethin started the Thruxton round with 81 points and went home with the same number but dropped down to third place. The nearest to these three was Scott on 72 points.

Tony Brise came from his home in Dartford to take part using Sid Taylor's Lola T332 that Evans had used at Snetterton, and Keith Holland was also there for the first time in the season, in a T330. Jones was also back with a Ford power plant in the back of a March 751. With the track breaking up, though, it looked unlikely that a race was going to happen, so instead of using the Grand Prix circuit, Don Truman, the Clerk of the Course, decided to run the meeting on the Club layout instead. After a short delay, practice produced a surprise when Dartford's finest drove a stunning lap in forty-four seconds to take pole position, with one of Belgium's best next to him, one-tenth of a second slower. Australia produced the third-placed driver half a second slower than the pole man, with the second Englishman, Gethin, a further tenth adrift in fourth. Edwards followed this quartet and was joined by Scott on row three. Sharing a time that was a full second slower than Brise were Purley and Ashley, who were to be found on row four. Completing the top ten came Holland and then Walkinshaw.

When the flag was waved to set them on their way, the customers at Paddock Hill saw Pilette first, followed by Brise, then Jones, then Purley and the remaining eleven drivers. The first three seemed to have the edge on the rest and a gap started to appear. Brise was determined to show his strength as was Jones, and both kept the pressure on Pilette. On lap nine Brise saw his chance as they came across the start line, and using Featherstone as a decoy, managed to take the lead leaving the backmarker between himself and his pursuers. Pilette used a similar strategy as a queue was forming with Purley at the head of it. Gethin entered the pits on lap twenty-one with what he thought was a steering problem, it was found to be fine, however, and he rejoined a few laps later. None of that bothered Jones, and once he was free of the lower order, he set about chasing Pilette once more. Pilette was having handling difficulties, though, and midway through the race he went into the pits and into retirement. Jones' next target was Brise, but there was a lot of daylight to catch up before he could make an effort to pass. Brise then suffered a puncture which helped Jones, and with fifteen of the sixty laps remaining, the Aussie had him in his sights. With the pit boards showing seven laps to go it wasn't so much a question of if the March would pass the ailing Lola, it was when. Four laps later they crested the rise at the end of the pit straight side-by-side, a slight contact knocked the local man slightly wide and his aggressor didn't need a second chance to press forward and go. As the laps ran down, Jones got quicker and set a new outright lap record before he took the chequered flag. Brise tried to fight back but the puncture hampered his efforts, although he did finish second, less than a second after Jones' triumph. With all of the remaining runners at least one lap down, Purley looked set for a visit to the podium, but a spin on oil and a lack of pressure of his car's own lubricant saw him retire before the end. This brought Edwards into third in an ill-handling car similar to that of Brise. Only four other cars were classified and these were driven by Holland, Ashley, Gethin and Leech in descending order, with the latter pair five and six laps down respectively.

Oulton Park Gold Cup was the prize for the Formula 5000 drivers when they visited the northwest again on 6 September 1975. Sadly, Brise wasn't present, but because of his strong showing at Brands Hatch he had found himself a seat in the last three rounds of the American series. Before that though, at the Italian Grand Prix, he was behind the wheel of an Embassy-Hill GH1 that qualified sixth but survived just one racing lap! Despite his absence in Cheshire, however, thirteen drivers did make the journey, and after his victory in Kent, Jones showed that he was quick here as well by setting the fastest qualifying lap. Gethin and Pilette were the next fastest followed by Ashley, who still had pins in his leg after the accident at Snetterton. In the car used in Kent and destined for Brise's US adventure, Schuppan was next. Purley was hoping to atone for his failure last time out and he sat next to Schuppan. Scott and Edwards made up the next row, the fourth. Walkinshaw failed to qualify after missing the session completely, further reducing the number of cars on the grid.

Although there was no snow to contend with this time, it had been raining, and it was a damp Foster's circuit that was used for the fifty-lap contest once again. Jones made his advantage count as they reached Old Hall and he left the rest to sort themselves out. As they approached Lodge Corner for the first time, Ashley ran over the kerbs and was passed by Purley, Schuppan and Edwards before he could move back onto to smoother ground. Gethin was also ahead of Pilette as the second lap began, but the positions were reversed partway through lap three. Scott was finding the conditions hard to handle and spun at Lodge, but he managed to save the car from the attraction of the barriers and rejoined at the end of the train. On lap seven Purley demoted both Pilette and Gethin as he grabbed second place, seemingly determined to catch Jones up at the front. Three laps later Purley became the leader when Jones retired after a conrod had split the engine block. Two laps after that, Gethin was pushed further down the order when both Schuppan and Edwards caught and passed his T400, with the latter car managing to get ahead of his fellow overtaker a bit later on the same lap. Schuppan got back in front, though, on lap twenty. A lap adrift of the top five were Ashley and Twaites, and even further behind were Turner, Leech, Scott and Robinson. Such was the lead that Purley created, he was able to pit to change tyres as conditions improved and a dry line started to appear. Pilette looked equally safe in second place, but with three laps remaining and with fresh tyres, Schuppan found a way past to finish over half a minute after Purley and forty-two seconds before the other T400 driver. Gethin was a couple of laps shy of the full distance but was still classified fourth, whilst Ashley took solace with fifth place followed by Edwards, Twaites and Robinson in that order.

*Back in Cheshire, Ian Ashley leads Richard Scott and a few others through Fosters. (Courtesy Pete Taylor)*

*At the Gold Cup meeting, Alan Jones leads Peter Gethin and the rest away from the line. (Courtesy Graham Petch)*

Guy Edwards had changed colours, though not sponsors. (Courtesy Graham Petch)

Lower down the order John Turner leads Trevor Twaites at Oulton Park. (Courtesy Pete Taylor)

*Peter Gethin tries to win the coveted Gold Cup. (Courtesy Graham Petch)*

*David Purley shows off his winnings! (Courtesy Pete Taylor)*

At the end of round twelve, the championship was still led by Ashley, but with only a 4-point lead over Gethin who was, in turn, a point ahead of Pilette. Edwards had 80 points whilst Purley, back to winning ways at Oulton, was fifth, 5 points behind Edwards. Scott's fortunes looked to be slipping as he was down in sixth with 72 points.

After a three week break, Silverstone was the venue for round thirteen of the championship on 28 September. Five more cars than at Oulton came to the grid, and those in the first two slots had a familiar look about them because they were headed by Jones and Pilette once again, the Australian setting a time two-tenths faster than his front row companion. Walkinshaw made his best qualification of the season in his March, and lined up immediately behind Jones' car from the same factory. Ashley, having taken pain-killing drugs but without the plaster cast he had been wearing the past few weeks, repeated his Cheshire feat by coming on to the grid in fourth spot. A new name to most Formula 5000 racegoers in the United Kingdom was that of Formula 3 pilot,

Ingo Hoffman, from Brazil, who turned up with a Chevron B28 borrowed from Dean and set a reasonably fast time to start fifth. He was due to drive in Emmerson and Wilson Fittipaldi's Copersucar Formula 1 team in 1976, and the drive was to give him a chance to experience some higher-powered cars. Gethin, Edwards, Scott, Evans who stood in for Spice and used the rebuilt Lola, as well as another returnee, Magee, made up the top ten. Richard Lloyd was due to drive Spice's car, but the deal for the drive fell through and Evans took it over.

Pilette found himself in a crisis as the lights changed; his car started to leak fuel and he was worried about the possibility of it igniting and decided against setting off. He realised too late that there wasn't a problem as Jones was already away in front. After the end of the first lap the Belgian pitted to sort the problem out, leaving Jones to lead Ashley, Purley and the rest. The Australian built his lead further by the next lap, and looked to have the race in the bag with only the remainder of the points-scoring positions to be sorted out. After ten laps, Jones was twenty seconds in the lead to Evans after Ashley had been forced to retire on lap eight. Purley came through to third after passing Edwards at Copse. For the following ten laps the dice of the race followed for second place, and it was enhanced when Evans slid coming out of the chicane on lap eleven. With the battle looking to go in favour of the Lola driver, and despite having the Chevron apparently stuck to the gearbox, it was the latter who was first across the line at the end of lap twenty-one with four laps remaining. At the end of the next tour, Edwards had closed the gap to Evans who was now playing the part Purley had endured previously and they crossed the line as one extremely long Formula 5000 car. Pilette was up to fifth at this point, despite his difficulty at the start, and on his way to enough points to give him the overall lead in the championship for the first time in 1975. Magee made his way up to sixth place and for the remaining few laps the top six runners didn't change, with Jones' advantage almost twenty-five seconds over Purley. Hoffman took seventh place when he got past Scott, whose Lola then fell away to finish outside the top ten after Turner, Robinson and Twaites also passed before the flag came out.

Only three rounds of the championship were left when the Formula 5000 circus arrived at Snetterton on 5 October. Pilette was looking to extend his championship hopes and with Gethin, he made it on the front row for the forty-lap race. Both set a qualifying time of 59.2 seconds, but as usual the first driver to have done so is deemed to have been the quicker, this time it was Pilette. Jones' car needed a new engine after Silverstone but he was still fast enough to line up on the grid in third position. Purley made it an all Ford-power second row. Ashley was only 3 points behind Pilette in the title chase and was on row three, desperate to not allow this to gap to grow too much. He had Edwards for company with Scott directly behind him and Hayje behind Edwards. Row five of the fourteen-car grid consisted of Magee and Hill. Hoffman returned to his Formula 3 seat and was winning the race at Oulton Park for his 'normal' class of car. A new name did appear, however, when the sometime saloon car driver from America, Bill Gubelmann, took over the seat that Evans had filled so well at Silverstone, Spice's Lola T332.

Gethin didn't get the start he wanted as his car came to an abrupt halt barely a quarter of a lap after the race began. This meant that Pilette had to do the hard work without the benefit of a team-mate to cover his back. It didn't seem to make much difference, though, as at the end of the lap he was two seconds in front of Purley who had Ashley breathing down his neck. Edwards was fourth, Jones fifth, and Magee sixth before the remainder of the field. On lap two, Purley was involved in an incident that left his car with a broken nose cone and damaged radiator, and at the end of the lap he called it a day. After a poor start Jones started to come back into the reckoning. He moved into second place by lap ten after some of those in front had been forced to retire or had had 'moments' out on the track. Hayje came up to fourth having disposed of Scott, but then he, too, was forced to retire after a head gasket blew, leaving Hill to fill the place he left. On lap twenty-eight, Jones' good run came to an end when the motor expired and he coasted to a halt. This meant that Pilette was well ahead and only ill fortune would prevent him from enhancing his title hopes. Edwards was now in second place almost the length of the circuit behind him. The bad luck that most of the second-placed cars had endured looked to have transferred to Pilette when his car appeared to be running on just seven cylinders towards the end. Such was his lead, however, that when the chequered flag came out at the end of the fortieth lap, he was the only one to have driven the full distance, and he set a new circuit lap record as well. Edwards held on to second with Scott third a lap or so down on the winner, with Hill and Gubelmann the only other two to be classified in the results.

For the penultimate round of the 1975 championship the teams travelled to Mallory Park. Evans reappeared in Scott's Lola T400 run by the Alan McKechnie Racing Team with Durex sponsorship, whilst Scott was behind the wheel of a T330, the car that Turner had driven earlier in the season with similar branding. The change occurred after the McKechnie team felt that recent results by Scott hadn't been good enough for him to remain in the seat of its car. Evans certainly seemed to prove its point, qualifying on the grid with just Purley and Pilette in front of him, having set an identical time to the points leader although he did so after Pilette. Edwards still had his eyes on the season's prize and he joined Evans on the second row. Jones and Gethin also set equal times and they lined up behind Evans and Edwards respectively. Ashley's bad luck continued but not before he'd set a time that gave him seventh spot, most of his session, however, had been spent in the pits with engine problems. Robinson joined him on row four. McGuire made a welcome return to the series and qualified ninth next to another returnee, Mike Wilds, in Hill's March. For his pains Scott started just outside of the top ten, in twelfth. Hoffman was back but he failed to start after he broke several valve springs on Dean's old Chevron during qualifying.

An accident involving Leech at Gerards on the warm-up lap delayed the start but when it came, it was Pilette that was first into that corner. Purley and Evans weren't too far behind him with a slight gap before Edwards, Gethin and Jones followed through. Ashley's hopes of the championship took a knock when he lost his visor on Stebbe Straight. The top three seemed to be having a race of their own leaving the rest to see what they could do; Jones was locked in battle with Gethin meaning Edwards was virtually alone in fourth place. On lap twenty Jones' efforts paid off as he passed Gethin at Gerards. In the battle ahead of them, Purley challenged Pilette a few times with Evans ready to pounce should either of them falter. After a further five laps, it was Evans' turn to show the crowd what he could do and he went through at the hairpin. Three laps after that, Gethin regained fifth place when he passed Jones at the same place. Purley wasn't happy to be third and harried Evans as the laps wound down. On lap forty-two of the allotted fifty, he came to the hairpin once again, closer to Evans than ever, and went for a gap that was virtually non-existent, making contact with the Lola and sending it into the air. This left Pilette unopposed on the way to the win that all but guaranteed him the title after Ashley failed to finish, although Edwards was mathematically still a contender. The damaged cars continued before Edwards and co arrived on the scene, but with five laps remaining, Purley was the first of them to pit. Evans managed to carry on but on the last lap didn't have enough to fend off Edwards and Jones, who had found another way to pass Gethin, before the flag came out. Purley rejoined and recorded fifth place, followed by Gethin, Wilds, Gubelmann, Magee and the deposed Scott. Also at the end it was announced that Evans' day's labour had equalled the circuit record that Ashley had set at the equivalent meeting in 1974.

The final meeting of the season was held at Brands Hatch, and with double points on offer the title had only one of two destinations, to Belgium with Pilette or to stay in England with Edwards. Ashley's hopes came to a more-than-sudden end when his team announced that he wouldn't be racing as it didn't have a suitable engine available for him or any other driver. Following the change in the layout at the Kent circuit's previous Formula 5000 meeting from Grand Prix to Club layout, this meeting changed too, from Club to Grand Prix configuration. Gethin declared it as his favourite circuit, and went and showed why on his way to pole position in a time that was lower than the official lap record. Pilette was also below that mark, and not for the first time this season he lined up alongside his team-mate. On the rows behind them another fourteen drivers and their cars were just as keen to make their mark, with the outgoing champion, Evans, the quickest of them; he had the first non-Chevrolet-powered car alongside him, the March 751 of Jones. The second Ford-engined car was on the third row with Purley aiming to make amends for his mistake at Mallory Park the previous week. Wilds was next to Purley back in his old car that Hill had bought and driven more than once during the season. Edwards' chances of taking the title from Pilette's grasp were hampered when he could only line-up seventh as he'd suffered handling problems throughout qualifying when he couldn't get the tyres of his Lola up to a suitable working temperature. McGuire was having similar troubles and set a time a little slower than Edwards, but still sat next door to him on the grid. Despite having their own problems in the session, completing the top ten were Walkinshaw and Magee in ninth and tenth respectively. Hoffman, Turner and Robinson were amongst the rest towards the back of the field.

The final race day of the season was bright, as was Pilette's start with Jones following him through before Gethin could get his act together, but the poleman did just enough to prevent him taking second place as they exited Paddock Hill corner. Evans led the chasing group with Wilds and Purley opening a slight gap before the remainder of the field came through. This was the order for the first couple of laps until Purley missed a gear at Druids and spun, and then had to wait until Edwards had passed him before rejoining. Pilette and Gethin circulated together, and on lap six swapped places with the double ex-champion streaking away from his colleague and the rest of the field. Jones and Evans then came closer to the Belgian than he

*Brands Hatch will do for Bob Evans. (Courtesy Graham Etheridge)*

probably would have liked, whilst Wilds was having to contend with the newly-advanced Edwards looming large in his mirrors. Purley was trying hard to get back into the leading group and in doing so, broke the existing lap record on his sixth trip around the circuit. Four laps later, Edwards' pressure on Wilds resulted him taking over the fifth place that would add to his points haul in his title quest. For the next five laps, though, all eyes were on the battle for second. At one time, Jones managed to wrest the place away from Pilette only to lose it when he, too, missed a gear at Southbank and saw his car pirouette a few times and the engine stall. Evans overtook Pilette shortly afterwards but then he also made a mistake as he went through Stirlings, although he managed to carry on a bit smarter than Jones. His indiscretion cost him third place as well as second, and he then set off after the new occupant of that spot, Wilds. Edwards' efforts came to nought when he discovered a misfire that couldn't be cured and he eventually recorded a 'DNF', his title hopes … gone! Purley's hopes of a race win disappeared when he ran wide trying to overtake Turner at Dingle Dell and he made hard contact with the barrier. So with fifteen laps remaining Gethin was where he wanted to be, in front, with Pilette, Wilds, Evans, Jones and Hoffman making up the top six. Turner and Robinson were the only other runners and it looked like that was going to be the finishing order. Evans, though, had other ideas, and he passed Wilds on lap twenty-five to go third. Gethin slowed to allow Pilette to catch him up, and they crossed the line just two-tenths apart and with the championship sealed in favour of the second-placed driver on the day. Jones completed thirty laps with a damaged gearbox as the flag fell, and although he had smashed the lap record before that, he wasn't classified as a finisher. Wilds luck ran out three laps from the end when his car ran out of fuel, but he pushed it across the line to record seventh place. The classified result therefore read as follows, first was Gethin, Pilette took second, Evans and Hoffman were third and fourth, Turner came in fifth and Robinson was sixth.

With Pilette taking his second championship crown and two drivers tied for tenth position, the top ten from the first and only ShellSPORT European Formula 5000 Championship looked like this at the end of the season:

| Position | Driver | Car | Engine | Points |
|---|---|---|---|---|
| 1 | Teddy Pilette | Lola T400 | 5.0 Chevrolet | 174 |
| 2 | Peter Gethin | Lola T400 | 5.0 Chevrolet | 143 |
| 3 | Guy Edwards | Lola T332 | 5.0 Chevrolet | 122 |
| 4 | Ian Ashley | Lola T330<br>Lola T400 | 5.0 Chevrolet<br>5.0 Chevrolet | 101 |
| 5 | David Purley | Chevron B30 | V6 Ford | 98 |
| 6 | Richard Scott | Lola T400<br>Lola T330 | 5.0 Chevrolet<br>5.0 Chevrolet | 85 |
| 7 | Alan Jones | Chevron B28<br>March 751 | 5.0 Chevrolet<br>V6 Ford | 64 |
| 7 | Bob Evans | Lola T332 | 5.0 Chevrolet | 64 |
| 9 | Brian Robinson | McLaren M19 | 5.0 Chevrolet | 49 |
| 10 | Vern Schuppan | Lola T332 | 5.0 Chevrolet | 30 |
| 10 | Gordon Spice | Lola T332 | 5.0 Chevrolet | 30 |

# CHAPTER 8

## A NEW COMBINATION OR THE END OF THE ROAD?

Formula 5000 cars continued to run in Europe during 1976, although the championship races they competed in weren't exclusively for these cars. Formula Atlantic cars joined the fourteen-race series that was sponsored once again by ShellSPORT, but rebadged as ShellSPORT 5000 European Championship. *Autosport* announced at the end of the previous season that the series would travel to nine events on circuits operated by Motor Circuit Developments, Thruxton, as well as Zolder, Zandvoort and Nürburgring. In the end, thirteen rounds were held, all within the UK as the European rounds were cancelled.

The regulations specified that all cars over two-litre engine capacity should use Formula 5000 tyres, whilst those below should use tyres more normally associated with the other formulae. Formula 1 and 2 cars that weren't being used in either of those two formulae were also eligible to compete. The series ran under what was known as Group 8 rules. Points were awarded to the top ten finishers as follows: 20-15-12-10-8-6-4-3-2-1. Prize money was also increased to cover the first twenty to finish the race.

A number of the drivers moved into other formulae as well. The Lincolnshire driver Ian Ashley replaced Bob Evans at the Stanley-BRM team despite his disappointing end to the 1975 Formula 5000 series. His first race for the team was the Brazilian Grand Prix that was held on 24 January where, regrettably, he failed to finish after an oil pump broke. By contrast, Evans was given a two-race contract to drive the John Player-sponsored Lotus 77. He lost that seat when Mario Andretti arrived, however. Another former driver from the European Formula 5000 series, Brett Lunger, was signed by John Surtees to drive his Formula 1 TS19. Both of these were to begin their new jobs from 6 March, the South African Grand Prix onwards, and finished tenth and eleventh respectively. The Stanley-BRM team wasn't present for that race and it was wound up shortly afterwards, leaving Ashley out on a limb. Moving out of single-seaters was Steve Thompson, who joined Andy Rouse in the Broadspeed-prepared Leyland Cars team in the RAC Touring Car Championship driving a Triumph Dolomite Sprint. Part-way through the season, though, he quit because of business commitments. The series also featured the erstwhile Formula 5000 drivers Gordon Spice, Tom Walkinshaw, and Chris Craft. Brian Redman was another trying a tin-top and in a

3-litre BMW CSL, he and Peter Gregg won the Daytona 24-Hour race at the end of January.

Coming into the ShellSPORT series was the former captain of the British Women's Olympic ski team, Divina Galica. Driving a Surtees TS16 that John Watson had used in the Formula 1 World Championship in 1975, Galica became the first British woman to drive a Grand Prix car. Returning to the series after his one-off outing in 1975 was Keith Holland, using a Formula 5000 Lola T400. Others who kept the faith were David Purley, who had switched his Chevron B30's engine to a 3.4-litre Ford power plant, Damien Magee in Alan Jones' year-old March 75A and Richard Scott, who this time used a 1.6-litre Modus M3 that was in Formula Atlantic spec. In a March 751, John Cannon also returned to the series that he had last competed in during 1972.

A fifty-lapper at Mallory Park was the opener to the new ShellSPORT series on 21 March 1976. The entry list for the race featured six Formula 1 cars, five from Formula 5000, eight that were more usually seen in Formula 2 and three from the 1975 Formula Atlantic series. Brian McGuire was listed as one of the drivers in a Formula 1 car, a Williams, but he didn't appear at the Leicestershire circuit. Setting the scene for the day, Purley took pole position in a time of 41.4 seconds that was the same time the lap record stood at. Almost a second slower than Purley were a pair of Formula 2 drivers, but qualifying for second and third places on the grid were Richard Robarts and Val Musetti. Magee was fourth fastest and completed the second row qualifiers. Cannon emerged for his first ever run at Mallory and was due to start in fifth. Another Formula 2 runner, Ray Mallock, joined the March 751 driver, and Scott equalled Mallock's time but started one place lower down the order. Galica's time of 43.8 seconds was somewhat slower than Purley, but she did enough to warrant the next place on the grid. John Wingfield in a Formula 2 Ralt with former Ecurie Ecosse pilot, Norman Dickson, for company, completed the top ten.

A mix-up at the start meant that the first three rows of cars that set off were not in qualifying order; Musetti assumed a front-row position with Cannon behind him, whilst Robarts and Purley had to carefully pick their way through to the front. Almost as soon as they had done so, the flag dropped and the race began. Musetti failed to react quickly enough, Mallock's reactions were better, and the two made contact before the race was a lap old. Mallock's car was written off and Musetti pitted to collect his thoughts before setting off into the race again. Purley, though, managed to get away from the melee followed by Magee, Robarts, Cannon and the rest. A major worry then entered Purley's mind when one of his front tyres started to blister, causing the car to understeer and allowing the next two to catch up. Magee was the nearest and looked to be able to pass when he liked but then back markers got in the way and Purley proved more adept at passing them. Purley seemed to be able to keep his car on the road despite its handling problems, and the winner's margin was 5.8 seconds to Magee. In third position, Robarts looked set to take that place, but on lap thirty-seven engine difficulties brought his race to a premature end. Cannon had already retired leaving Scott as the man who took the third step on the podium one lap down. Wingfield and Bill Gubelmann were fourth and fifth in that order having driven the same number of laps as Scott. Dickson was the next man to cross the line after completing forty-eight of the fifty trips around the circuit, and Galica and John Calvert completed the classified runners. The top ten were augmented by Musetti and Chris Featherstone back in his McRae GM1, the latter only driving for twenty-one tours, but they were unclassified and failed to earn any points.

One week later the championship moved over to the Norfolk circuit, Snetterton, for forty laps of the 1.917-mile track. Tony Rouff became the latest import from America to take part in the series using a Formula 2 Boxer car that had a Ford BDX engine, although he had raced in the

UK since 1973 when he won the Formula 3 race that supported the British Grand Prix that year. John Cannon was also back in the UK using the March that Ashley drove in 1975, and he put the car on pole position underlying his own performance if not that of the field, which only had twelve cars on the grid. Purley was second fastest in the Chevron that was backed by his father's company, LEC Refrigeration. Magee was another March driver, a 751, and he was the fastest man on row two. McGuire was present in his ex-Formula 1 Williams FW04 this time, and he lined up next to the Irishman. Scott and Musetti were on row three. Gubelmann should have had Mallock for company on row four, but the crank broke on Ray's car after he had set the eighth fastest time, ruling him out of the race. After the qualifying sessions, Rouff emerged ninth quickest with only Emilio de Vilotta, Galica and Robinson behind him. Featherstone set a time just outside the qualifying time limit but was allowed to start anyway. At the start, Cannon stalled on the grid as the flag fell. Purley also had his problems and his over-revving engine allowed Magee to lead through Riches until Purley composed himself and went in front before the first lap ended. These two pulled ahead of McGuire and Scott and the rest of the runners including Cannon, who managed to find his gears after most of the field had passed him on the start-finish straight. Magee was trying desperately to get ahead of Purley, but also had Cannon and Scott to contend with behind him after McGuire fell away and dropped down to sixth place on lap six. Cannon took third place away from Scott three laps later, and two laps after that there was a new leader, Magee. McGuire's woes increased at the end of that lap when the clutch on his car burned out. Gubelmann was up to fifth, albeit some way back, but this became fourth after Scott became a visitor to the pits on lap seventeen with a broken gear linkage. Three laps later and with twenty to go, Purley was trying to get back in front but Magee was equally keen to keep him behind. Cannon's chances went west two laps later when his car came to an abrupt halt before the lap came to an end. Purley's pressure triumphed on lap twenty-four when he passed Magee going in to Riches, but his car started to vibrate badly and his race came to an

*Keith Holland came back in 1976 to see what he could do. (Courtesy Norman Hayes)*

end with just two laps remaining. He had done enough by then to finish fourth. Up at the front, though, Magee was back at the top of the field followed by Gubelmann and Rouff who were a lap down when the chequered flag was shown. De Vilotta and Galica had been having their own race, the Spaniard winning that particular duel, and they were the only others to be classified in the results. In winning, Magee equalled the outright lap record.

On 16 April, Keith Holland joined the ShellSPORT Championship for the next round at Oulton Park using the Durex-sponsored Lola T400 that had seen action at the hands of both Bob Evans and Scott in 1975. Lella Lombardi was back as well, but she used a 3.0-litre-engined Shadow DN1 numbered 37 instead of the 5.0-litre Lola she had driven in her previous campaign. Alan Jones was present in a Lola T330. After qualifying, his mount was fourth fastest, whilst up at the front was the car that he had raced and put on pole at the same venue in September 1975, but with Magee at the wheel this time. Also in front of him were fellow Australian, McGuire, and Purley. Alongside him on a similar qualifying time was Musetti. Cannon was to have been on row three, six-tenths of a second slower, but a broken crown and pinion couldn't be fixed in time for the race. With a pair of drivers, Scott and Holland, a further two-tenths adrift, row three had a gap when the drivers lined up for the race. Completing the top ten were Lombardi, on the same time as this last pair, and John Wingfield in a Ralt RT1, who was a shade under half a second slower.

Wingfield was the first to retire from the fifty-lap contest when a driveshaft broke with just one-tenth of the race completed. After leading early on, McGuire followed him three laps later with a slipping clutch problem. This started on the third lap and meant that the lead was taken by Purley, with Magee and Jones trying their hardest to get on terms. Alo Lawler was out racing in a Chevron B29, but he spun on his way into Druids meaning that the leader slowed so as not to be collected by the failing car or driver! With Purley slower than he had been all race, Magee and Jones soon caught up and the number seven car was passed at Lodge by the pair of them before the lap ran out. Jones' manoeuvre was a little more hurried than that of Magee, and he made contact with Purley's car and dislodged its nosecone. With the pair of them dictating the pace it looked like a close race until lap twenty when Jones' car broke a rear upright and he retired to the pits a lap later. Before that de Vilotta spun going into Lodge, and after hitting the barrier, he was unable to rejoin. At half-distance Magee's nearest challenger was the film and television stuntman, Musetti, with Holland and Scott a little farther back. Jim Crawford, in a 1.6-litre Chevron B29, lay fifth, with Scotsman Norman Dickson's Modus 3 in close attendance and Galica not too far away from him, either. Purley was on a charge as he'd had to pit after his tussle with Jones, and he was up to seventh. Musetti lost second place when his 2-litre March 752 jumped out of gear entering Lodge corner a little later on, thus allowing Holland, Scott, Crawford and Purley, who'd found his way past Galica, to climb higher up the order. The latter pair swapped positions before the flag came out but they couldn't improve any further. Holland was the only unlapped driver in the race although he was over fifty-eight seconds down on Magee's time. Crawford became airborne when he and Robinson made contact as the B29 tried to put a lap on the Tynesider. Both continued, but the mishap allowed Purley to jump yet another place and Crawford eventually finished fifth. Musetti was one place worse off, with Jeremy Rossiter seventh, Robinson eighth, a recovered Lawler in ninth and the Brabham BT36 pilot, Bob Howlings, scoring the last championship point in tenth position. The fastest lap time of the race was shared by Jones, Magee and Purley after travelling round the Foster's circuit in fifty-five seconds flat, an average of 108.26mph.

*Right: Waiting to go I – Alan Jones in the pits. (Author's collection)*

*Far right: Waiting to go II – Teddy Pilette in the pits. (Author's collection)*

*Already gone, Guy Edwards with a new sponsor at Brands Hatch. (Author's collection)*

With only three days in between rounds three and four, the series moved to Kent, with Brands Hatch playing host to the fourth round of the ShellSPORT 5000 Championship on Easter Monday. After a healthy field at Oulton though, only eighteen cars were present for this event. Fastest of them all was Jones in a car that Tom Belso had used in an earlier season. Cannon was the next speediest driver using a March that had also been campaigned previously. Both cars had Chevrolet V8 power plants in deference to the second row occupants, Purley and Magee, who both had a Ford V6 engine in their car. Musetti was fifth fastest and used a Swindon BDG engine in his March 752, but he was over a second slower than Jones. Chevrolet V8-power returned to the top ten when Holland joined Musetti on row three. Exactly two seconds slower than Jones were Wingfield and Scott in their BDG- and BDA-engined Ralt and Modus cars respectively. Completing the first ten qualifiers were Williams and Crawford, both of whom drove BDA-powered Formula Atlantic cars.

Three warm-up laps were allowed to the competitors as it was found that their tyres hadn't achieved sufficient heat to allow them to maximise their grip. Even after that, Wingfield had to start from the pits, but Jones wasn't bothered and set off into a lead that he never lost. Magee and Purley got ahead of Cannon but it was the second of this pair that was the nearest to Jones as the first lap came to a close. The top three held station for the whole of the sixty laps with Holland initially in fourth place, and the deposed second-grid-spot man, Cannon, trying to get back on terms in fifth. Musetti had also been relegated from his starting slot and he was circulating in sixth place in the early stages of the race. Lap after lap went by with Jones lowering the record as they were ticked off, passing almost the whole field into the bargain. Purley was the only unlapped runner as the flag fell, almost fourteen and a half seconds down. Cannon took fourth place from Holland around one-third distance as the Lola driver was nursing a car with a slow puncture. This problem meant that the best he could do was to finish eighth, and brought Rossiter, Dickson and Scott into the places between him and Cannon. Completing the top ten were Lombardi and de Vilotta. Musetti's race was spoiled after his car lost all its water thanks to a hole in the radiator, but he was classified as eleventh.

After a six week lay-off the championship resumed on 31 May at Thruxton. Mike Wilds had returned but Cannon had gone back across the Atlantic to compete in the North American Formula 5000 series which also featured Brian Redman, Peter Gethin and Teddy Pilette. Jones had been involved in a controversial Spanish Grand Prix where he finished ninth on the road but classified a place higher following James Hunt's disqualification for having an over-wide oil cooler system on the McLaren M23 that he drove, and he, too, was an absentee from this race. The Australian also drove a Surtees TS19 in Belgium on 16 May, and scored a couple of Formula 1 World Championship points when finishing fifth. Back in England though, all the cars had to be resilenced as they were found to be over the allowed noise level when they tested prior to the meeting. Quietened down in qualifying, the pole position was taken by Purley who circulated the Andover circuit almost a full second faster than his 'shadow' of the season so far, Magee. McGuire was third fastest with John Nicholson in a Formula 2 March 752 in fourth. Holland and Musetti were separated by four-tenths of a second on row three, but were around two seconds slower than the pole-sitter. Wilds marked his return by putting his ex-works Formula 1 Shadow DN3 on the grid in the seventh place. Gubelmann was eighth and Crawford qualified ninth but was unable to take part in the race as the engine on his Chevron B29 was misfiring badly. This left Galica alone on row five but with eight other cars behind her.

*Teddy Pilette got out of the pits eventually. (Author's collection)*

*Mike Wilds was at Mallory Park. (Author's collection)*

*So was David Purley. (Author's collection)*

The weather was dreadful as Purley led the field on a couple of warm-up laps, and it didn't improve throughout the thirty-lap contest. Magee didn't start from his qualifying spot, though, as he had limped into the pits with a waterlogged engine before the start of the race only to enter the fray when it was five laps old. Gubelmann had made a great start and was up in third with Wilds being sprayed violently in fourth place, but before the end of the opening lap their positions were reversed. Gubelmann's race pace slowed, and by the end of the next tour he had been passed by Galica and was being challenged for fifth place by Dennis Leech in a Chevron B28. The two in front were disputing second place that became the property, albeit temporarily, of Wilds. Despite severe pressure from Galica, Nicholson regained the place on lap twenty-one as Wilds' car started to make horrible noises as it, too, was beginning to become very wet. Wilds managed to keep both the car running and the Olympian behind him for the remaining laps, and got his car home in third place. In front, though, Purley looked comfortable in the lead until he had a moment on the final trip around the Hampshire circuit, but his lead was sufficient to enable him to recover and finish almost twenty seconds before Nicholson. Galica took fourth place, over six seconds after Wilds but almost eleven before Leech. Holland dropped Gubelmann earlier in the race and he was sixth, two seconds in front of the March 732 driver. Musetti and Jim Kelly completed the classified finishers with the latter in a Trojan T101. Magee completed the race but he hadn't been able to catch up any of his lost laps and was therefore unclassified.

Round six of the championship was held at Brands Hatch on 20 June, and it saw the return of Guy Edwards in an Ensign N174 who made a great impression when he qualified on pole, eight-tenths of a second faster than Purley. Musetti was over a second slower than Purley and qualified third but he snapped a cam belt on his March 751 and, as the car wasn't able to be repaired in time, had to qualify his Formula 2 March 742 out of session and start from the back of the grid. Following this problem McGuire was all alone on row two in another ex-Grand Prix car, a Williams FW04. Row three was made up of two cars with an identical qualifying time of 57.2 seconds, driven by Magee and Wilds, whilst the two on the next row also had the same time, 57.8 seconds this time, with de Vilotta and Galica in the drivers seat. Leech was ninth, over half a second slower, and a full second behind him was Holland who completed the top ten.

Edwards lost out at the start when his Formula 1 car's wheels overspun which allowed Purley to go in front. He was followed by Magee who also took advantage of Edwards' mishap, although the Ensign didn't lose any more time and he chased this pair down Paddock Hill. Holland had also made a great start and he was breathing down the neck of Edwards as the lap came to a close. Wilds was receiving close attention from Dickson, who had come through from row eight in the Modus that was more usually seen in Formula 2 races, and the Scotsman's team-mate Scott was also close. Magee briefly held the lead only for Purley to reassert himself on lap ten. Musetti was also rapidly climbing through the field to put those in front under pressure, by lap twelve though his race was over after he crashed out. Holland overtook Edwards on the next lap but he spun three laps later and although he managed to restart, the Ensign sailed past to regain the placing. Holland's race ended when he was forced to retire with rear suspension failure. On lap thirty-three Edwards relinquished third position again when he had to pit with a puncture in one of the rear tyres, but the engine wouldn't start again and that was his work finished for the day. With Purley and Magee out of sight, it was now McGuire who assumed the place that would give him the lowest podium step after the chequered flag was shown at the end of the fiftieth trip, even though he'd completed only forty-nine. Wilds closed up on him throughout the last few laps, and finished about eight seconds down at the end. De Vilotta was another lap adrift and he finished two places better than he had started, with his fellow row four inhabitant, Galica, just behind him. Phil Sharpe in another Modus was seventh, Brian Robinson was eighth with Scott in ninth and Kelly in tenth completing the top ten runners. For all of his early prowess, Dickson completed only half the race after a collision with Mike King bent the steering arm on his car. The victory gave Purley a 7-point lead over Magee in the championship so far.

Mallory Park became the next venue to host a round of the ShellSPORT 5000 European Championship a week after the Thruxton event. Edwards was in the list of entrants but didn't appear at the track. Purley underlined his title hopes by putting his Chevron B30 on pole after setting a time of forty-two seconds in qualifying. Just two-tenths behind, and enjoying his best qualification of the season so far, Scott was in the M3 version of the Modus that he and Dickson both controlled. Musetti's 752 had been repaired and this time he was in the grid space allotted to the third fastest driver. He, too, was two-tenths down on the man immediately quicker than him, although he was behind Purley on the grid. Holland was next to Musetti. Scott's team-mate was next fastest, sharing the time and row three with Magee. Gubelmann and the returning Rouff shared the next row after travelling around the Leicestershire circuit in a shade over forty-three seconds. Wilds and Galica made up the top ten.

Drama unfolded at the start of the race when Scott's car failed to move off the grid as it had a flat battery and Purley accelerated very slowly as his car's clutch had been adjusted after the warm-up lap. This allowed Holland to get ahead of the pack before the title leader could get going, although that didn't take long and Purley was the next to show at Gerards. Magee took Musetti's place in third, but the Italian-sounding Briton did appear next. Scott finally managed to get going and he was fifth, one place ahead of the other M3 pilot. Going into the Esses on lap two it was Purley who hit the front, despite Holland trying his best to keep him behind. Further back, Gubelmann put Rouff a place further down the order as he came through to take seventh, although he then lost the position to Galica a couple of laps later. Wilds was on a charge as well, and he, too, overtook the American's March just before the Esses on lap three. As the Shadow went past, however, Gubelmann clipped its rear wheel, rode over it and sent it rolling. The American's car was launched into the air and hit the bank. Wilds emerged unscathed although the car was a write-off, but Gubelmann was taken to the local hospital and placed into intensive care with head injuries. Suffice to say the race was red-flagged and made into a two-part affair.

Part two saw the cars line up on the grid in the finishing order of the first, meaning that once again Purley was on pole. Magee should have been on the fourth grid slot but failed to appear as there was a problem with the engine on his March 751 that couldn't be repaired. Once again Holland got the jump on Purley when the race started, but once again the Esses was the place where Purley reasserted himself to take a lead that he never lost in the remaining thirty-four laps. Holland kept the pressure on but couldn't gain enough momentum to retake the lead. He was similarly untroubled until Musetti caught up and started to show his intent, but Musetti also had Scott, a rapid Modus driver, on his tail. This pressure from Scott told on lap twenty-two, and Musetti spun at the hairpin, although he managed to rejoin without falling any further down the order than fourth. Scott, though, fell out of the order altogether two laps later when the fuel pressure on the M3 disappeared. Galica showed that she was no slouch when she was the only other unlapped runner as the flag dropped. Rouff was lapped but completed the allotted thirty-four laps and was fifth in the end. Dickson was sixth with a new name and Phil Dowsett was seventh, followed by the Oulton Park regular Formula Fordster, Ken Bailey. Another driver from the northwest of England, Alo Lawler, and Emilio de Vilotta were ninth and tenth in that order.

There was a long break before the next round of the series, and a few of the championship drivers found themselves alternative employment in the British Grand Prix at Brands Hatch on 18 July. These included Galica in a Surtees TS19, Edwards in a Hesketh 308D and Magee behind the wheel of a Brabham BT44B. Wilds was listed as a reserve to drive the Shadow DN3B. In the end, however, Galica failed to qualify, Edwards was shunted at the start and failed to complete a lap, Magee's drive was taken over by Lella Lombardi at the last minute (who also failed to qualify), and Wilds wasn't required. James Hunt won the race. Purley also announced a spot of extra-curricular activity when he told *Autosport* readers that he would try to set the world land speed record in a Rolls-Royce aero-engined car.

The first day of August 1976 saw proceedings shift to Norfolk, with Snetterton hosting round eight. Twenty-one drivers came to the circuit although only twenty made it to the thirty-lap race. The top three all set a qualifying time of exactly one minute, with Holland being the first one to set it and therefore sit on pole position. Purley wasn't too far away, though, and he was next to the Lola T400 driver. Completing the trio and third on the grid was Magee. Wilds' car had been replaced by an Ensign N174, but in the end he appeared in another Shadow DN3 and was sufficiently quick to line up alongside Magee. A full second slower than the first three came Scott, who was pipped to fifth position by Richard Robarts' March 762. This pair had a Formula 2 car and a Formula 1 car directly behind them, the first of them being a March 742 driven by Ray Mallock. McGuire was in the Formula 1 car, his often-seen Williams. Nicholson and Dickson completed the top ten, whilst Bernard de Dryver made his championship debut and he drove a car similar to Mallock from the fifteenth spot.

Magee's race was over before the end of the first lap when he crashed into the bank at Russell whilst chasing Wilds and Holland, who led the pack. These two carried on in front on the second lap, with a gap to Robarts and another to Mallock and then Scott. Purley had spun on the first lap but recovered to sit in sixth place as the race progressed, and he moved up a place on lap six. Robarts was doing well in third but his hard work became undone when, three laps after Purley passed Scott, he had to pit with a split tyre. Shortly afterwards Purley was third when he out-braked Mallock on the entry to Russell. Holland stretched a lead over the rest of the field with Wilds dropping into the clutches of Purley, but the Shadow driver wasn't about to be caught easily. On lap seventeen, however, Wilds couldn't rebut the challenge any longer, and the B30 got by. On lap twenty of the scheduled thirty, Holland still had Purley behind him but Purley was getting ever closer. Wilds and Mallock were a little way back but ahead of the rest of the field. With four laps to go, these two swapped places as the Shadow started to have fuel surge problems. Holland and Purley were close and collided on the penultimate lap as the latter tried to pass for the lead. Both stopped on the spot and only got going again after Mallock, Wilds and Scott had passed them both. Holland limped home with a puncture to record fourth place, Galica was the nearest to him in fifth, with Purley doing enough to beat Nicholson to sixth. Robarts, Leech and de Dryver were eighth, ninth and tenth respectively.

The eighth running of the 'Evening News Trophy' at Brands Hatch was held on 30 August, Bank Holiday Monday, and was also round nine of the championship with thirty-five laps of the full circuit to navigate. Twelve counties were represented. Bob Evans made a return to the series driving a McLaren M25 that another former Formula 5000 driver, David Hepworth, entered. Once again Wilds had two cars entered, and this time he used the Ensign. Only three proved to be quicker than him, one of them was inevitably Purley, another was Holland, and the future Formula 1 and Indy Car racer, Eddie Cheever, was the other. Evans qualified fifth with Galica next, and seventh place was gained by Ted Wentz with the same time as Galica. Robarts was a little slower but did enough to register eighth. Australian Bob Muir and Hans Binder both drove Chevron B35s, and they were ninth and tenth in that order. Binder was more usually seen in this car in the European Formula 2 Championship and had driven in an Ensign in his home Formula 1 race, the Austrian Grand Prix. Magee used a Penske PC3 that 'Boy' Hayje used at the Dutch Grand Prix earlier in the season, but could only qualify mid-grid for this race.

With thirty-six cars qualifying for the race it was the biggest grid of the season so far, although when it formed, Roy Baker's March 758 left a hole on one of the lower rows. The race was stopped at the end of the first lap after a crash at Clark Curve involved Ian Grob in a Formula 2 Modus and another newcomer, the European VW Gold Cup Formula Super Vee Championship leading competitor, Mikka Arpiainen. The drivers were unhurt but the catch fencing was so badly damaged it took about three-quarters of an hour before the action could recommence. Grob was unable to restart, leaving another space on the line. Purley made the best start as expected, but Wilds got in front of the rest only to have a puncture force him to pit at the end of the second of the racing laps. This gave second place back to Holland, but Cheever lost out to Evans as the cars completed their first tour. As things settled down Purley looked secure in the lead, Holland looked similarly safe in second place and Evans and Cheever were fighting for third. Wentz, Binder, Mallock, Galica and Nicholson were the members of the next group who chased for fifth. On lap sixteen Magee joined the chasing pack and was through to eighth place. Three laps later he was seventh, seemingly in control of those immediately in front of him, and he took advantage of their weakness to come up to fourth as the flag fell. Holland dropped out before the end with rear suspension failure five laps before the close. Purley, though, wasn't bothered by this or by Magee's charge and went on to win by over half a minute. Evans was the closest to him, with Cheever less than three seconds down in third. The top ten was completed by Arpiainen, Binder, Andy Sutcliffe, Muir, Galica and Wentz, with only the latter not having completed the full race distance of thirty-five laps. The championship standings leaving the Kent circuit showed Purley on 141 points at the top, 49 points ahead of Magee who was 43 in front of Holland. Galica was the closest to Holland on 42 points.

Thruxton held its second Group 8 meeting of the season on 12 September, with twenty-eight runners starting a thirty-lap contest. McGuire took his first pole position of the season but had Purley next to him on the front row. Brian Henton joined the runners and made a wonderful start to his career in the series when he qualified third fastest in a Formula Atlantic Boxer PR276, although his time was the same as the one Purley had recorded. Musetti was fourth fastest with Mallock, Sutcliffe, Wilds, Nicholson, Dickson and Wingfield making up the ten quickest runners.

*At Thruxton, Brian McGuire, David Purley and Val Musetti lead the way. (Author's collection)*

*Damien Magee was also keen to do well in Hampshire. (Author's collection)*

As the grid formed, Mallock stuttered to the line only to stall as the race began. Everyone managed to avoid him but Derek Cook in a Chevron B27 was hit and he cannoned into the stricken Mallock ending the race for each of them there and then. Up at the front, Purley had outgunned McGuire and taken the lead, but the Williams driver saw a way to overtake at the complex and he held his nerve as he squeezed back into first place. Wilds was third followed by Sutcliffe, Musetti, Evans and Magee in that order as the first lap ended. Tragedy followed on the next lap, though, when Wingfield careered off the road and hit a marshal's post side-on that sent breeze blocks flying into the air. The whiplash effect snapped the drivers' neck and that ended his life. The race continued as no one knew the extent of the accident, and McGuire pressed on in front with Purley trying to keep in touch. After ten laps, however, the drive shaft on Purley's car snapped and his race was over. Wilds assumed the place that Purley had left vacant, although he had Sutcliffe and Musetti snapping in his wheel tracks. Evans had Magee breathing down his neck for fifth place which Magee took, only to lose out when he spun at the chicane, but Evans then lost out permanently when he retired to the pits with a blown piston. McGuire was so far in front that the battle for second place became the focal point for the paying customers, with first of all Sutcliffe passing Wilds, then Musetti doing likewise, and the pair of them trying to pass one another. Magee was lurking in the shadows and he overtook Wilds on lap twenty-two and then surprised the other pair by getting in front of them on the next tour. The top two continued to the flag in that order, and McGuire won by over thirty seconds before Magee. Musetti overcame Sutcliffe before the end to take the final podium place. Wilds finished fifth with Holland coming home sixth, and Galica, de Vilotta, de Dryver and Leech sailed across the line in seventh, eighth, ninth and tenth respectively.

The twenty-third Oulton Park Gold Cup was round eleven of the championship, with a forty-lap race on the Fosters circuit. The previous race winner, McGuire, entered the race but failed to start after his car had engine problems during qualifying. The Modus M3 cars of Dickson and Scott also failed to appear. Edwards and Henton set the quickest time in qualifying, and on a 3x2x3 grid it was the ex-John Watson/Ian Ashley Formula 1 Brabham BT42/44 of Edwards that sat on pole position. Henton was still in his Formula 2 Boxer. Almost a second slower was Magee but he completed the front row. Holland and Musetti were the two on the second row, with the former two seconds slower than the pole-sitter and the latter a further two-tenths behind. Geoff Friswell and McGuire qualified fifth and sixth but both failed to make it to the race; Friswell had a coming together with Musetti at Clay Hill during the untimed warm-up session and McGuire blew a gearbox in the same period. This left de Dryver alone on the third row. Galica and Cook made up row four, and the final three drivers of the top ten were Andy Barton, Purley and Bailey in descending order.

Henton made a fabulous start and led the field into Old Hall for the first of the forty trips around the shorter Cheshire track. Magee also got in front of Edwards whilst Holland was fourth with Musetti and Cook having a coming together as the future car dealer responded quickly when the starter's flag fell. That dropped the pair down to fifth and seventh, with the Chevron driver ahead of the March and with de Dryver's Formula 2 version of the March between them. Purley was playing the percentage game, he was down in eighth as the lap came to an end hoping to gain the points he needed to clinch the title, and gained a place without any effort when Magee came a cropper on the second lap. He got it wrong at Clay Hill, hit the barrier and retired. At one-quarter of the distance Henton's lead was looking vulnerable, but backmarkers protected him from Edwards until one lap before the next quarter was completed. As they passed the pits it was Formula 1 power at the head of the field for the crowd at Old Hall to see. Six laps later, though, Edwards almost lost the lot when he came up to lap Cook and the two made contact, sending the leader into the air. Luckily the car landed right side up and pointing in the right direction, and he carried on despite the attentions of Henton, Holland and the rest. The three of them continued for the rest of the race in that order ensuring Edwards won the Gold Cup in 1976. Musetti crossed the line in fourth, soaked in petrol after a fuel line became detached, and when Purley managed to pass a spinning Galica at Lodge before the end, his fifth place meant the 1976 title was his. Galica recovered to finish sixth as she had so much in hand to Barton, Cyd Williams and Bailey. Although the nearest car to her on the track was that of de Dryver, he was a lap behind, but he still finished tenth at the end of the race.

*Dennis Leech drove a F5000 car for a while, as well as his saloon car. (Author's collection)*

*Keith Holland changed his car to this one later in the year. (Courtesy Pete Taylor)*

*Brian McGuire was keen to show off his Williams-backed car. (Courtesy Pete Taylor)*

*David Purley used Ford power. (Courtesy Pete Taylor)*

Although Purley had already secured the championship there were still two rounds remaining, with both of them being held at Brands Hatch. Before the first of these, on 24 October, Rouff and some of the others who took part in selected rounds of the ShellSPORT series went to Cheshire to compete in the final round of the Indylantic series at Oulton Park. Rouff was the winner of the race but it was Wentz who took the championship for the season.

Coming into the seat of the Penske that Magee had used in the previous three rounds was Derek Bell. His prowess put him on the second grid slot next to Holland's Lola. Henton continued to qualify well and he was in between the pair of them but on the row behind, although he blew an engine when he tried to go a bit quicker. He had Robarts for company when the race began. Behind them lay Mallock and McGuire. Grob's car had been rebuilt following its last visit to Kent, and he lined up with Purley on row four. Row five saw de Dryver and Galica close together again, ninth and tenth fastest respectively. Friswell started this time but the best he could manage was row nine, better than Edwards, however, whose qualifying performance was disappointing and after spinning into the Armco at Graham Hill Bend, he was on the twelfth row.

Using the Grand Prix circuit for twenty-four laps, twenty-four cars lined up on the grid. The change of the light from red to green saw Bell make a glorious start with Robarts looking to follow him through Paddock Hill Bend, but Holland had other ideas and stopped his advance. Purley shot through to fifth place behind Henton and the other three but ahead of the other nineteen runners. McGuire made a terrible start and was the last to show. After ten laps the order looked to be settled, with no difference in the top five from the opening lap. Mallock stuck to sixth place but Edwards was climbing through the field and looked good in seventh after passing Grob. Robarts and Henton seemed to be having a race of their own with the former seemingly having the upper hand. Bell started to have gear selection problems five laps before the end and a change of leader looked inevitable. This came on the next lap when the Lola of Holland swept by at the opening corner. Purley also had a moment on the same lap, and he dropped behind Mallock and Edwards. Galica spun her Surtees at the corner named after her car's manufacturer a little later, but although she carried on at that point, she failed to finish in the top ten. On the last lap Bell had his own moment at Druids; Roy Baker spun his Formula 2 March in front of him and, in taking to the grass to evade the car, he missed a gear and allowed Robarts and Henton to pass, but the latter went in too tight and the two collided. Henton's car produced an enormous smoke screen after he broke an oil cooler, but amazingly they both continued and passed the line in the order they had been in for most of the race. Bell nursed his car across the line behind the pair of them. Edwards was on his own in sixth, followed by Mallock, Grob, Purley, de Driver and de Vilotta to complete the points-paying positions.

The final round on 7 November formed part of the annual Formula Ford Festival in a meeting that was billed as a 'Tribute to James Hunt', and the man who had just become the Formula 1 World Champion in a McLaren was there to sign autographs and give rides around the circuit. Bell continued in the Penske but couldn't do enough to stop the returning Cheever taking pole position in a Formula 2 Ralt RT1 that was supplied by Ron Dennis on the Club circuit. Some kind of ironic coincidence, perhaps? Back to qualifying, though, and Purley and Bell both travelled round in fifty seconds, four-tenths shy of the time set by Cheever, but it was Purley who set the time first and was therefore on the front row with the Italian-American. Next to Bell was Robarts who was similarly four-tenths slower than his second row rival. Sharing a time a further two-tenths adrift and sharing row three were de Villota and Holland. Galica was the only other driver who recorded a time of less than fifty-one seconds, and she had Mallock for company on the next row. Rouff equalled the future Vauxhall British Touring Car team principal, but he was in the ninth grid space. Completing the last top ten of the season was Peter Wardle, driving the ex-Tom Belso/Galica Surtees TS15 that bore the number '208' after the Radio Luxembourg station frequency that had been their principal sponsor when they used the car.

A wet track greeted the twenty competitors when they came to line up for the intended forty-lap contest. Jim Crawford was amongst them, behind the wheel of a Chevron B34 that he had entered for himself, the no-shows, though, were Lawler, McGuire and Henton. Because of the track conditions, several warm-up laps were driven before the Clerk of the Course and Purley went round in a road car to decide whether it was safe to allow the race to go on. Having made a positive decision, it was the champion-elect who sent the spray billowing into everyone's face as proceedings began, with Cheever spinning his wheels and allowing Robarts to slot into second place. Bell came through to second, though, as he approached Clearways for the first time. By then Cheever had got his act together, and it was the Ralt that came through to start lap two in fourth place with Mallock very close behind. De Vilotta was next, very aware of the closing presence of Holland and Galica. The train held station until lap nine when Bell decided to exert some more pressure on Purley, at Druids this paid off and he went through to assume the lead. Two laps later the pair had lapped everyone up to and including de Vilotta and they came up behind Mallock. Bell went to overtake on the outside but was unable to pass before Purley, and he found himself back in second. These two carried on in this order for the rest of the race, and with Bell slipping back, Purley had an easy ride to the flag with just backmarkers to contend with. As the light was fading and the night was drawing in, Cheever closed up to Robarts but was unable to pass before the flag came out after just thirty laps. Holland spun before the end at Clearways but was safe in fifth, whilst Wilds came through ahead of de Vilotta and Galica, who lost ground with a spin of her own at Graham Hill Bend that dropped her to tenth. Between de Vilotta and Galica was Crawford. His second race in the series had been more successful than his first in round five when failed to start, as this time he crossed the line in eighth. Rouff scored another 2 points for finishing ninth.

At the end of the season the top ten of the ShellSPORT European 5000 Championship looked like this:

| Position | Driver | Car | Engine | Points |
|---|---|---|---|---|
| 1 | David Purley | Chevron B30 | 3.0 Ford GAA | 172 |
| 2 | Damien Magee | March 751<br>Penske PC3 | 3.4 Ford DFV<br>3.0 Ford DFV | 107 |
| 3 | Keith Holland | Lola T400 | 5.0 Chevrolet | 95 |
| 4 | Divina Galica | Surtees TS16 | 3.0 Ford DFV | 57 |
| 5 | Mike Wilds | Shadow DN3<br>Ensign N174 | 3.0 Ford DFV<br>3.0 Ford DFV | 51 |
| 6 | Val Musetti | March 73B<br>March 752 | 3.0 Ford DFV | 43 |
| 7 | Richard Scott | Modus M3 | 1.6 Ford BDA | 42 |
| 8 | Brian McGuire | Williams FW04 | 3.0 Ford DFV | 32 |
| 9 | Richard Robarts | March 763 | 2.0 Hart 420R | 30 |
| 10 | Guy Edwards | Ensign N174<br>Brabham BT42 | 3.0 Ford DFV<br>3.0 Ford DFV | 28 |

Although Formula 5000 machines continued to run on racetracks and hillclimbs in the UK in the years that followed, with a decreasing number of cars, Group 8 racing largely became the domain of Formula Atlantic and Formula 2 cars. The 1977 championship was renamed the ShellSPORT International Championship. In later years, the Aurora organisation brought some of the older Formula 1 cars together to create the British Formula 1 Championship that ran from 1978 until 1980. I don't propose to go into details of these events, although some fine races occurred in those times.

A few of the contemporary cars were included as part of the FORCE series in 2003, and included a few race wins for their drivers, most notably Edwin Jowsey's performances driving a Lola T400 at Donington Park over the late May Bank Holiday weekend; he won both races from pole position. On the same day, Ian Giles used a car that was one of Dan Gurney's Eagle FA74 team, but the best he could do was to finish third in race one. He made amends, though, when he won one of the races held at Dijon in July of that year, by a shade over a tenth of a second. Others taking part were Nick Rini and Mike Scott in a Lola T300 apiece, Ean Pugh who used David Prophet's old McLaren M10B, Anthony Goddard behind the wheel of a Surtees TS11, whilst driving Tom Belso's Lola T332 on Le Mans' Bugatti circuit was Frank Lyons.

*A comeback for F5000? Edwin Jowsey at Oulton Park in 2004. (Courtesy Ken Grey)*

# CHAPTER 9
## A RACE OF THEIR OWN?

Formula 5000 cars came back to the country's racetracks with a vengeance in 2004 after a few had made guest appearances the previous year. The Derek Bell Trophy was instrumental in returning many of the cars to prominence, and it is my intention to show in the following chapters how they once again became a force on the racetracks of Great Britain. The events – more of a series of individual races rather than a championship – started on 11 April at Donington Park. Somewhat reminiscent of the old Group 8 days, a mix of nineteen cars arrived to take part. Eight were Formula 5000 motors that formed Class A of the entry. These included David Woods in a car that Ulf Norinder had driven when Formula 5000 first came into being, a Lola T142, Frank Lyons and his wife, Judy, were on the grid in the ex-Tom Belso Lola T332 and Brian Redman McLaren M18 respectively, and Simon Hadfield was also present in a Trojan T101 that had once seen action in the hands of John Watson and Willie Green. Mike Scott and Anthony Goddard were in the race, having switched from FORCE events, but using the same cars as they had in 2003. The latter pair of Keith Norris, in a Chevron B28 that Peter Gethin once had charge of, and Steve Fitzsimmons in an ex-Max Stewart Lola T400, completed the octet. The rest were once again a mix of cars, including Formula Atlantic, Formula 2, and even a Formula Ford 2000.

A damp track greeted the Formula 5000 contingent and its assorted colleagues when qualifying opened. Fastest of all was Hadfield, whose time of 1 minute 7.9 seconds was over seven seconds faster than the next quickest Formula 5000 car, that of Fitzsimmons, who could only qualify fourth. Scott was four places farther back and should have had Frank Lyons for company directly behind, but a blown engine at the Old Hairpin spoiled Lyons' weekend and he exited from the race. The other Formula 5000 cars occupied grid slots sixteen to nineteen in the order Norris, Goddard, Wood and Judy Lyons.

Fourteen laps were given to the race and Hadfield made his intentions clear as he blasted away from the line into Redgate, and a demonstration of how to lead an entire race. Lapping the whole field into the bargain, he took victory by almost fifty seconds and set a fastest lap of over 150mph. There was a fight for second between Stuart Tilley, in a Formula Atlantic Modus M1, and Tim Barrington's Formula 2 Lola T240. This pair were a lot closer at the finish than Hadfield had been to them, just over six-tenths the margin in Tilley's favour. Not that they had it all their own way, as Fitzsimmons' Lola T400 was in close attendance for the early part of the race, but at the end he was over half a minute behind them both. Scott was the next to cross the line after passing the former seventies Formula 5000 runner, Patrick Sumner, who drove a Kitchiner K4B that had been designed by Tony Kitchiner of K3A notoriety. Norris was twelfth, Wood fifteenth but Judy Lyons was sadly unclassified.

Round two of the series was held at Silverstone on 6 June as part of the two-day Historic Festival, and in contrast to the season opener, hot sunshine greeted an expanded field of thirty-one entrants for qualifying. This time an additional six drivers joined the ranks of the Formula 5000 'brigade', Edwin Jowsey, Mike Wrigley, Tim Barry, Ian Giles, John Bladon and Peter Leigh-Davis. The latter used another of Gethin's former drives, one that Reine Wissell had also been found in, another McLaren M10B, whilst Bladon drove an ex-Mike Hailwood Surtees TS5B that had been used in Formula 1 races by the former car and motorcycle ace. Hadfield changed from the Trojan that had brought him success at Donington to the last Chevron ever built, a B37. Woods, though, was missing this time. Once again it was Hadfield whose style lent itself best to the circuit and he took pole position yet again, but this time with only a fraction more than two seconds advantage over the next driver, Giles, in the FA74 Eagle that he had used to take to a win and two third place finishes in FORCE events in 2003. Jowsey made up for lost time as well when he recorded a second slower than Giles, but quick enough to line up third on the grid. Wrigley suffered a similar fate to that of Frank Lyons at Donington; after he and his Lola T332 had set their qualifying lap the engine blew up and his fourth grid slot became vacant. Frank was out in an ex-James Hunt Formula 1 McLaren M26, and he and Bladon took fifth and sixth places in that order. Fitzsimmons was the next fastest of this group but he was four places behind Bladon. Scott was eleventh and the next Formula 5000 driver was found in the bay marked out for the seventeenth qualifier, who on this day was Norris. Leigh-Davis' car that was often a winner in 1970 when Gethin drove it, was a disappointing twenty-second fastest.

When it came to the race it was Jowsey who out-dragged the whole field, but only as far as Becketts when Hadfield wrested the lead from the younger man. Leigh-Davis' misery was complete when, on lap four, he spun at Luffield and then stalled the engine of his McLaren and was unable to restart it so retired it there. Goddard retired to the pits at the end of the fifth tour, and on the seventh, Bladon joined in the race after spending all that time in the pits having a blocked fuel filter problem sorted. Jowsey appeared to be heading for second place in his first Formula 5000 drive of the year, but a misfiring engine soon dashed those hopes and he retired at the end of lap eight leaving Giles in second place, over forty seconds behind the leader. Frank Lyons was about a second or so in Giles' wake and on lap eleven he crept by at Priory, but the Eagle driver retook the place on the next lap. Lyons started to drop back and after twelve of the scheduled fifteen laps he, too, disappeared off the timing screens and back into his garage with an electrical problem. Giles carried on and at the end was the only unlapped runner but only just, he was over 1 minute 22 seconds behind the victor when he took the flag after Hadfield. Third place went to another Chevron driver, Alain de Wagter, in a B48. Scott was the third of his class to finish when he crossed the line, almost twenty seconds after the Formula 2 car.

Just over a month passed before the next round of the series when Brands Hatch became the venue. On 18 July it was go-go-go in Kent for the battle that was held on the Grand Prix circuit. Twenty-seven cars took part in the race, of which nine were members of the Formula 5000 Drivers' Association. James Denty brought Jock Russell's old Lotus 70 along for his first race in the series. Also joining the group was

Michael Schryver, who used the Trojan T101 that Hadfield had successfully campaigned at the opener of the season. Scott, Wrigley, Norris, Barry, Fitzsimmons and Hadfield returned in Formula 5000 cars. Judy Lyons drove a Formula 1 Surtees TS9 that John Love had previously used in March 1972 at the South African Grand Prix for Team Gunston, but he finished out of the points in sixteenth. Judy's husband, Frank, took part in a Formula 2 Chevron B29. Schryver showed his intentions when he led from start to finish to win the opening race of the day, a Historic Formula Ford race that also featured Jowsey.

Hadfield set the pole position time on a damp track with Denty alongside him, with two and a half seconds being the difference between the pair. A pair of Mikes should have made up the second row, with Schryver being faster than his peer man, Wrigley, and a similar gap between them, but when the racers came to the start the latter was missing from the grid. Hadfield also created a gap when he decided to change tyres before the race started, as the weather had changed from wet to dry and he decided to go out on slicks. The gaps gave Schryver the chance to take the lead with Denty slotting in behind him and a pair of non-Formula 5000 entrants, Stuart Tilley and Marcus Pye, in third and fourth respectively. Barry's March 76A was fifth at the end of the opener, the third of the Formula 5000 class, but he had a con-rod fail on the next lap and was forced to call it a day. Denty's solid start also came to nought two laps later, when an electrical fault brought his race to an end at Dingle Dell. Hadfield had joined the event in last position as the whole field went through on the opening lap. He started to pick his way through the cars and, by lap six, he was up to seventh. Not that that was the end of his charge, however, and he was in fourth three laps later and keen to catch those in front, lapping quicker than the rest of the field. Tilley and Pye continued in the remaining podium places but Hadfield's tyre choice had proved beneficial, and on the penultimate lap he decided that he wanted to be there as well and he powered his way past the pair of them. Pye edged out Tilley for the third spot as the race ran down and they made their way to the line. As the cars took the flag, the F5000 dice of the race between the Lola cars of Scott and Fitzsimmons was settled in preference of the latter in a T400, when the T300 driven by his rival had a rear tyre start to deflate as they rounded Clearways for the eleventh time. This gave Fitzsimmons eleventh place overall, and Scott then dropped a further place as Tony Dunderdale also passed him in his March 742. Norris followed Scott home in fourteenth in a Chevron B28. Despite being over thirty-eight seconds behind Schryver, Hadfield had set the fastest race lap, over five seconds faster than the victor.

Round four of the Derek Bell Trophy series was also set as part of the Oulton Park Gold Cup meeting over the August Bank Holiday weekend of 29-30 August 2004. Once again, twenty-seven cars were present to compete for the points and the associated prize money although sadly, only four Formula 5000 cars took part. These were driven by Scott, Norris, Hadfield and the returning Jowsey. Qualifying was truncated when red flags brought it to an unscheduled stop after the drivers had completed just four laps. The restart only lasted two more before they came out again, due to Hadfield hitting the barriers at Clay Hill and damaging his car. He had failed to take pole position on this occasion after Martin O'Connell managed to record a time of a fraction over two minutes in a Formula Atlantic-spec Lotus 59/69 hybrid. Hadfield was second quickest, some seven seconds or so slower, but his accident meant that he failed to compete in the race as no spares could be found for his Chevron. The next fastest Formula 5000 car was that of Norris in his ex-Gethin B28, but he lined up eleventh. Frank Lyons was behind the wheel of an ex-James Hunt Hesketh 308E this time but although a member of the Formula 5000 Drivers'

Association, this was a Formula 1 car. He was directly in front of Norris, in ninth overall. Scott was fifteenth whilst Jowsey's return was marked with disappointment when he started two places behind him, seventeenth on the grid.

The twenty-minute race got under way on a very greasy track, and O'Connell took advantage of his grid placing and led as the pack entered Old Hall for the first time. Stuart Tilley in a Modus Formula 3 car led the way behind him, with Andy Middlehurst third in a Lotus 69 single-seater. Former Rothmans Formula 5000 pilot, Sumner, in a Kitchener K4B, was up in fourth place. Of the current Formula 5000 contingent it was Jowsey who was faring better than the rest as he improved his grid slot of seventeenth and charged up to eleventh place as the field approached Knicker Brook on the opening lap. Middlehurst followed O'Connell across the line at the end of the lap, and Frank Lyons was also improving his chances of victory as he was fourth behind the now-deposed Tilley. Jowsey continued to make progress; he was eighth and looked likely to make even more progress towards victory. At the end of the next tour, Frank Lyons was ahead of Tilley and Jowsey was about to go through in front of the Modus as well. In the middle of the field Scott was tenth in his Lola, which soon became eighth when the race was another lap older, but then John Bladon, who had retaken Amnon Needham, spun at Knicker Brook. Needham, having no-where to go, ran over the nose of Bladon's Surtees and both retired on the spot, blocking the track and bringing the red flag out.

A new ten-minute race started after the debris was cleared up and once again it was O'Connell who was seen first by the large crowd assembled at the first corner. Tilley was second again this time with Frank Lyons, Middlehurst and Jowsey making up the rest of the top five, slotting in behind the leading pair. Middlehurst's Lotus was fastest of the trio, even faster than Tilley as he came past the pits at the end of the new first lap with O'Connell in his sights as well. Jowsey spun at Hill Top on the second trip past after a rear brake failure, and although he managed to rejoin, he sadly retired at the end of the lap. Norris now moved up to eighth and was catching Scott who realised his intentions and, on lap five, responded by passing both Steve Worrad, in a Formula 2 Brabham BT30 and Sumner, achieving fifth position on the road. As the leader, O'Connell crossed the line at the end of the next lap, the chequered flag was shown and he was declared the winner. Frank Lyons was second, the leading Class A runner, but Scott, in sixth place, was the top Formula 5000 driver. Norris was one place behind, the only finisher of the larger cars. Judy Lyons brought her Formula 1 Surtees TS9 home in eighteenth place.

Mallory Park was the next to host a round of the Derek Bell Trophy on 3 October 2004 with a disappointingly small field of sixteen entrants taking part, only two of which were Formula 5000 cars. Hadfield's Lola T330 had been repaired and it was he who headed the time sheets at the end of qualifying. As the only other Formula 5000 driver, Scott drove a T300, and the best he could do was to line up in ninth place. Both Lyons partners were present, with Frank back in the Chevron B29 for a change. Judy was behind the wheel of a McLaren M18 that she used at the opening round, although sadly she failed to start the race as an oil leak was discovered after she completed three laps in practice.

Wet weather greeted the racers once more, although Hadfield had not made the same mistakes as he had in Cheshire and he took up the pole for the proposed fifteen-minute race. He was out-dragged at the start by Tilley, however, and had to settle into second place as the contest began, but pressurised Tilley for the lead throughout the second lap. On lap three this paid off, and as the cars crossed the line to start the fourth trip around the Leicestershire circuit, it was the T330 driver who was in front and was never headed as he led to complete the seventeen laps before the flag signalled the end of the race. Scott finished a lap down, seventh out of twelve finishers.

The final round of the series was held on the National circuit at Silverstone just under two weeks later, and three more cars took part than at Mallory Park. Nine members of the Formula 5000 Drivers' Association were listed amongst them but in the end, seven were on the track for qualifying. Giles completed just ten laps in his Gurney Eagle FA74 but proved to be the fastest of them all, just over three-tenths of a second quicker than Frank Lyons who was in yet another different car, a Lola T330/332 hybrid that had been used by Tom Belso in previous years. Jowsey was back and he was four-tenths of a second behind Frank and third on the grid. Another Formula 5000 entry, Denty in Jock Russell's old Lotus 70, had Andrew Marler separating him from the top three. Scott sat on the third row. Norris used Peter Gethin's old Chevron B28 but only completed a disappointing six laps and was down in sixteenth place on the grid. Hadfield, however, was unavailable to take part in a series he looked to have sewn up earlier in the season.

The weather at the start of the race was worse than the competitors had faced at the previous two rounds and two green-flag laps were given to the runners. As the lights changed, the cars at the front of the grid tried to put down their power, but just spun their wheels. They inched forwards and began to pick up momentum led by pole man Giles from Frank Lyons and Jowsey, but another car struck the back of Jowsey's which set off a chain reaction resulting in seven cars being damaged. This blocked the track and the red flags came out without a racing lap being completed. The worsening weather conditions, and the time needed to clear the track due to the heavy damage to some of the cars, meant that the race was abandoned, bringing the season to a damp and for some, expensive end.

# CHAPTER 10

## ANOTHER BELL 'RINGING SESSION'

Donington was once again the venue for the opening event of the Derek Bell Trophy season, and a cold Easter Sunday, 27 March 2005, was the date set for it. Sixteen cars were on hand for the fifteen-minute race to see who would take the latest winner's trophy home, four of which were from the ranks of Formula 5000 stock. These were driven by David Wood and Simon Hadfield in a Lola T142 and a Chevron B37 respectively, whilst Tim Barry and Ian Chiles returned in the cars they had used in 2004. The B37 had been driven by Peter Gethin in its heyday, whilst Wood's car had previously been driven by the South African driver, Jackie Pretorius. Frank Lyons completed the Class A runners, but he drove a Formula 1 Hesketh 308E that Rupert Keegan had once used.

On a damp track it was Giles' Eagle that took pole position after qualifying, a fraction over three-tenths quicker than the ex-Gethin car alongside him. Lyons' car was midway down on the grid with Barry's March 76A in eleventh position, whilst Wood was a disappointing sixteenth and last of the runners. Conditions hadn't improved when the cars appeared for the race that was delayed after Steve Worrad's ex-Rolf Stommelen Brabham BT30 went off during the warm-up lap. As they got under way, however, the field, led by Hadfield, entered Redgate and the midfield bunch became involved in a mass accident that resulted in the race being red-flagged. Barry, Chris Ball, Tim Barrington, Ian Jacobs, Mike Campbell-Cole and Peter Richards were all caught up in the incident. Barry's F5000 March 76A suffered the heaviest damage, mainly to the suspension and monocoque, whilst Chris Ball's Brabham BT28 lost a front wheel and suspension, and the sole Invitation class runner, Peter Richards, in a Delta, would also take no further part in the event.

The delay seemed to affect Giles more than the rest and, almost immediately, Hadfield once again took control of the race in what the Clerk of the Course described as 'dreary conditions'. At the end of what turned out to be the first of eight laps, he was already almost two seconds ahead of the whole field that had Giles at its head. Giles, though, was keen to regain the position he thought was rightfully his and the deficit was cut in half by the end of the next tour. Although Giles was circulating less than two-tenths slower at the end of the next lap, Hadfield responded and was a fraction over a second ahead. For lap four Giles reacted as quickly as he had on lap two and made up the difference, and a great race was seen as these two fought for the lead. On the next trip, though, the Eagle driver tried a little too hard and slid off at Starkey's; he attempted to retrieve the situation but by then, two other cars had passed him and he was relegated to fourth place. Lyons was out to prove a point, too, and he managed to get up to seventh position on lap six but, with the conditions deteriorating rapidly, he spun his Hesketh at Redgate only to rejoin a little farther back. Two laps later the chequered flag came out, with Hadfield the first to see it fly. Formula Atlantic pilot Stuart Tilley was next, and as James Murray had fallen victim to the recovering Giles, it was the latter that claimed the final podium place. Wood was the only other Formula 5000 driver to see the flag when he crossed the line in twelfth, the last of the field.

Three weeks later the Derek Bell Trophy circus moved into East Anglia, and Snetterton was the venue for the next competition. A pair of Lola T142s driven by Wood and Will Tomkins travelled to take part as half of the Class A runners, the other two were Mr and Mrs Lyons in the familiar Hesketh and Surtees TS9 respectively. It was Frank who sat on pole position in front of nine other cars and their drivers as qualifying came to an end, and at the end of the fifteen-minute, thirteen-lap race he was also at the top of the result sheet, the only one from his group to be classified as well.

North Yorkshire, and the Croft circuit became the latest venue to host a contest from the series on 21 May. This time Frank Lyons took the wheel of a Lola T332 that Tom Belso had used in earlier years, but he was unable to stop Giles' Eagle taking pole position. Lyons, though, was less than a second slower, and alongside him on the ten-car grid. Judy Lyons completed Class A in the McLaren M18 that her husband had used previously. When the time to race arrived, Frank sat alone on row one as Giles' car had water in its oil supply and he decided that it was unsafe to race and withdrew. Judy Lyons also failed to appear on the grid. Mr Lyons, though, took full advantage of his colleague's absence and led from lights to flag, although he didn't have it all his own way. First of all, Stuart Tilley, in a Modus M1, filled the T332's mirrors, then David Coplowe in a March 712 tried to join them. The challenge of the latter, though, became less of a problem after lap six as the March began to fall back. As the top two continued in close proximity to one another, it was the male Lyons who saw the flag before the rest of the field, having completed his fourteenth trip around the circuit. A little over seven-tenths later, Tilley recorded victory in Class C, whilst in third place, Coplowe gained maximum points for Class B but was over fifty-two seconds behind Tilley.

The Formula 5000 entry was appreciably better when the last clash for the Derek Bell Trophy arrived at Brands Hatch for the weekend of 23-24 July 2005. In a field of thirty-four cars, twenty fell into Class A with many of these having had a Formula 5000 pedigree of some sort. Three of them, including Tim Barry's ex-Steve Thompson Trojan T101, the McLaren M10B driven by David Prophet in its heyday but now with Ean Pugh at the wheel, and Giles' Gurney Eagle were absent though when qualifying began. Despite this, the Brands Hatch faithful present saw the biggest gathering of Formula 5000 machinery in the UK since the ShellSPORT Championship days. Hadfield was back on the entry list in a Chevron B37 with a definite 1975 style, using the colours of Count van der Straaten that Peter Gethin and Teddy Pilette's cars had been seen in. It was Hadfield who was found at the top of the time sheets following a session that saw him record an average speed of 93.59mph. Mike Wrigley's Lola T332 was the second fastest of his class and he found himself directly behind Hadfield on the grid. Sandwiched between the two bigger cars was Martin O'Connell in a Lotus 59/69, just over eighth-tenths slower than the pole man but with roughly the same gap to Wrigley. James Denty was back in a Lotus 70 that had once seen action with Jock Russell behind the wheel, and he was fourth quickest. Jowsey was another to return and his Lola T400 was found as the leading row four contestant. Stewart Lush and John Crawford from New Zealand each brought a car that one of their fellow countrymen, Graham McRae, had used, the McRae GM1. Lush was the most successful of this pair after he joined Frank Lyons on row eight. Lyons continued in the T332. Crawford was on the twenty-first grid slot.

Using the full Grand Prix circuit the cars had a rolling start, and it was the top four from the grid that the crowd saw first entering Paddock Hill Bend, but with Denty and O'Connell having switched places. By the end of the first lap, though, Jowsey had stormed through into second place behind Hadfield, with Denty now down in fifth. O'Connell spun on lap two at Dingle Dell meaning that those immediately behind, Wrigley and Denty, had to take brisk avoiding action, and this meant that the Lotus driver had to take to the grass. He wasn't as tidy as he would have liked to have been and he spun into the barriers, bringing about his retirement there and then. Wrigley continued in the third place that O'Connell had vacated. Despite his lack of experience at the Kent circuit, Crawford was driving extremely well and by the end of the second tour he was up to tenth. By the sixth tour, a number of runners had been lapped and Jowsey was falling back with a troublesome clutch, bringing him into the reach of Wrigley; he was duly passed when he retired into the pits as the lap came to an end. With Hadfield comfortably ahead, Wrigley settled into the position he never lost for the remaining seven trips around the Kent countryside. Ian Jacobs in a March 742 came into third, but he had James Murray at the controls of a Brabham BT36 that Silvio Moser had used in Formula 2 outings harrying him throughout the next three laps. A Lola T332 did likewise to Murray. This was Frank Lyons, and on lap eleven the Irishman made a move to successfully overtake Murray. Later on the same lap he made his claim for the final step on the podium, and as the cars emerged from the wooded area of the track, it was the Lola that appeared in front. With the chequered flag imminent it was all Frank could do to keep the pair he deposed in check behind him. At the end of the thirteenth trip, however, the flag did appear, and a first 1-2-3 for Formula 5000 cars since 1975 had been achieved. The two behind were Formula 2 cars, so that brought a very satisfied Crawford home fourth in class, sixth overall.

The trend continued a week later when twenty-three Formula 5000 cars appeared at Silverstone for a double helping of Derek Bell Trophy racing as part of the Silverstone Classic meeting. In all, forty-one cars took part in the practice session for the first event. All were allowed to take part. At the head of the grid was Hadfield with Jowsey alongside him. Wrigley once again qualified third, with Formula 2 runner Christian Fischer for company, and Frank Lyons was on row three with Michael Schryver as his 'row-mate'. Belgian Alain de Wagter in a Surtees TS16 was joined on row four by Denty in his now-repaired Lotus 70. The top ten was completed by Marcus Pye, in a Lola T330, and Crawford in his GM1.

A rolling start ensured that tyres, engines and drivers were prepared when the lights went out to signal the start of the twenty-minute race that equated to twelve laps. First to show into Copse was Hadfield followed by Jowsey, Wrigley, Fischer, Frank Lyons and another thirty-six cars and their drivers. The first overtaking manoeuvre occurred shortly afterwards at Hangar Straight, as Lyons pressed his right foot harder than Fischer and moved up a place. The top five continued in their places as the first couple of laps were crossed off, but going over the line the next time it was Wrigley who was second, and the rest also moved up a place as Jowsey pulled into the pits with gear selection problems. Although he rejoined later, he gave up the chase on lap seven and gave his mechanics more time to work things out for the second race. Jowsey's initial visit moved Pye up to fifth but on the very next tour he was relegated back to sixth when Giles' Eagle passed by. Things became worse for the journalist-driver when he was further demoted by Denty on lap five. The next lap, and the dice of the race, ensued with these two squabbling over sixth place. First it was Denty, then Pye, then Denty again, but the last pass only came about after his rival was forced to retire with the gear selector broken on his T330. Denty then set about his next quarry, Giles, and caught him at Luffield on lap eight, only to spin his effort as he exited the complex that dropped him to eighth position, leaving Crawford to fill the position he had left. Schryver made giant strides to recover the Trojan that John Watson and Willie Green had driven previously, and was up to eighth by this time. Lyons was passed by Fischer's March 772 on the next trip round, and Schryver came through to take fifth place away from Giles on lap ten. With only a single lap of the twelve to go, Hadfield had the race in his pocket, whilst the rest of the top six held station to finish in the order of Wrigley, Fischer, Lyons, Schryver and Giles.

As the rolling start crossed the line for the second twenty-minute race, it was clear to the rest of the field that Hadfield, in his red, white and blue Chevron, was looking to add another victory to his tally for the season. Wrigley followed through with Pye, Martin Stretton in a Formula 2 March 712M, and Frank Lyons in close formation behind. By the end of the lap, however, Lyons had got into third place displacing both Stretton and Pye who had also exchanged places. Following his problems of race one, Jowsey started from the very back of the grid. By the end of the opening lap, however, his pace had brought him through to twenty-fifth. Giles came steaming through the field ahead of everyone except the top four when the race was two laps old. Jowsey's gear selection difficulties resurfaced on this tour; he was only able to use fourth and he called it a day. Schryver also pulled into the pits and retired his T101. So with Hadfield seemingly in control at the front, the race settled into some form of order with no one troubling the top six until Crawford looked likely to do so. He then found Denty looming large in his mirrors and had to take defensive action to preserve his seventh placing. On lap six, Lyons had similar problems with an advancing Stretton, and the battle was resolved when the March driver squeezed by to steal the third place away from the Lola driver. As the laps counted down it was clear that only mechanical gremlins would prevent Hadfield from taking victory number two of the weekend. Crawford got in front of Pye before such problems started to affect the English driver, who eventually retired on the penultimate lap with a lack of fuel pressure in a Lola that had seen action with Clive Santo during the Rothman's Championship days. With less than one lap to go, Denty elevated himself to sixth when he got in front of Peter Dunn in Clive Baker's old March, a 73A. The five in front of Denty were, from first to fifth, Hadfield, Wrigley, Stretton, Lyons, and Crawford who, like his fellow Kiwi, Graham McRae, all those years ago, was starting to make a name for himself in the UK.

Another double-header occurred for the next outing when the cars appeared at the Oulton Park Gold Cup meeting over the August Bank Holiday on 27-29 of the month. Sadly, only six Formula 5000 cars took part in a twenty-six-car field. One of them, a Surtees TS8 driven by John Monson, had last been seen in Cheshire driven by the late Mike Hailwood, whilst Nick Shrigley-Fiegl brought along Teddy Pilette's old Chevron B28. During testing, Giles' Eagle sustained damage to its engine and went no further all weekend, thus reducing the entry further. Patrick Sumner returned to the field in a Kitchiner K4B that was outside the class where he had previously raced in the 1970s.

Starting from pole position for the first of the two twenty-minute contests was, somewhat predictably, Hadfield, but he had a Formula 1 car that Val Musetti had used in the Aurora series, an Ensign MN177, driven on this day by

John Crowson, next to him. Wrigley was the next best placed Formula 5000 driver when he lined up on row two, fourth fastest. Frank Lyons was four places behind Wrigley, whilst Monson's debut started on the sixth row. Completing the Formula 5000 contingent were Mike Scott on row eight and Shrigley-Fiegl on thirteen.

Hadfield continued his fine run of form by leading the cars across the start-finish line at the end the opening tour, and was followed closely by Crowson, Wrigley and the rest as he took another lights-to-flag victory. Wrigley's joy evaporated at the end of the second, though, when he retired with a broken inlet valve that in turn caused severe damage to the Chevrolet engine of his Lola. Crowson was the next to disappear from the timekeepers' screen when the car without fourth or fifth gear coasted to a halt at Knicker Brook. This brought Formula 2 driver, Fischer, up to second place which he held on to until the end. Third and fourth places were taken by non-Formula 5000 drivers, Steve Hartley in a car that Frank Lyons had driven in 2004, the Hesketh 308C, and O'Connell in his familiar Lotus. Lyons himself recorded fifth place, over half a second down on the winner. Scott was the only other driver of Formula 5000 machinery when he completed the top ten over a full second behind Lyons.

*Frank Lyons shows what some people had missed from his earlier years. (Courtesy Ken Grey)*

*Ian Jacobs was amongst the new drivers in old cars. (Courtesy Ken Grey)*

*Opposite page:*

*Top: The battles were just as intense; here, James Murray defends his line against Chris Sharples. (Courtesy Ken Grey)*

*Left: Another lady driver in a F5000 car, Josephine Sebastian this time. (Courtesy Ken Grey)*

*Right: Simon Hadfield always did well in 2005; here he is in a familiar-looking Chevron. (Courtesy Ken Grey)*

7
BP
27

63

40
GETHIN
40

Frank Lyons also performed well during the season. (Courtesy Ken Grey)

John Monson, on his way to Lodge Corner, Oulton Park. (Author's collection)

With the grid positions of race two being determined by the finishing positions of the previous day's race, the thirteen-lapper went ahead on the Bank Holiday Monday afternoon. The Formula 5000 field was reduced following Scott and Monson's withdrawals, but Wrigley came out in a Chevron B29 after the engine he blew up the day before was written-off. As the nineteen-car field crossed the line again, Hadfield repeated his previous form; going into Old Hall he had Fischer directly behind him, who in turn was being monitored by Frank Lyons. At the end of the next tour it was a battle at the front between Hadfield and Fischer, with Lyons dropping off slightly but being chased by O'Connell. The Lotus pilot fought a way past two laps later, and that looked to be the order until lap eight when Ian Jacobs, driving a BMW-powered March 742, came alongside at The Avenue and then passed as they appeared at Cascades. On the next lap Lyons then lost out to another Formula 2 car, a Lotus 69 driven by Andy Middlehurst, but later on in the same lap he managed to reassert his car's superior torque when he retook the place. With laps running out, Fischer kept Hadfield in his sights but was unable to prevent him recording a second double win in successive meetings. O'Connell and Jacobs took third and fourth respectively, whilst Lyons had to settle for his second fifth placing of the weekend. No other Formula 5000 cars were in the top ten on this occasion.

One of the other races in Cheshire was for open-wheeled Chevron cars, and some of those taking part were from Derek Bennet's stable of Formula 5000 vehicles. Amongst them was Hadfield's B37 but this time it was Pye at the wheel, and driving Pye's Formula 2 B40 was Hadfield. The switch of car didn't prevent Hadfield recording the first hat trick of wins seen at the circuit for many years, however, and Fischer recorded a triple of second places. Pye was the leading Formula 5000 driver in this event when he inherited third place after Gareth Burnett retired his B40 on lap seven. Brian Redman was also present at the circuit where he had cut his teeth, but he took control of a Formula 2 B42 for this race rather than one of the bigger cars that he had campaigned during the 1969 and 1970 seasons. The multi-skilled driver did challenge Pye for fourth place before Burnett's demise, though, and so was classified in that place at the end of the race.

The next date on the calendar for the Derek Bell Trophy was 10 September 2005, and Thruxton was the venue for a single race this time. A disappointing field of only sixteen cars included just three from the Formula 5000 ranks. Two of these were the husband and wife partnership of Frank and Judy Lyons in their Lola T332 and McLaren M18 respectively. The pair was joined by Scott in his Lola T300. Tim Barry in Steve Thompson's old Trojan T102 had hoped to swell their ranks by another twenty-five per cent, but in the end the car refused to start and he withdrew from the event. Frank Lyons was the leading qualifier from his class but he was upstaged by three other drivers, two from Class B, Chris Lillingston-Price in a Tecno T70 that was a Formula 2 car and Ian Jacobs' March 742. At the pole, though, was Class C runner, Stuart Tilley, in a Modus M1 that had been a Formula Atlantic car in period. Scott was eighth fastest, seven seconds or so slower than Frank who in turn was almost two seconds behind Tilley. Judy Lyons took up the last grid slot, over a minute slower than her other half, but she enjoyed her time in the car!

The pace car peeled off into the pits at the end of the formation lap and Frank Lyons shot through to take the lead, and as the race got under way, it was clear that this track was suited to Formula 5000 cars. Tilley filed in behind, with Jacobs slotted in next before the rest came through Allard. Jacobs then passed Tilley as the second lap evolved and went about catching the leader, Lyons. He achieved this and passed him before the end of the lap. At the end of that lap, Judy gave up her interest as her M18 was overheating. With Jacobs pulling away the battle was for second place, and eventually on the fourth trip around the Hampshire circuit, Tilley outbraked Mr Lyons going into the Chicane and he stole the place back. Chris Sharples in a Formula Atlantic Chevron B29 was going well and he came into fourth place after Chris Lillingston-Price retired with a broken drive shaft. Lap eight didn't see any changes in the top four, but a little further down the order Scott started a move to take fifth place away from Peter Shaw in a Brabham BT35 that came to fruition on the next lap at Allard. With three laps remaining, Lyons had increased the gap to Sharples with the two ahead of him edging away but with Tilley getting closer to Jacobs. The order remained set, though, and when the chequered flag came out it was Jacobs who saw it first, over five seconds ahead of his closest pursuer. Twenty-three seconds or so later, Lyons saw it to record a class win. Sharples and Scott were fourth and fifth respectively out of only ten finishers.

The final round of 2005 took place at Silverstone on 15 October and this time four Formula 5000 cars took part in the warm and sunny event. Stalwarts of the series Frank and Judy Lyons were amongst them, and the former was rewarded for his efforts when he took pole position ahead of the twelve other drivers. Jacobs and Tilley were second and third in that order, with Scott the next Formula 5000 driver in fourth despite a cracked exhaust hampering his time. Mike Gatt made twelfth position when his Buick-powered Techcraft Brabham BT21 went round the track somewhat slowly, taking twelve seconds longer than the pole-sitter. Judy Lyons was alone on the back of the grid, almost eighteen seconds adrift of Gatt.

The race was given fifteen minutes on Silverstone's Club circuit, which meant that sixteen laps would need to be completed before a winner could be declared. Judy Lyons' thirteenth grid position turned out to be an unlucky number for her as her race lasted barely a single lap! The water pressure on her ex-Brian Redman McLaren rose significantly and she decided it wasn't worth risking the engine. None of this deterred her husband from capitalising on his pole position, however, as he led the field through on the opening lap in just over a minute. His time on the second lap was almost two seconds less than that, and it reduced by around half a second more on lap three, generally hovering around the fifty-eight-second mark throughout the race. Needless to say there was no one who could match his pace, and he recorded another victory in the 2005 season. Behind him Jacobs, and James Diffey in a Lotus 69, fought for second place, with Tilley also on hand to capitalise on any mistakes either of them made. Jacobs looked to have the measure of them both, though, until a slight error at Luffield as the flag appeared for Lyons allowed both pursuers to leapfrog the winner from the previous meeting and pick up the podium places, with Diffey one step higher than Tilley. Scott registered fifth, whilst Gatt was a 'DNF' after retiring at the end of lap five.

The 2005 season was mixed; sometimes the grids were very good but some were also very poor, and this detracted from the racing. On days where there were twenty or more cars competing, generally some excitement was seen but on other occasions the racing became processional. Whatever the number, however, Hadfield and Frank Lyons both enjoyed their wins, and both men hoped that in 2006 the formula would see an improvement both in terms of numbers and in the quality of the racing.

# CHAPTER II
## LIFE WITH THE LYONS

The 2006 series opened at the same venue as the previous two had, Donington Park, with twenty-three cars on the grid after a qualifying session that saw Simon Hadfield start where he had left off at his last race of 2005, on pole. Driving a Lola T300 that had seen action in the USAC series at the hands of Gus Hutchinson, he was over half a second quicker than his nearest rival, Martin Stretton, in a Formula 2 March 712. The next best placed Formula 5000 car was another Lola, a T332 driven by Frank Lyons, in fourth place on the grid. This was the car that Brett Lunger had used whilst competing for the American championship in 1974. Ahead of the 2006 series director was another March, a 761 that Arturo Merzario had driven during the 1977 Formula 1 series. John Monson used a Surtees TS8 to capture the ninth grid slot, whilst Michael Scott made it a trio of Lolas when he drove his T300 eleventh fastest of the field.

The start was delayed due to a shift in the weather conditions from dry to wet, and many drivers took advantage of this time to change tyres. The duration of the race then became twelve minutes instead of the planned fifteen. Lyons got the right line going into Redgate as the race began, and managed to muscle past Stretton but wasn't quite quick enough to pass the pole man, Hadfield. The T300 driver held on and led as the lap unfolded with all the drama going on behind him. Keith Norman's Brabham BT35 spun into the gravel at the first corner, and Stretton was also passed by Stuart Tilley, back in his Modus M1, before the end of the lap. One of former Formula 5000 favourite David Purley's old Formula 2 cars was present amongst the pack, a March 742 driven by Mark Dwyer; it had been placed at the tail end of the grid after failing to record a qualifying lap. Dwyer showed he was comfortable in the car, however, by gaining six places by the end of the first tour and another five at the end of the next. Up at the front, though, Tilley had jumped into second place after Lyons had got into a bit of a tangle at the Old Hairpin and lost three places before rejoining. Hadfield continued to pull away, and he looked like repeating his win at the track where he won the opening round of the 2005 season. Dwyer, though, continued his charge and looked as though he could also have a say in where the spoils of victory would end up. At the end of lap five the old Purley car was up in fifth position and gaining. He caught and passed Lyons after the T332 spun again, and then by the end of lap seven he had done something similar to Stretton, who was now back in third place, and also deposed Tilley to take second.

With the clock running down, the big question was whether he could deprive Hadfield of the win after coming from the very back. As both cars appeared at Coppice on the ninth and final time, the March driver made his move, and as they came from under the Dunlop Bridge he pulled away from his rival from there to the finish line. In the end he was a fraction over one-and-a-half seconds faster. Stretton and Tilley were over ten seconds behind, the pair of them in third and fourth respectively. Lyons came through some twenty seconds later in fifth, but second in his class, and Scott failed to finish.

Another Bank Holiday weekend, May Day on 7 May, saw the cars return to Kent for the next instalment of the Derek Bell Trophy. This time twenty-four drivers were present to contest the twenty-minute race, and that included seven from the Formula 5000 ranks. Series director Frank Lyons yielded control of his Lola T332 to former Formula 5000 driver and 1978 Aurora British Formula 1 Champion, Tony Trimmer. This proved to be quite beneficial as after just eight qualifying laps it was his name that was at the top of the time sheets with a time of 1 minute 26.52 seconds. Mike Wrigley made his first appearance of the series as well, and he showed the crowd what he was made of when he came to the grid alongside Trimmer in a Hesketh 308C. Lyons used the Gurney Eagle that Ian Giles had driven in the years that saw a resurgence in Formula 5000 cars, and showed a quick turn of pace by lining up third. Peter Dunn made a Class A quartet at the front when he took his ex-Clive Baker March 73A round in a time that was a fraction under three seconds slower than that set by Trimmer. Donington victor, Dwyer, was the next fastest, with Tilley in the next berth to him. Peter Gethin's old Chevron B28 was driven by Monson and he lined up twelfth. Gethin's old team-mate, Teddy Pilette, had a similar old mount that was driven by Bob Birrell, but the best he could do was to start from twentieth. Hadfield was unavailable to take part.

Monson came a cropper on the formation lap when an upright broke on his B28 as he passed through Druids and that was his race over. Lyons made the best start of the field, though, and it was the light blue Eagle that led the way for almost the entire lap. Trimmer wasn't too keen on that, however, and as they emerged from Graham Hill Bend it was the T332 that was in front. Dunn was behind Lyons in third place, with Dwyer the highest of the non-Formula 5000 runners next up. Mark Griffiths in a Surtees TS15 had come through from ninth to fifth at the end of the opener, but by the time the second lap was complete he had been passed by Tilley. With the order looking settled the question was whether Trimmer could add another victory to his CV, and the answer was in the affirmative after he completed fourteen laps over twenty-six seconds in front of Lyons. Dunn was in third place around nineteen seconds further back. Dwyer was fourth, Tilley and Griffiths were fifth and sixth respectively.

The fortieth anniversary of the HSCC was celebrated at Silverstone two weeks later, but a lot of the cars failed to attend as the event clashed with the Historic Grand Prix of Monaco weekend. In fact, only two Formula 5000 cars enrolled when the call for entries was made. These were the Trojan T103 of Barry and the Lola T330 of Pye. In all, only eight cars made the journey to the Northamptonshire circuit. Pye made it on to the front row alongside Tilley but over two seconds worse off. Barry endured a torrid practice session and started from row four in the second-to-last grid slot. The race started in atrocious weather and after three incidents the red flag was shown and it was abandoned.

The weekend of 3-4 June 2006 was a much better-attended contest, with eight Formula 5000 cars coming on to the grid; a few of the others needed repairs following incidents they were involved in whilst abroad. The entrants of the pair of Derek Bell Trophy races held on the day were swelled by the addition of a couple of

Kiwi drivers, Steve Ward and Stan Redmond. Ward used Lyons' ex-Lunger Lola T332 whilst Redmond was found behind the wheel of the old Clive Santo version of the same car. Neither of these drivers, however, made an impression on the top ten in qualifying for the first race, although Redmond did give the marshals something to do when he spun out at Dingle Dell. Ward also kept the attention of those watching when gearing difficulties saw his car spin at Druids before the classification for the first race was established. Hadfield was one who returned, whilst Trimmer was also a welcome addition to the ranks. It was these two who opened the race on the front row with the veteran having to settle for second spot. Making a first appearance in his ex-Mike Hailwood Surtees TS8 was Simon Diffey. Also in Class A was a TS19 driven by David Coplowe. This pair was ninth and tenth respectively.

The drivers were given sixteen laps to show what they could do, and as they went round on their rolling start lap, the Trojan T102 of Barry pulled off before he had a racing lap under his belt. At the front Hadfield and Trimmer kept it close, and as they emerged over the crest it was the Chevron B37 that led from the Lola T332. T101 Trojan driver, Michael Schryver, was the next man to show, closely followed by the male of the Lyons family, then Dwyer and the impressive-starting Coplowe who had Diffey in close attendance. On the second lap, Diffey got ahead of Coplowe, whilst in front Trimmer's T332 became clutchless. Seven laps later Schryver decided it was time to have a go at Trimmer and his timing appeared to be just right as he was the first of the pair to emerge from Graham Hill Bend, although Trimmer's car did have a puncture. With these two involved in a tussle for second place, Hadfield took advantage to pull away. On the next tour Coplowe decided to call it a day, at least for this race. Dwyer came into fourth place after displacing Lyons on the penultimate lap after the latter had been suffering from the close attention of the Class B March driver for much of the race. Diffey took sixth position after Lyons refused to yield yet another placing. With Trimmer well out of reach, the top six circulated in strict formation, and when the chequered flag came out to a very wet field, it was Hadfield that was the name on the top of the time sheets. Indeed, in the top ten at the end just two non-Class A cars were included in the race result.

With that result determining the grid for race two, it was no surprise that Hadfield was on pole. A couple of additional laps were run in this one but with Hadfield as dominant as he had been in race one, in reality the battle was for second place. As the lights changed, however, it was Schryver who led into the first corner, but Hadfield asserted himself before the end of the lap. Trimmer and Lyons squabbled over third place, which was settled to some degree on the next lap when Trimmer went in front of Schryver but Lyons was unable to pass the previous race's runner-up. Edmond spun out just as he had done on the previous day, this time at Clearways on lap seven. Trimmer suddenly found himself short of gears on the eighth tour, and he decided to retire; this brought both Schryver and Lyons up a place that they never lost. Dwyer repeated his first race, and was the first Class B driver to cross the line, with Diffey and Alistair Morrison behind him the only others to complete the full race distance. Coplowe completed one fewer than the required number of laps in taking ninth whilst Ward was tenth after having driven seventeen laps as well. Barry managed to keep his car in the race this time, although he was the last classified finisher in thirteenth after only completing fifteen of the scheduled eighteen laps.

Another pair of races was held at Snetterton on the opening weekend of 1-2 July. Only ten cars took part in the opening qualifying session, however, with just five from Class A, four from Class B and one from C. Frank Lyons was in his T330 and, with Denty back in his Lotus 70, the pair managed to set an average time that exceeded 100mph in qualifying. The Lola pilot, though, was almost half a second quicker. Despite spinning with a puncture, Monson was fifth fastest to qualify when he took a Chevron B28 round the Norfolk circuit almost six seconds slower than Lyons. All of the hard work, however, was undone when the battery fell out of the pole man's car before the end of the opening lap. This gave the Lotus 70 – that carried the number seventy – a free run to the flag for the entire twenty-two laps. Dwyer took second place overall as well as the Class B victory. For his troubles, Monson was the next best placed of the big car drivers, but he lost one place from his grid position and was a lap shy of the five in front of him.

For the second race, which was held on the Sunday, Frank Lyons made sure that everything was secure as he started from row five of the grid. With Denty in the old Jock Russell Lotus on pole, Frank was going to have his work cut out. This time Monson sat out the race but his car was used by Diffey, whilst New Zealand was represented by Ward in another of Brett Lunger's former mounts, a Lola T330/332. The latter started just in front of Frank whilst the B28 was one place behind. Despite the obvious gap, Lyons got up to third before the first lap was complete and that was improved during lap three. Diffey was also doing well as he was fourth by the time the field crossed the finish line at the end of that lap. With Denty and Lyons up front it looked as if the Lotus was going to record a second win, but as they appeared on the Revett Straight, a puncture put paid to that aspiration and the only thing Denty could do was park safely. Lyons breezed past and took a somewhat fortunate win. Diffey continued to make progress throughout, and it was the Chevron that recorded second place almost fifty-five seconds after the Lola. Third place went to Dwyer, just in front of Ward.

The third double-header of the season followed Snetterton over the weekend of 28-30 July 2006, as part of the Silverstone 'Classic' meeting. With a thirty-seven-car grid, a bumper group of Formula 5000 cars were on show, including a few that hadn't been seen on the track since their heyday. One such example was a Len Terry-designed Leda LT25 that Trevor Taylor had driven; on this occasion, however, it wasn't the former Lotus Formula 1 driver at the helm but Ian Jacobs. Neil Glover had acquired a Formula 5000 Lola T300 from Scott instead of his usual Formula 2 Brabham BT30 that Alan Rollinson had used in period, and that Glover had also used earlier in the season.

With the top twelve all exceeding an average speed of over 100mph, it was an exciting twenty minute practice session. At the end of it, Martin Stretton took pole after completing just six laps in a March 712 that had been used in Formula 2 races. In trying to go that little bit quicker, however, Stretton met a slower runner at Bridge and was left with nowhere to go, and he crashed into the barriers rendering his chances of making the race very slim. Hadfield completed seven more laps than Stretton and he put the Class A former Gus Hutchinson Lola T300 next to the Class B runner on the front row. Frank Lyons was one place further back in the Gurney Eagle that his wife Judy had used in earlier contests, with Diffey back in his Surtees TS8 in fifth. Sandwiched between this pair was a Fittipaldi Formula 1 car driven by Stephen Allen. Glover's Formula 5000 debut started from twenty-seventh after ten laps, whilst in the Leda, Jacobs completed only four laps and started from thirty-fifth.

With a gap on the grid where Stretton ought to have been, Lyons thought he had a good chance to lead going into Copse, but Hadfield was equally determined to keep him behind and it was the T300 that led from the Eagle as they came into view. Allen was third, and a Class B Lola T360 driven by Steve Maxted followed with Diffey in his wake before the rest of the field streamed through. Lyons' race came to an abrupt halt at the end of lap four, though, when he was forced to pit with his car's engine smoking due to a failed rocker cover gasket. This brought Allen up to second and Maxted into third whilst Dunn, in a March 73A, moved into the place Maxted had vacated as he had passed Diffey earlier. The Surtees slipped back a further place on the next lap when Paul Drayson's March 712 found a way to pass. With the battle of the race seeming to be for second, Hadfield looked to be untroubled at the front, and after twelve laps he crossed the line over fifteen seconds before anyone else. Maxted exerted a bit of muscle at three-quarter distance, and he got in front of Allen to take the runner-up spot that he held onto until he, too, was shown the chequered flag. Allen's misery was compounded as he was forced to retire at the end of lap ten with falling fuel pressure in his rare Formula 1 car. Dunn then took over in third and was largely untroubled as he made it to the final step on the overall podium. Diffey was a further fifteen seconds behind in fourth place.

With the grid for race two determined by the finishing positions of the first, thirty-five cars started the race, with Hadfield on pole as a reward for his win. Frank Lyons, however, started from the back row. Hadfield led the way on the opening lap leaving the rest to fight it out for the minor placings, and the first of these initially was Dunn who had Maxted and Diffey closest to him. By the end of the lap, however, Diffey had got ahead of the pair in front of him, but Dunn managed to repass the Surtees driver on lap seven and he crossed the line in second place over thirteen seconds after the winner, Hadfield. Diffey hung on to third place despite Lyons making up lots of ground from his lowly starting place. The latter was less than four seconds behind his rival as the flag was shown, making it a 1-2-3-4 for Formula 5000 cars.

*Well and truly back – Mark Dwyer at Oulton Park. (Courtesy Ken Grey)*

*A pair of Chevrons: John Monson leads John Holmes. (Courtesy Ken Grey)*

*A great start: Frank Lyons, Mark Dwyer and Christian Fischer leave the line. (Courtesy Ken Grey)*

*Battle of the ladies; Josephine Sebastian leads Judy Lyons. (Courtesy Ken Grey)*

*Mr Lyons! (Courtesy Ken Grey)*

*Rob Harvey looks to be in a hurry! (Courtesy Ken Grey)*

*Judy Lyons waves her thanks to the marshals (as always). (Author's collection)*

Oulton Park's now traditional date of the August Bank Holiday weekend for its Gold Cup meeting was next to feature on the calendars of a number of Derek Bell Trophy entrants. Eighteen cars in all contested the first of the two races held over the course of the meeting, and almost a third of them were Formula 5000 cars. The Lyons couple were joined by a Chevron B28 originally driven by Peter Gethin, but this time it was Monson at the wheel. Nick Shrigley-Fiegl was present in a Lola T300 that had been driven abroad previously, whilst another Lola T300 was also there. This one was driven by another lady driver, Josephine Sebastian with David Hobbs having been the driver in bygone days. After a practice in damp conditions the best time was driven by Frank Lyons, but he could only go fast enough to achieve fifth on the grid. One row back, but lining up in eighth, was Monson. Shrigley-Feigl was the next best and he started from row six. The other two cars lined up on the back row, row nine, with Ms Sebastian second from the back and Mrs Lyons behind her.

When the race started it was sunny, but the weather forecast wasn't good and so whoever used the right tyre combination would prove to be the best in the ten-lap race. Chevron B25 driver, Christian Fischer, was on pole, and he made the best possible start as he led the pack into Old Hall. The first couple of laps passed and Fischer looked in command, but Frank Lyons looked to bring his T332 into contention after coming through to fourth on the opener and then third at the end of lap two. By then, though, Fischer had slipped out of contention when he parked his car at Old Hall with the gear lever in his hand but not attached to his car! This meant that passing Maxted was Lyons' target, and this was achieved as the two of them came over Hill Top on the way to Knicker Brook, and he set off into the lead that he never lost for the remaining seven laps. Maxted seemed to have second place in his pocket but his car became stuck in third gear and started to drop down the field, and was fifth on lap seven which was then sixth on the next lap. The gap to his nearest rival, however, was sufficient to enable him to hang on to that place until the flag came out to signal the end of the race. Passing him as he was dropping through the field were Dwyer, Amanda Whitaker, Sandy Watson and latterly Shrigley-Feigl. This quartet shuffled before the end of the race, too, as Dwyer's car was firing on just three cylinders, causing him to drop down the order to come home fourth before the end. Formula Atlantic class drivers Watson and Whitaker travelled quickly for the remainder of the race, with Watson passing the girl from Newton Aycliffe on the last lap. The second Formula 5000 car to finish was the one driven by Monson, but the best he could do was to finish eleventh overall. The two Formula 5000 ladies, Sebastian and Lyons, were fourteenth and fifteenth respectively.

Race two came on the following day and the weather was dry when Frank Lyons led the field around the International circuit. Five laps were added to the race distance, and the Essex-based Irishman looked in control throughout the whole race, although the margin of his lead was constantly chipped away. Dwyer came through to steal second place from Watson at the first corner. Maxted also got ahead of the runner-up from race one, allowing him to challenge Dwyer. Maxted pressed Dwyer hard to take second, but Dwyer wasn't so keen to let him get through and the two made contact before the corner unwound. This sent the March 742 spinning out, although he collected the car and rejoined lower down the order, and Maxted carried on in second. After starting from the very back of the grid, Fischer was beginning to make an impact on the pack and at the end of lap five, there was only Maxted and Lyons ahead of him. Three laps later Fischer was up to second when Maxted's race was over and he retired his Lola T360 just before Cascades with gear selection problems. This brought Dwyer back into the podium placings, albeit some distance behind Fischer, but with Watson trying to get on there, too. As the race became shorter, Fischer brought the gap between himself and Lyons down to just over a second with a couple of laps remaining, but Frank responded. As he crossed the line for the final time the margin was almost eleven seconds to the T332 driver. Dwyer was over half a minute behind in third, and he in turn had twenty-two seconds in hand to fourth-placed Whitaker. She had capitalised, taking the Class C win when Watson's almost fuel-less Chevron stuttered at Deer Leap just before the flag. Monson was once again the second Formula 5000 driver to finish in eighth, and the other two ladies were the last to finish again, Sebastian thirteenth and Judy Lyons fourteenth.

Brands Hatch was the venue for the next and penultimate meeting for the Derek Bell Trophy drivers on 10 September. There were only three Formula 5000 cars taking part in Class A, with Barry being the only non-Lyons driver again in the Trojan T102 that Keith Holland and Steve Thompson had used during the 1970s. Of the Lyons partnership, Frank was in the Lola T332 that he had loaned to Trimmer for a few of the races earlier in the season, whilst Judy was using the Gurney Eagle that Giles had used in early days of the HSCC's involvement with these cars. Maxted was also there in the T360, and it was he who placed his motor on pole position with Mr Lyons next to him. The others from Class A were on the back row, with Barry being one place better off than Mrs Lyons.

The race was given fifteen minutes on the Indy circuit, which in the end translated to nineteen laps. Maxted crossed the line first as the pace car pulled clear, but by the time the field reached Paddock Hill Bend it was his colleague from the front row, Lyons, who led on the way up to Druids. Lyons, Maxted, Dwyer, Tilley and Chris Sharples completed a very close top half dozen as the first lap came to an end. This top six became a top three, however, at the end of the next tour, as Tilley and the other two became detached, although well ahead of the rest of the pack. There was a slight change, though, as Dwyer was now in second place. As the race wore on the top three cars looked inseparable and settled in their order until Maxted tried to get back in front of Dwyer, but on lap nine the attempt ended in tears as Maxted tried to pass at Druids. Contact between the cars sent them both spinning and neither was able to rejoin. Lyons was unbothered by the accident and stretched out a lead that he never lost for the remainder of the race. The main beneficiary of the incident, however, was Tilley, and there was a big gap before the HSCC Chairman, Sharples, in a Formula Atlantic spec-Chevron B29, was seen in third place. As the chequered flag came out it was Lyons who made it three in a row, winning by over twenty-five seconds.

The final meeting for the Derek Bell Trophy was held on 21 October 2006 at the home of the British Racing Drivers Club, Silverstone, using the National circuit layout. Six Formula 5000 cars made the trip – the three from Brands Hatch were joined by Monson, Wrigley and Glover – and it was the second of these, Wrigley, who set the fastest time in qualifying for the fifteen-minute race that was held in the afternoon. Frank Lyons was second fastest once again. Glover also had a good return to the fold when he put his Lola T300 onto the grid in the fourth slot. Monson achieved eighth, and Barry and Judy Lyons were at the back again, but this time separated by Peter Meyrick's Reynard SF79 Formula Ford 2000.

As the fifteen-minute race began, it was Frank Lyons who took the lead with Wrigley tucked in behind him. Barry made great strides and he was up to sixth as the lap wore on, but the race was stopped before the lap could be completed after one of the smaller cars had gone off at the start line and was deemed to be in a dangerous position. The race was restarted and given twelve minutes duration, with the first start declared null and void. Wrigley kept Lyons in his starting place on this occasion, and Dwyer was next. The two Formula 5000 Lolas started to pull away from the rest of the field with Frank unable to do anything about Wrigley until he made a mistake selecting third gear on lap six at Becketts and the Irishman pulled in front of his rival. Wrigley wasn't about to give up, though, and he chased hard, finally getting back in front on lap ten at Maggots. Lyons couldn't pull out anything more and had to settle for second place, less than half a second behind. Third place was claimed by a lonely Dwyer. Monson was third in his class this time, fifth overall. Judy Lyons was the only other Formula 5000 to complete the race after Barry and Glover failed to finish.

# CHAPTER 12

## OUT IN EUROPE AGAIN – BRIEFLY!

Six meetings were held in the UK for the Derek Bell Trophy series in 2007, but a race for Formula 5000 cars was also held at the Historic Grand Prix meeting at Pau. The Formula 5000 class was renamed Class B and split into two, B1 for cars that were built before 1972, and B2 for younger cars. As had occurred in the past few years, these were seen for the first time when the opener was once again held at Donington on 15 April.

Nine Formula 5000 cars were on the grid, of which three were in Class B1, but only one had raced in the United Kingdom during the Rothmans European Championship days, a Surtees TS8 used by Mike Hailwood. This time the driver was Stephen Gibson. The other two were Lola T300s that had featured in the USAC series during the early 1970s, Mike Wrigley drove one and Bruce Fullerton the other. Frank Lyons brought along another ex-USAC runner to join Class B2, a Lola T400 that Al Unser had driven in the USA. The others in that class were the Lolas – Neil Glover's T332, Simon Hadfield's T330 and Judy Lyons' T330/332 – and the Chevrons of John Monson and Anthony Taylor, who drove a B28 and B24 respectively.

Heading the time sheets at the end of the fifteen-minute qualifying period, however, was a familiar name in a familiar car; Hadfield had completed ten laps in his Huntingdon-built car. His time of 1 minute 6.276 seconds was almost three-quarters of a second quicker than his nearest rival, Andrew Meyrick, in a March 782 that was previously used as a Formula 2 car. Andrew's father, Peter, was also in a 782, and he was fifth on the grid. The next fastest Formula 5000 car was driven by Glover, over five-and-a-half seconds slower than Hadfield, and he had another four cars in front of him on the grid. Next fastest of the big guns was Frank Lyons who was over nine seconds slower than the pole-sitter, but he suffered engine problems during the session and only completed two laps. Slower than the rest was Wrigley, and he, too, had a short session before a problem with the car forced him to pit and attempt to put matters right before going into the race.

The race was the same duration as the practice session and, as the cars crossed the line on the opening lap on their rolling start, it was Hadfield that was the first to see Redgate, followed by Meyrick Junior. The March driver, however, was in front when the field came round to pass the pits to start his second lap. These two continued to circulate in tandem with Hadfield in a Meyrick sandwich as it was Peter Meyrick who was directly behind him. Both seemed unable to match the younger Meyrick's pace, but Hadfield was still the nearest to him as the laps wore down. Hadfield did manage to head the two Meyricks temporarily on lap seven, but the junior member of the family pushed back ahead before they passed the pits on the same lap. Four laps later, though, it was Hadfield that crossed the line first as they had made contact whilst trying to get past some backmarkers and the March had come off worst. Although out of the race on the spot, the Formula 5000 driver did manage to compose himself and continue the run to the chequered flag three laps later. The older Meyrick saw this happening from afar but he didn't let it faze him and he crossed the line in second place. Mark Dwyer came through from a grid position of twenty-one to finish third, albeit over a minute behind, the only other unlapped driver. Monson was second in the Formula 5000 class but the best he could do was to be sixth overall. Fullerton was third in his class but he, too, was someway down the order in twelfth. Frank Lyons and Gibson were the only other two classed as finishers when they were three laps down in fourteenth and fifteenth respectively.

Eight Formula 5000 cars appeared to take part at the next meeting for the Derek Bell Trophy race at Silverstone on 12 May. Sadly, Ian Jacobs' Leda LT27 failed to appear on the grid after his engine seized during testing on the day before the race. Dwyer was now in one of the B2 Class cars, the Lola T400 that Edwin Jowsey had used in earlier years, and he was joined in that class by Frank and Judy Lyons, Hadfield and Tim Barry. Fullerton and Gibson arrived in the B1 Class. With the weather turning and becoming atrocious, a number of cars had to change tyres during the fifteen-minute qualifying session, which obviously reduced the number of laps they could fit in. Peter Meyrick drove the most laps, five, and took the pole position in his March 782. On second grid slot was Hadfield, who completed four laps. Frank Lyons was next fastest after he, too, had completed four tours of the International circuit. Fullerton lined up twelfth, with Gibson, Barry and Judy Lyons occupying the last grid positions.

The weather had improved by the time the eighteen cars came to the track to be led around by the pace car and start their eleven-lap race. Peter Meyrick's car refused to start, however, and he was forced to retire without completing a racing lap. This gave Hadfield the chance to set off relatively unopposed, and he managed to complete the race without seeing anyone else in front of him except backmarkers. Into second place came Frank Lyons, but he was overtaken by Dwyer on lap two and he dropped down to third. On lap five this pair was joined, at a similar pace, by Formula Atlantic class Lyncar 001 driver Nick Overall, but he was almost a lap down so they didn't lose any places. Gibson went into fifth place on lap seven with Chris Lillingston-Price in a Formula 2 Tecno T70 BDA spoiling the chance of a symmetrical Formula 5000 1-2-3-4 finish, but this became a possibility on the next lap when the Surtees got ahead. Class B2 and Lola runners, Hadfield, Dwyer and Lyons, all managed to pass Gibson before the end, although it was Gibson whose heroics gave him the Class B1 win despite finishing fourth on the road.

Snetterton was booked to hold a double-header on the weekend of 9-10 June, but two weeks before that a number of the regulars visited Pau to compete in a two-race weekend at the seventh Historic Grand Prix meeting. In both contests, eleven Formula 5000 cars and drivers took part and the winner was the same after both; Hadfield, who drove untroubled in his Chevron B37. Michael Schryver and Frank Lyons in their Trojan T101 and Lola T332 respectively joined Hadfield on the podium after the first race, but after ten laps were completed in the second it was James Denty who replaced Lyons on the third step. After starting from fourth on the grid, Denty completed only four laps in the first race after misfiring engine problems beset his Lotus 70. These were repaired in time for the second race.

Back in England, eight Formula 5000 cars went to Snetterton but this time only three appeared in Class B1 and each one was a Lola T300. These were driven by Nick Shrigley-Feigl, Josephine Sebastian and Fullerton. The Class B2 runners were regular members: the Lyons couple, Dwyer, Barry and Simon Diffey in his Chevron B28 that Peter Gethin had used in the car's heyday. Leading the way after qualifying was Frank Lyons who completed ten laps before the session was brought to an end. Dwyer completed three laps fewer and he was alongside the Essex-based Irishman although almost one-and-a-half seconds slower than his rival. Diffey managed sixteen laps in a time that was 2.7 seconds slower than Lyons, and he managed to come through to take third overall. Shrigley-Feigl snatched sixth place and he was just one place ahead of Fullerton. Judy Lyons, back in the Gurney Eagle, and Sebastian, in that order, were found in fifteenth and sixteenth grid slots.

A mix-up at the start when the red lights failed to go out sent the cars on a second rolling start lap, but the pole man wasn't upset by any of this as he powered into Riches for the first of seventeen laps. Dwyer and Diffey were the next to show, and they held Matt Watts in a Brabham BT29 Formula Atlantic car and Shrigley-Feigl behind them, but with a gap before the rest appeared. These were also the top five at the end of the second, third and fourth laps, but after the fifth was completed, Dwyer fell out of the classification as he lost his drive shaft during the sixth. The top four were untroubled for the rest of the race and finished in the following order: Frank Lyons, who grabbed the win in Lincolnshire for the second year in a row, Diffey, Watts and Shrigley-Feigl, the latter being a lap down on the other three. Fullerton was seventh and Sebastian was the only other Formula 5000 driver to finish after Mrs Lyons retired with a flat battery four laps shy of the race distance.

With the finishing positions of the first race determining the grid positions for the second, Mr Lyons had a good chance of recording a brace. The race took place the following day, and this time twenty-one laps were given to the field that featured only twelve cars in total. Seven of these vehicles were the Formula 5000 contingent that started the earlier contest and included Dwyer's repaired T400. This time the lights did their job and the cars set off correctly with Lyons again leading the pack into the opening corner. Diffey was second this time as he didn't have Dwyer to contend with ... yet! Sebastian was almost the first to go when she spun her Lola on the opening lap at the Bomb Hole, but she recovered and set off again after the rest of the field passed her, including the advancing Dwyer. By the end of the lap he was fourth, and two laps later he was right behind Diffey. Sebastian was also gaining places but her ambitions were thwarted when she was forced to retire in tenth place at the end of lap eleven with no oil pressure. The Bomb Hole became a Lola magnet as it was also the scene of Shrigley-Feigl's demise as he lost the exhaust of his T300 on lap sixteen. None of this appeared to be bothering the top three, however, as Lyons reeled lap after lap in the lead. The battle for second between Diffey and Dwyer was intensifying, though, until three laps from the end when the Chevron driver pulled his car off the track with an empty petrol tank. Dwyer couldn't believe his luck but didn't have sufficient time or pace to challenge Frank ahead of him, and he finished over twenty-two seconds behind as the flag was shown to him. Watts' strong run in the first race was repeated with another third position. This time, Judy Lyons was the top female Formula 5000 driver when she took the penultimate chequered flag of the race in seventh, two places behind Fullerton and one ahead of Neil Bowman's Class D Merlyn.

The Brands Hatch Festival meeting over the weekend of 30 July-1 August was where Formula 5000 machinery could be viewed next, and twelve cars turned up to see what their drivers could do. This time the Leda that Trevor Taylor had used in the past was available to Jacobs, whilst Peter Dunn came along with Clive Baker's old March 73A. During a rain-soaked qualifying there was only one car faster and it was a Formula 2 March 782 that had seen action with Jean Pierre Jarier at the wheel, but this time Sean Walker was the driver. Frank Lyons took the wheel of his usual Lola and was over four seconds slower than Walker when the grid sheet was published, and he was found on row three alongside Trimmer, half a second faster in a similar T332. Denty and Glover were immediately behind this pair, whilst two rows back were another couple of Formula 5000 cars, a Chevron B28 driven by Diffey and Marcus Pye in another T332.

*Top: Out of Paddock Hill, Brands Hatch, Neil Glover leads the pack. (Courtesy Ken Grey)*

*Motor racing correspondent Marcus Pye was there, too. (Courtesy Ken Grey)*

*After some years, Tony Trimmer came back to F5000 in Kent. (Courtesy Ken Grey)*

*In a car rarely seen outside of the USA, Frank Lyons used a Lola T332 during 2007. (Courtesy Ken Grey)*

*Bruce Fullerton was another in an American race car. (Courtesy Ken Grey)*

*Sean Walker leads ex-BTCC driver Anthony Reid across the line. (Courtesy Ken Grey)*

The light rain continued, and when the scheduled twenty-minute race started, Dunn got in front of Walker. Before the race was less than a lap old, however, the Formula 2 car was in front followed by the Leda and then Dwyer, who in turn had Trimmer behind, and Diffey and Glover had both found a way past Lyons and were fourth and fifth respectively. Lyons' car was suffering with a misfire and it was costing him places, and a couple of laps later he had slipped back to ninth position. Trimmer disposed of Dwyer as both cars passed the pits side-by-side, only for the Formula 5000 pilot to be the bravest as they went into the first corner on the track. A few laps later with Dunn safely in second place, Diffey also found a way to pass Dwyer, although no one seemed able to compete with the man in front of them all. Lap nine, though, saw the heavens open and it was clear that the race was over due to the state of the track. It was also the time for a red flag to be shown which was just as well for Dunn as he went spinning out as he slowed down after taking the flag. Walker tried to get back on terms following Dunn's pass on what transpired to be the final lap, and in the end he was just over seven-tenths down. Sixteen seconds after Walker, Trimmer crossed the line to join the podium group. Diffey was a further fourteen adrift but he was classified fourth before Dwyer. Glover finished sixth overall, around three seconds in front of Denty. Frank Lyons was next to finish, who in turn wasn't too far, just a single one-thousandth of a second, in front of Pye. Jacobs completed the top ten.

The second race of the weekend saw improved weather conditions, although it was very windy. Jacobs' race was over before it began, though, as he suffered electrical problems on the green flag lap and he pitted and retired his Len Terry-designed vehicle. Trimmer got in front of Walker and, with only Dunn ahead of him, set about trying to win the race on the opening lap. The second- and third-placed drivers made contact before the end of the lap as they passed through Graham Hill Bend and with each going off the track on opposite sides, the marshals had their work cut out. With both in dangerous positions, the safety car was deployed on lap two as the cars were removed to a place where they were considered to be out of harm's way. The safety car then came into the pits at the end of lap five and the race began again with Dunn once more at the head of the queue. Diffey was second whilst the fight for third was far from over, with Dwyer passing Glover as the race became alive once more. Pye had Frank Lyons behind him in the battle for fifth. Too much time had elapsed, however, and only three more racing laps were seen by the crowd, and the racers maintained this order as the flag was shown to them. Dunn's winning margin this time was a shade over three seconds.

Cheshire became the next stop on the Derek Bell Trophy tour, and at the Gold Cup meeting held over the late summer Bank Holiday of 25-27 August, there was another pair of races. The first was twenty-five minutes long and, disappointingly, only seven Formula 5000 cars turned up. The quickest of these in qualifying was, somewhat unsurprisingly, Frank Lyons on board a Lola T400. This was the car that Al Unser Snr and Mario Andretti had used in the USAC series of times gone by. In the car he acquired from Wrigley, Glover was just over half a second slower than Frank and one place worse off, fourth on the grid. Dwyer graduated to a Lola T400 that Jowsey had used previously, and he started sixth. Twentieth and twenty-first on the grid were Judy Lyons and Anthony Taylor, propping up the rest of the field.

As the twenty-five-minute race got under way there were only nineteen cars on the grid after a couple of non-Formula 5000 cars dropped out. None of this was a problem to Frank Lyons, the first to show, followed by Dwyer and then Glover before the rest came into view. This trio started the second lap as well until Dwyer accidentally switched the petrol pump off on his way through Cascades, allowing Glover to take second place away from him. Glover saw a chance to win and he started to put Lyons under pressure as they reached Knicker Brook, but the positions remained unchanged as they came through Lodge Corner to finish the lap. Dwyer managed to restart his engine and he crossed the line in fifth place, and he was two places better off at the end of the next, having disposed of a couple of non-Formula 5000 competitors in between times. Dwyer was closest to Lyons at the end of lap four, though, after he'd muscled past Glover and then tried a move on Frank as they went down The Avenue on the next tour. Dwyer's T400 was the first one seen at Lakeside, indicating that his move had worked, and he held the lead as they finished the lap. Lyons wasn't about to surrender meekly, but his efforts only succeeded in bringing grief to the Essex-based driver as he spun at Knicker Brook for the sixth time. Although he rejoined in fourth, his Lola had lost its nose which was subsequently hit by Glover who took the second race position. Lyons, though, dropped another place on lap eight as his car had little or no road-holding ability thanks to his 'lost' nose. One of the Invitation class cars, a Formula 2 Toleman that Derek Warwick had driven for the former car transporters team in period but now with Terry Fisher in charge, passed Lyons and then Glover to take second three laps later, but he was forced to retire within a couple of laps of that manoeuvre with an over-hot motor. Glover reclaimed the position he had been forced to give up, but Lyons was passed by John Holmes in a Formula 2 March 772P and, as with the rest, he stayed in that place until the race drew to a close.

The second of the weekend's contests for Derek Bell Trophy racers was five minutes shorter than the first, and featured three fewer cars. Lyons lined up on the grid with a hastily-repaired nose cone, meaning that at least the car would stay on the road better than it had towards the end of the previous day's race. Next to Holmes though, Dwyer was looking to complete a double for the weekend, while Glover, in the third slot, wanted

*In Cheshire, Mark Dwyer had a new car ... (Courtesy Ken Grey)*

*... and so did Frank Lyons. (Courtesy Ken Grey)*

*Mrs Lyons used a Gurney Eagle. (Courtesy Ken Grey)*

*Top left: Anthony Taylor brought a Chevron back to its spiritual home, Oulton Park. (Courtesy Pete Taylor)*

*Top right: Neil Bowman also had a blue car, but it wasn't one of Derek Bennett's designs. (Courtesy Pete Taylor)*

*Neil Glover proved red cars aren't always Ferraris. (Author's collection)*

a piece of the action as well. It was these latter two who were in front going into Old Hall on lap one. Holmes managed to keep Lyons at bay but only for a short time as it was the Lola that was third to cross the line at the end of the opening lap. The leader, though, seemed in charge, and left Glover and Lyons in his wake to fight it out for the runner-up spot but with Holmes seemingly having to fight off a cooled-down Toleman driven by Fisher, he had other things on his mind, so this pair was left to fight for second place themselves. Lyons eventually took the place on lap five when he passed his rival at the scene of his lost nose the previous day. Glover was further demoted two laps later when the Toleman that was now fourth also passed him. Fisher must have been doing something special because, as the cars reappeared on the start-finish straight, he was also ahead of Lyons at the end of the same lap. The top four remained the same for the next two laps but then Fisher nearly threw it all away on lap ten at Druids as he went across the grass and gravel allowing the two Formula 5000 drivers to pass as he collected his car without spinning out. Two laps remained and, in the end, it was the three Lola cars that crossed the line before any of the rest, ensuring a Formula 5000 whitewash for the second time in 2007.

Seven Formula 5000 cars and their drivers went to Silverstone in Northamptonshire to take part in the next race for the Derek Bell Trophy series on 20 October. The crowd saw six Lolas and the Gurney Eagle, piloted by Frank and Judy Lyons, Fullerton, Dwyer, Glover, Schryver and Monson, join seventeen other motors and drivers to see who could win the final contest of 2007. After a qualifying session that was run under a threatening sky that didn't actually produce any rain, it was Schryver who emerged as the quickest of the septet, but he was only third on the grid. Richard Eyre in a Ralt RT1 and Peter Williams' March 761 were quicker, with the latter the quickest of all. Dwyer and Glover, in that order, made up row three whilst Frank Lyons was immediately behind Dwyer. Monson was on row five, tenth fastest, and Judy Lyons was on the twelfth ranking, almost twenty seconds off the pace of Williams.

The race started with Williams leading as the cars entered Copse. Dwyer moved in front of Schryver, but so did another Formula 2 March driver, Jeremy Smith, so Dwyer was fourth. That was bettered as the lap came to an end, though, and he crossed the line second with Glover looking promising in fourth. Lyons had the top four and the now-deposed Smith ahead of him in sixth place. Schryver spun his car at Luffield and fell farther back to twelfth as he recovered whilst the cars streamed by. Two laps later he was two places better off and on a charge, however, and this brought him into eighth on the next tour. This was also when Frank got ahead of Smith to bring himself into fifth place. Schryver continued to make progress and he was sixth by the end of lap six with that looking to be his final achievement, but drama was to come. On lap thirteen Eyre came through in sixth with his car misfiring, having lost out to Glover, Frank Lyons and Smith. The Ralt driver did not complete lap fourteen as he ran out of fuel on the circuit before reaching the pits. On the next lap, Frank Lyons out-ran Glover through Woodcote to finally get ahead to take third place. When they reached Maggots, however, as Frank braked he spun on oil and the positions were reversed. Smith and Schryver also benefited from Frank's spin as they, too, got through before he could set off again. So it was that after sixteen laps, the flag came out for Williams to take victory ahead of Dwyer and Glover. Frank recovered his car to record a sixth-place finish, Monson was eighth, Fullerton tenth and Judy Lyons eighteenth.

So such as it was, 2007 saw the renaissance of Formula 5000 cars on the tracks of the United Kingdom and they have become a favourite of many spectators. The Derek Bell Trophy races bring back the days of the Group 8 ShellSPORT series, how long will it take before the Rothmans series makes a similar comeback with just Formula 5000 cars involved? Until that day, long may they continue to come back in whatever form … I enjoy seeing them set the tracks alight, I hope you do, too!

***Lola T70***
*John Starkey*

*The definitive racing and development history of one of Britain's most important sports racing cars. Includes international competition history and completely revised individual chassis histories of T70, T160 & T165.*

*• Hardback • 25x20.7cm • £45.00**
*• 192 pages • 200 colour & b&w photos*
*• ISBN: 978-1-84584-189-8*

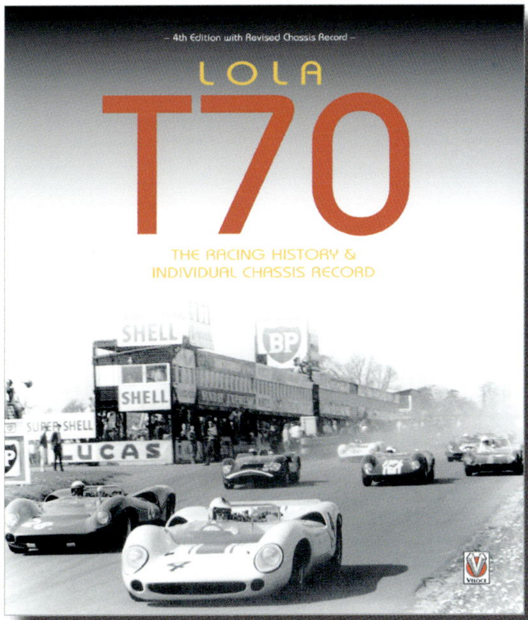

***Forza Minardi!***
*Simon Vigar*

*After 20 years of glorious 'failure,' the best-loved team in Formula One is consigned to the history books, but deserves one of its own. This is the one and only inside account, with exclusive, frank and comprehensive interviews with bosses, drivers and engineers. 145 unique colour photos complete this revelatory tale.*

*• Hardback • 25x25cm • £24.99**
*• 160 pages • 145 colour photos*
*• ISBN: 978-1-845841-60-7*

***Alpine & Renault***
*Roy Smith*

*The inside story of the first turbocharged Grand Prix car from concept to Grand Prix victory. Contains interviews with the men of the time, reports on every race, and over 400 photos and illustrations.*

*• Hardback • 25x25cm • £45.00**
*• 240 pages • 400+ colour & b&w pictures*
*• ISBN: 978-1-845841-77-5*

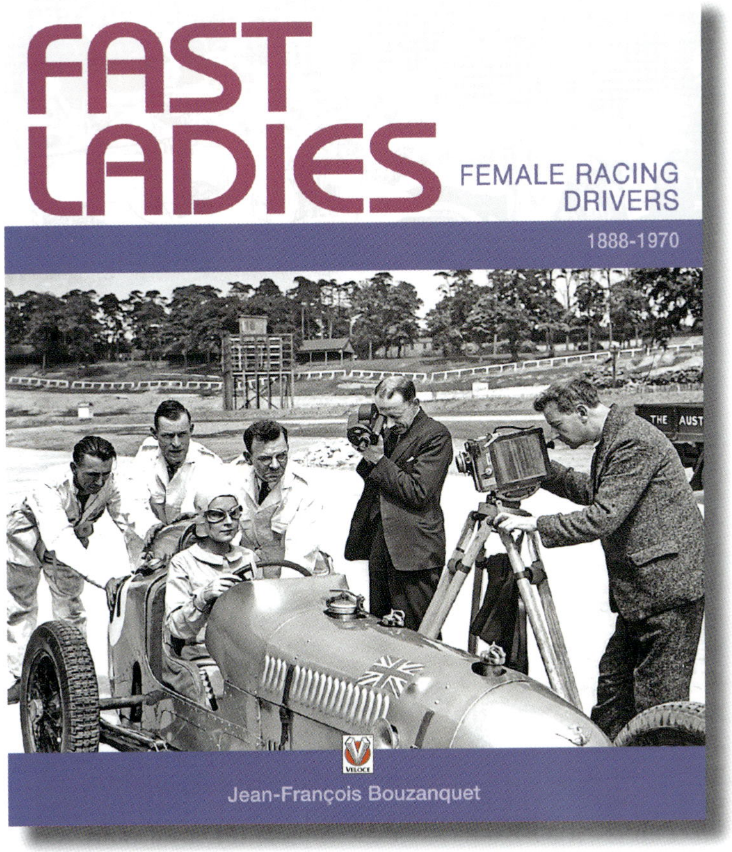


**_Fast Ladies – Female racing drivers_**
*Jean François Bouzanquet*

*A veritable saga of female determination to sweep aside male resistance in the inner circles of the motoring world, with a wealth of illustrations spanning almost a century of motor racing. Features over forty unique portraits of some of the daring, brave women who took part in speed records events, rallies and Grand Prix races.*

*• Hardback • 23.9x29cm • £29.99**
*• 176 pages • 400+ colour and b&w photos*
*• ISBN: 978-1-84584-225-3*

**_The Toleman Story_**
*Christopher Hilton*

*Small, unfashionable, short of money, and the last of its kind to become a force in Grand Prix racing. The story of Toleman is not only fascinating and improbable, it has never been told before – until now, and through the eyes of the people who lived it, making this a very special record indeed!*

*• Hardback • 25x25cm • £37.50**
*• 208 pages • 200+ colour & b&w photos*
*• IBSN: 978-1-84584-217-8*

For more information on these and other great Veloce books:
visit www.veloce.co.uk • email info@veloce.co.uk • or call +44 (0)1305 260068
* p+p extra, price subject to change

# INDEX

JORGENS
Marty
74